LEVINAS AND THE
CRISIS OF HUMANISM

CLAIRE ELISE KATZ

LEVINAS AND THE CRISIS OF HUMANISM

INDIANA UNIVERSITY PRESS

Bloomington and Indianapolis

This book is a publication of

Indiana University Press
601 North Morton Street
Bloomington, Indiana 47404-3797 USA

iupress.indiana.edu

Telephone orders   800-842-6796
Fax orders   812-855-7931

Library of Congress Cataloging-in-Publication Data

Katz, Claire Elise, [date]
    Levinas and the crisis of humanism / Claire Elise Katz.
        p. cm.
    Includes bibliographical references and index.
    ISBN 978-0-253-00762-9 (cloth : alk. paper) — ISBN 978-0-253-00765-0 (pbk. : alk.
paper) — ISBN 978-0-253-00767-4 (electronic book) 1. Lévinas, Emmanuel. 2. Education—
Philosophy. 3. Humanities—Philosophy. I. Title.
    B2430.L484K37 2012
    144—dc23

                                                                2012026292

1 2 3 4 5 18 17 16 15 14 13

To Dan, for everything
and to our daughters
Olivia and Evie
Deuteronomy 22:3

Here I am; send me (Isaiah 6:8)

But in truth I know nothing about education except this: that the greatest and the most important difficulty known to human learning seems to lie in that area which treats how to bring up children and how to educate them.

—Michel de Montaigne, "On educating children"

This crippling of individuals I consider the worst evil of capitalism. Our whole educational system suffers from this evil. An exaggerated competitive attitude is inculcated into the student, who is trained to worship acquisitive success as a preparation for his future career. I am convinced there is only one way to eliminate these grave evils, namely through the establishment of a socialist economy, accompanied by an educational system which would be oriented toward social goals. In such an economy, the means of production are owned by society itself and are utilised in a planned fashion. A planned economy, which adjusts production to the needs of the community, would distribute the work to be done among all those able to work and would guarantee a livelihood to every man, woman and child. The education of the individual, in addition to promoting his own innate abilities, would attempt to develop in him a sense of responsibility for his fellow-men in place of the glorification of power and success in our present society.

—Albert Einstein, "On Education" (1949)

And here I am not speaking of the elite among us who were real Resistants, but of all Frenchmen who, at every hour of the night and day throughout four years, answered NO. But the very cruelty of the enemy drove us to the extremities of this condition by forcing us to ask ourselves questions that one never considers in time of peace . . . Resistance was a true democracy: for the soldier as for the commander, the same danger, the same forsakenness, the same total responsibility, the same absolute liberty within discipline. Thus, in darkness and in blood, a Republic was established, the strongest of Republics. Each of its citizens knew that he owed himself to all and that he could count only on himself alone. Each of them, in complete isolation, fulfilled his responsibility and his role in history.

—Jean-Paul Sartre, "The Republic of Silence"

Contents

Preface

In many ways, I have been writing this book since I was an undergraduate discussing education with my grandparents when I shared Friday night dinners with them. My grandfather, z"l, a retired college professor and a fan of John Dewey's philosophy of education, was a formidable interlocutor. My grandmother, with an advanced degree in library science from Columbia University, could hold her own. It was around their kitchen table that they pressed me to reflect on the college education I pursued. From my freshman year, which began with my interest in computer science, to my senior year, when I completed a degree in philosophy, my grandparents watched me transform from a student interested in mathematical puzzles to a citizen engaged in the world, obsessed with questions about ethics and justice, fascinated by philosophical problems, and convinced, even if naïvely so, that education was the answer to all of the world's ills.

Influenced by these discussions, I traded my interest in law to pursue the Master's degree in the Philosophy for Children program. I remain convinced of the program's ability to improve critical thinking and engage young people in philosophical questions such that they are able to find meaning in the world around them and the lives they live. But I am no more convinced that this program is sufficient to make children "better people," where "better" means more ethical, or that my own humanities education made me or any other humanities student a better person.

Engaging the humanities might enable us to be more reflective, to ask critical questions, to consider different perspectives, and to think more creatively. I do not believe, however, that it creates the desire or establishes the motivation for us *to act* ethically or justly. Yet, the view that the humanities do in fact accomplish this task has become part of humanities education rhetoric. Moreover, this view frames the narrative that is often told to those who are responsible for funding—and frequently suspicious of—higher education. The aim of this book is not to provide a manifesto for or against the humanities. Rather, I wish to take a step back and examine what informs the way an individual might receive that education. Who is this person before she engages the humanities?

When I teach Emmanuel Levinas's philosophical project, the question my students ask me repeatedly is the following: How does one become the ethical subject that Levinas describes? Some might say this is the wrong question to ask. The question presumes that the strict phenomenological reading is limited and that Levinas is not simply describing who we are. After reading his essays on Jewish education alongside his philosophical project, I remain convinced that my students' question is precisely the right question to ask. How indeed does someone become an ethical subject?

This book attempts to answer that question by first examining the role that Levinas's essays on Jewish education play in understanding his larger philosophical project. I then consider why Levinas turns to Jewish education and not a classical humanities education to answer this question. There are two simultaneous and possibly competing visions of ethical subjectivity. On the one hand, Levinas is interested in the ethical subject who will not be a murderous self in the first place. Yet, on the other, he is also interested in the person who, like the prophet, will not only see injustice but also cry out against it.

The seeds of this project were planted many years ago, but the trajectory of the project shifted when life events provided the intersection for theory and practice. Several years after I completed my PhD, I was confronted with just such a situation. We do not often get to see our friends' or colleagues' mettle tested. Depending on how they respond, it can be inspiring or disappointing. The department in which I was a faculty member had imploded. A colleague had been harassing graduate students. My department head reported his behavior to the university Affirmative Action office. About ten days later, he—not the person doing the harassing—was summarily relieved of his headship position. The department fell into chaos and then suffered a series of humiliations including being called "whiners" by upper administration for demanding that something be done about the bad behavior in the department (one can only wonder about the future success of K–12 programs to stop bullying when those with the highest degrees in education call those who speak out against such behavior "whiners").

I was not yet tenured at the time and I was pregnant with my second baby. I was terrified that my husband (also my tenured colleague) and I might lose our jobs: how would we support ourselves, our two-year-old daughter, and the new baby we would have that fall? Yet, this battle that continued for the next two years also asked me to consider who I am and what kind of person I want to be. Who will my daughters see when they look at me? These are not easy questions to ask of ourselves. Looking back, I remember moments of which I am proud, where I stood strong, where I spoke out, and defended my colleagues. But there were also moments where I fell short, where I thought I had "caved." The fight in the university had infected our home and the relationship with our kids—it was time to stop. But we felt that the actions we took to protect our family had also betrayed our friends and colleagues, or at the very least, let them down. The real disappointment, however, was the lack of support and the deafening silence from the larger academic community.

Are injustices that are close to us harder to see? Are they harder to act upon? I remain convinced that for Levinas ethical subjectivity comprises both parts: to see the injustice, to recognize it as such, is to be moved not only to speak out but also to act. His ethical project responds to the Shoah in which he not only lost members of his family but in which the world saw extraordinary cruelty unleashed. Many courageous people risked their lives to save others, but far more stood by and watched. We are in bad faith if we justify our inaction by using the Shoah as a litmus test for all evil. Unlike Milgram and Zimbardo, Levinas is less concerned with how easily we become the bystander, or even the perpetrator, than he is concerned with how ethical subjectivity can be achieved. If the argument of my book is correct, our task is to ask what kind of education would be comparable to the one he describes.

I am grateful for all that my grandparents shared with me in those discussions around their kitchen table. I have no doubt that the roots of my intellectual interest in these questions are found in those conversations. I am frequently reminded of their own courage in the challenges they faced as Jews growing up in the American South. I recall how their lives taught me about ethics and justice when I remember the experience I described above, an experience that shaped me not only as a philosopher and an academic colleague, but also as a mother, a wife, and a friend. I am drawn to European philosophy precisely because it exposes the everyday challenges of what it means to be human: to be engaged in an ethical life where we cannot recuse ourselves from responsibility or from making choices, and the consequences of those choices often have damaging effects on those we care about most. My own perceived failures motivated me to ask what it means to raise daughters who will stand up for others, who will defend the victim, and who will stand against the bully. It is not enough simply not to do harm but one must also stop others who commit it.

Acknowledgments

I have been writing this book for many years, and I have been thinking about the themes that occupy its pages for many years longer. The list of people to thank is numerous. My undergraduate teachers, Tom Benson, John Titchener, and Craig Vasey, who first encouraged me to pursue the Master's degree in the Philosophy for Children program, nurtured my theoretical interest in education. Mat Lipman and Ann-Margaret Sharp, my teachers in the Philosophy for Children program, influenced my approach to the relationship between educational theory and political theory. Mat was particularly inspiring as a teacher who truly believed that a program like Philosophy for Children could bring about a revolution in democratic thinking through a radical approach to education. These extraordinary teachers first set me on this path not only through their encouragement but also by their example as teachers.

Earlier versions of this material were published in the following places and I wish to thank those journals and presses for their kind permission to reprint this material: "Educating the Solitary Man: Levinas, Rousseau, and the Return to Jewish Wisdom," *Levinas Studies: An Annual Review* 2 (Pittsburgh, PA: Duquesne University Press, 2007), 133–152; "Turning toward the Other," in *Totality and Infinity at 50*, ed. Scott Davidson and Diane Perpich (Pittsburgh, PA: Duquesne University Press, 2012), 209–226; "Thus Spoke Zarathustra; Thus Listened the Rabbis: Philosophy, Education, and the Cycle of Enlightenment," *New Nietzsche Studies*, ed. David B. Allison, Babette Babich, and Debra Bergoffen; "Thus Spoke Zarathustra, Thus Listened the Rabbis: Philosophy, Education, and the Cycle of Enlightenment," from *Nietzsche and Levinas*, ed. Jill Stauffer and Bettina Bergo, © 2009 Columbia University Press. Material from chapter 1 originally appeared in "The Presence of the Other is a Presence that Teaches," in *Journal of Jewish Thought and Philosophy*. Material from chapter 3 originally appeared in "Before the face of God one must not go with empty hands: Transcendence and Levinas's Prophetic Consciousness," in *Philosophy Today*. Material from chapter 4 originally appeared in "Jew-Greek redux," in *philoSophia* and in a forthcoming review of Michael Fagenblat, *A Covenant of Creatures*, in *Shofar*. Material from chapter 5 appeared in "The Stirrings of a Stubborn and Difficult Freedom," in *Journal of French and Francophone Philosophy*. Material from chapter 6 originally appeared in "Levinas—Between Philosophy and Rhetoric," in *Philosophy and Rhetoric*. Material from chapter 7 originally appeared in "On a word and a prayer," in the *Journal for the Society of Textual Reasoning* and in "'The Eternal Irony of the Community': Prophecy, Patriotism, and the Dixie Chicks," in *Shofar*. I would like to thank Art Resource for use of the cover image.

I am especially grateful for two groups whose intellectual company I have enjoyed for many years: The Levinas Research Seminar and the North American Levinas Society. I would like to thank, in particular, Deborah Achtenberg, Andrew Ball, Dennis Beach, Bettina Bergo, Scott Davidson, John Drabinski, Oona Eisenstadt, Chris Fox, Octavian Gabor, Lisa Guenther, Sandor Goodhart, Michael Gottsegen, the Hansel family, James Hatley, Dara Hill, Dana Hollander, Greg Kaplan, Martin Kavka, Dan Kline, Jacob Meskin, Sol Neely, Monica Osborne, Michael Paradiso-Michau, Diane Perpich, William Simmons, Jill Stauffer, Rebecca Weir. Their feedback on my work over the years sharpened my thinking.

Words will simply fail to express the special thanks I owe to Martin Kavka, whom I met when I completed the manuscript for my first book over ten years ago. Martin is the kind of friend and colleague everyone should have—his intellectual acuity and clever wit have sustained me in a profession that sometimes seems to lack both. He generously read my work—many times—and provided invaluable feedback. His insistence that I pursue this project and his affirmation that what I was doing was important provided the encouragement I needed especially when the doubts threatened to take over.

The support of senior colleagues who encouraged me in this project confirms why academia, in spite of all of its flaws, is a truly special place to work: Doug Anderson, Annette Aronowicz, Leora Batnitzky, Andrew Benjamin, Deborah Bergoffen, Robert Bernasconi, Catherine Chalier, Tina Chanter, Richard A. Cohen, Steve Crowell, Veronique Foti, Robert Gibbs, Emily Grosholz, Susannah Heschel, Debra Nails, Peter Ochs, Kelly Oliver, Hilary Putnam, Hava Samuelson, Norbert Samuelson, John Seery, Anthony Steinbock, Cynthia Willett.

Several colleagues invited me to share my work with their academic community. Their feedback helped with the development of my argument: Robert Abzug, Roberto Alejandro, Jeffrey Bernstein, Jeffrey Bloechl, Miriam Bodian, Zachary Braiterman, William Edelglass, Randy Friedman, Eric Nelson, Sarah Pessin, Randi Rashkover, Janet Rumfelt, Carl Sachs, Susan Shapiro, Jules Simon, Matt Story, Iain Thomson.

Jean-Claude Kuperminc, the director of the AIU (Alliance Israélite Universelle) library, was an invaluable resource. His staff in the archive assembled a box of materials that spanned the time when Levinas was the director of the ENIO (École Normale Israélite Orientale). The glimpse into this part of Levinas's life and career provided a unique perspective on his work.

During the 2011–12 academic year I had the good fortune to participate in the Copeland Colloquium at Amherst College. The year focused on this theme: "The Future of the Humanities in the Age of Instrumental Reason." No small question with no easy answers. But the discussions stayed with me long after the hour-long lunch discussions ended. This group introduced me to a set of readings and ideas I might never have encountered otherwise. I cannot express my appreciation to them enough: Jay Caplan, Jennifer Cayer, Thomas Dumm, Catherine Epstein, Anne-Lise Francois, Maria Heim, Leah Hewitt, Premesh Lalu, Ruth Miller, Andrew Poe, Austin Sarat, Teresa Shawcross, Adam Sitze, Lucia Suarez, Christopher van den Berg, Boris Wolfson. The dean of the college, Gregory Call, coordinated the fellowship, and Megan Estes coordinated everything else! We were welcomed into the Amherst community by a number of people: Roberto Alejandro, Suzanne and Chris Baxter, Shmuel Bolozky, Mary Lysakowski, Dan Gordon, Karen Remmler, Jody Rosenbloom, Susan Shapiro. My faculty sponsor, Maria Heim, was a joy to work with. Catherine Epstein and Dan Gordon warmly invited my family into their home to celebrate the cycle of Jewish holidays. Wildwood Elementary School strengthened my confidence in public schools. Sandra Brown, Cyd Champoux, Elizabeth Elder, Naihsin Kuo, and Nick Yaffe created an ideal learning environment and they graciously welcomed my children into it. The students at Wildwood never made either of my daughters feel like "the new kid."

My friends, colleagues, and students at Texas A&M have made the last five years of research and teaching more joyful than I could have imagined: Nandini Bhattacharya, Elizabeth and Eric Blodgett, Cynthia Bouton, Kimberly Brown, Karin Doerr and Rene Garcia, Marian Eide, Margaret Ezell, Jeff Engel, Kate Carte Engel, Ted George, Joe and Nancy Golsan, Micah Greenstein, Stefanie Harris, Jimmie Killingsworth, John McDermott, Patricia McDermott, Kathryn McKenzie, Mary Meagher, Claudia Nelson, Kirsten Pullen, Linda Radzik, Kristi Sweet, Jyotsna Vaid, Apostolos Vasilakis, Joan Wolf. I am especially grateful for conversations with the three colleagues who shared a fellowship semester at the Glasscock Center for Humanities Research: April Hatfield, Leah DeVun, and Robert Shandley. Jim Rosenheim, the past director of the Center, encouraged us to host an event that would be most beneficial for feedback on our work. The four outside scholars we invited provided tremendous comments and suggestions. Kathleen Perry Long offered several important suggestions. Along with Jim, Donnalee Dox, the past associate director of the Center, has supported my work since I arrived at Texas A&M. Everyone should be so lucky to have such generous colleagues. The Texas A&M philosophy department and the Women's and Gender Studies program provided financial support for this project in addition to a collegial atmosphere in which to work. My project benefited from a Faculty Development Leave in Spring 2010. Support offered by Associate Dean Mike Stephenson enabled me to complete a full draft of the manuscript. Provost Karan Watson and Antonio Cepeda-Benito and the Dean's office in the College of Liberal Arts made it possible for me to take advantage of the Copeland Colloquium Fellowship at Amherst College. Charles Johnson, the former dean of the College of Liberal Arts, provided me with a research year during which I wrote the material that formed two chapters of the book. In his position in the office of the Vice President for Research, Charlie supported my project through the Program to Enhance Scholarly and Creative Activities. Through a semester-long grant-writing workshop, the director of that workshop, Phyllis McBride, taught me how to write a grant proposal and in the process showed me what my project was about. I was the recipient of a Cornerstone Faculty Fellowship through the College of Liberal Arts, which has provided financial support for this project. My mentor, Pam Matthews, is always a source of wisdom and good humor. The students in my undergraduate philosophy of education class in Fall 2009 and my graduate seminar on Levinas in Spring 2011 helped me refine my argument.

I began working with Dee Mortensen at Indiana University Press eleven years ago when she accepted for publication the manuscript for my first book. Dee is an editor extraordinaire and I have benefited from her guidance over the years. I am delighted and privileged to work with her again. A special thanks to Nancy Lightfoot and Marvin Keenan for shepherding the manuscript through production, and my copyeditor, Hila Ratzabi, whose keen eye helped bring this manuscript to its final form. The staff at Indiana University Press produce beautiful books.

My aunt and uncle—Betsy Brill and Ken Kobre—made an otherwise dreary week in January in the AIU archive much less dreary. Mitchell Aboulafia and Cathy Kemp will always set the courage bar high and I would not wish for it to be any other way. I am fortunate to have the friendship of Constance Weaver and Alan Block, Lourdes Cantu, Cary Fraser, Valerie Loichot, Pam Roth, Lynette Wright.

My deepest gratitude is to and for my family—my husband, Dan Conway, and our children, Olivia and Evie. Dan, who is in many ways the inspiration behind this book, is a stalwart defender of those who are vulnerable. With justice always as his guide, he earns my admiration every day. Enduring many years of my working on this book, my daughters have learned that there might be nothing worse than having a mother who cares so deeply about education. The abstract work of writing about education does not translate as neatly as one might hope into the practical act of parenting. Thus, I fear the most significant lesson they have learned is that "just a minute" really means "in at least an hour." I am fortunate that they have indulged my lapses in parenting with patience, understanding, and humor. I am forever grateful for the uninterrupted time to work that my husband helps make possible. Yet, it is also the interruptions that remind me why this project was so important to me in the first place.

Abbreviations

AT   *Alterity and Transcendence.* Trans. Michael B. Smith. New York: Columbia University Press, 1999. Translation of *AeT*.

BJ   "Being Jewish." Trans. Mary Beth Mader, *Continental Philosophy Review* 40, no. 3 (July 2007): 205–210.

BPW   *Basic Philosophical Writings.* Ed. Adriaan Peperzak, Simon Critchley, and Robert Bernasconi. Bloomington: Indiana University Press, 1996.

BV   *Beyond the Verse: Talmudic Readings and Lectures.* Trans. Gary D. Mole. Bloomington: Indiana University Press, 1994. Translation of *AV*.

CPP   *Collected Philosophical Papers.* Trans. Alphonso Lingis. Pittsburgh: Duquesne University Press, 1998.

DEH   *Discovering Existence with Husserl.* Trans. R. Cohen and M. Smith. Evanston, IL: Northwestern University Press, 1998.

DF   *Difficult Freedom: Essays on Judaism.* Trans. Seán Hand. Baltimore, MD: Johns Hopkins University Press, 1990. Translation of *DL*.

EE   *Existence and Existents.* Trans. Alphonso Lingis. Pittsburgh: Duquesne University Press, 2001. Translation of *EAE*.

"Existentialism," "Existentialism and Anti-Semitism." Trans. Denis Hollier and Rosalind Krauss, *Translation (October Magazine)* 87 (Winter 1999): 27–31.

EI   *Ethics and Infinity.* Trans. Richard A. Cohen. Pittsburgh: Duquesne University Press, 1985. Translation of *EeI*.

EN   *Entre Nous. Thinking-of-the-Other.* Trans. M. Smith and B. Harshov. New York: Columbia University Press, 1998. Translation of *En*.

GCM   *Of God Who Comes to Mind.* Trans. Bettina Bergo. Palo Alto, CA: Stanford University Press, 1998. Translation of *DVI*.

GDT   *God, Death, and Time.* Trans. Bettina Bergo. Palo Alto, CA: Stanford University Press, 2000.

"Hitlerism," "Some Reflections on the Philosophy of Hitlerism." Trans. Seán Hand. *Critical Inquiry* no. 17: 63–71. "Quelques Réflexions sur la Philosophie de L'Hitlérisme," *Esprit* 2 (1934): 199-208.

HO   *Humanism of the Other.* Trans. Nidra Poller. Urbana: University of Illinois Press, 2003. Translation of *HAH*.

IR   *Is It Righteous to Be? Interviews with Emmanuel Levinas.* Ed. Jill Robbins. Stanford, CA: Stanford University Press, 2001.

ITN   *In the Time of the Nations.* Trans. Michael B. Smith. Bloomington: Indiana University Press, 1994. Translation of *HN.*

LR   *The Levinas Reader.* Ed. Seán Hand. Oxford: Basil Blackwell, 1989.

NT   *Nine Talmudic Readings.* Trans. Annette Aronowicz. Bloomington: Indiana University Press, 1994.

NTR   *The New Talmudic Readings.* Trans. R. A. Cohen. Pittsburgh: Duquesne University Press, 1999.

OB   *Otherwise Than Being or Beyond Essence.* Trans. Alphonso Lingis. Pittsburgh: Duquesne University Press, 1998. Translation of *AE.*

OE   *On Escape.* Trans. Bettina Bergo. Palo Alto, CA: Stanford University Press, 2003. Translation of *De.*

OS   *Outside the Subject.* Trans. Michael B. Smith. Stanford, CA: Stanford University Press, 1996. Translation of *HS.*

PN   *Proper Names.* Trans. Michael B. Smith. Palo Alto, CA: Stanford University Press, 1996. Translation of *NP.*

TI   *Totality and Infinity.* Trans. Alphonso Lingis. Pittsburgh: Duquesne University Press, 1969. Translation of *TeI.*

TIH   *The Theory of Intuition in Husserl's Phenomenology.* Trans. André Orianne. 2nd ed. Evanston, IL: Northwestern University Press, 1973.

TO   *Time and the Other.* Trans. Richard A. Cohen. Pittsburgh: Duquesne University Press, 1987.

UH   *Unforeseen History.* Trans. Nidra Poller. Urbana: University of Illinois Press, 2004. Translation of *IH.*

Levinas's Works in French

"L'inspiration religieuse de l'Alliance." *Paix et Droit* 15, no. 8 (October 1935): 4.

"L'actualité de Maïmonide." *Paix et Droit* no. 4 (1935): 6–7.

"La réouverture de l'Ecole Normale Israélite Orientale." *Cahiers l'Alliance Israélite Universelle* no. 9 (July 1946): 1–2.

"L'École Normale Israélite Orientale." *Cahiers de l'Alliance Israélite Universelle* no. 34 (September-October 1961): 9–10.

Unpublished correspondence in the files of the Alliance Israelite Universelle, 1962.

"M. Emmanuel Levinas invite de l'Universite Catholique de Louvain." *Cahiers de l'Alliance Isaélite Universelle* no. 139 (January 1963): 5.

AE	*Autrement qu'être ou au-delà de l'essence.* The Hague: Martinus Nijhoff, 1974.
AeT	*Altérité et transcendence.* Paris: Fata Morgana, 1995.
AV	*L'au-delà du verset.* Paris: Minuit, 1982.
CC	*Carnets de Captivité et autres inédits, Oeuvres 1.* Ed. Rodolphe Calin and Catherine Chalier. Paris: Grasset, 2010.
De	*De l'evasion.* Paris: Fata Morgana, 1982.
DL	*Difficile liberté. Essais sur le judaïsme.* 2nd ed. Paris: A. Michel, 1976.
DVI	*De Dieu qui vient à l'idée.* Paris: J. Vrin, 1982.
EAE	*De l'existence à l'existant.* 2nd ed. Paris: J. Vrin, 1978.
EDE	*En découvrant l'existence avec Husserl et Heidegger.* 3rd ed. Paris: J. Vrin, 1974.
EeI	*Ethique et infini.* Paris: Fayard, 1982.
Ej	"Être Juif." *Confluences* nos. 15–17 (1947 année 7): 253–264. Reprinted in *Cahiers d'Etude Lévinassiennes,* 2003, Numéro 1, 99–106.
En	*Entre nous. Essais sur le penser-à-l'autre.* Paris: Grasset, 1991.
HAH	*Humanisme de l'autre home.* Montpellier: Fata Morgana, 1972.
HN	*A l'heure des nations.* Paris: Éditions de Minuit, 1988.
HS	*Hors sujet.* Cognac: Fata Morgana, 1987.
IH	*Les imprévus de l'histoire.* Cognac: Fata Morgana, 1994.
NP	*Noms propres.* Montpellier: Fata Morgana, 1976.
PS	*Parole et Silence et autres conferences inédites au Collège philosophique. Ouevres 2.* Ed. Rodolphe Calin and Catherine Chalier. Paris: Grasset, 2011.
TeI	*Totalité et infini: Essai sur l'extériorité.* The Hague: Martinus Nijhoff, 1961.

LEVINAS AND THE
CRISIS OF HUMANISM

Introduction

Learning is a good medicine: but no medicine is powerful enough
to preserve itself from taint and corruption independently of defects
in the jar that it is kept in. One man sees clearly but does not see
straight: consequently he sees what is good but fails to follow it; he sees
knowledge and does not use it.

—Michel de Montaigne

[Freedom] is a philosophical problem, but philosophy does not
concern itself with children. It leaves them to pedagogy where they're
not in very good hands. Philosophy has forgotten about children.

—Bernard Schlink, *The Reader*

Responding to the atrocities of the Holocaust, the critical theorist Theodor
Adorno declares in a 1966 radio interview that "the premier demand upon all
education is that Auschwitz not happen again."[1] A provocative statement, it
is also revealing. His directive connects him to Emmanuel Levinas insofar as
each presents education as that which will—and must—mitigate the possibility
of evil that surrounds us. In so doing it also betrays the spectacular failure of
education to humanize us in spite of its promise to do so. The aim of this book
is to trace Levinas's philosophical project, which describes a radical revision of
ethical subjectivity, and the necessary role his essays on Jewish education play
in the success of that project.

*   *   *

In September 2009 I attended a conference on teaching philosophy to children, an area in which I hold a Masters of Arts and Teaching. In one session
we were asked to discuss a personal account of an ordinary university professor
who lived during Nazi Germany. This professor had not thought of the events
taking place around him as "any of his affair." Only when he heard his young son
refer to the "Jewish swine" did it occur to him that maybe he had been wrong in
his initial assessment of his responsibility. Upon moving into these small groups
we were given a set of questions to consider, including these: Why did the professor not speak out? If one person had spoken out, how could that have made
a difference? Was the professor indifferent? Is indifference wrong? If your life
is at risk, do you still have an obligation to help? The most common response,
"No, we don't have an obligation if there is a risk to life or livelihood," left me
puzzled. I tried to explain to the other participants that we do have an obliga-

tion to others even if we choose to do otherwise. I did not mean to suggest that there might not be conflicting obligations including a direct or indirect obligation to protect or feed our own families.[2] Rather, my point was that even if I save my own child, my obligation to others is not eliminated or canceled.[3]

It was nearly impossible to persuade the other participants that even when competing obligations impinge on us, there is rarely the one correct choice, if only we could reason better to find it. It was harder still to persuade them that the question at hand is not "which action is correct?" but rather "how do I defend 'my place in the sun'?" The conversation turned from competing obligations to the more difficult conversation over a perception of competing "rights." At this point, another participant and I pointed out that the language of competing rights has become conflated with competing ethical obligations, which in turn distracts us from an originary ethical responsibility for the Other. Returning our attention to this obligation for the Other motivates Emmanuel Levinas's approach to ethics.[4]

In Levinas's view, the language of rights has covered over any conception of a more basic obligation to our responsibility for another, a responsibility which Levinas claims is one from which I cannot recuse myself. It claims me prior to my ability to make a choice. For Levinas, the assumption of "my place in the sun" gives way to "whose place in the sun takes precedence?" and inevitably leads to war. Indeed, even to pose the question in this manner already frames the discussion toward life and ethics as a zero-sum game: my place in the sun is in competition with yours. His ethical project then requires us to reframe our view of subjectivity in order to draw the ethical landscape as something other than a fight for what is rightfully mine. If ethics were about developing the self in relationship to another for whom I am responsible, whose life comes before mine, my claim to that place in the sun is put into question from the start.

* * *

"How does someone develop ethically?" This question occupies the eighteenth-century philosopher Jean-Jacques Rousseau in several of his writings. In his *Second Discourse* (1755), Rousseau offers two principles of human nature as a counter to Hobbes's claim that we have only the innate sense of self-preservation. If that were the case, Rousseau concludes, we would be monsters. But we are not. He offers then a second principle, which is "an innate repugnance to see his fellow suffer."[5] But having an innate repugnance to seeing my fellow suffer will not alone keep me from being a monster in a different sense. In this essay and later in his *Social Contract* (1762), Rousseau expresses his concerns with the development of an intellect that is not anchored by a good character.

Several years after publishing his *Second Discourse*, Rousseau struggles with this same problem in *Émile* (1762), his treatise on education. Yet here, he offers an attempt at an educational project that will mitigate those concerns. I will return to *Émile* in chapter 2, but it is worth noting briefly what is at stake in this book. In the voice of the tutor, Rousseau describes the problem of moral development. He repeats his claim that we are born with an innate repugnance to suffering and he warns us that as a result of this aversion there are different possible responses to another's misery: we can pity the other person and then turn toward him in an attempt to alleviate his pain; or, we can compare ourselves to the other person, silently expressing gratitude that we are "not like her." The latter response might lead us to position ourselves so that we do not have to see her suffering.[6] For Rousseau's tutor, the task is to help the child develop the proper response to suffering so that unlike the stereotypical image of the philosopher, Émile does not sit in his study while ignoring the cries outside of those who suffer.

Like Rousseau, nearly every major philosopher in the history of philosophy, extending as far back as Plato, either wrote an independent treatise on philosophy of education or included a version of it in their larger philosophical project: in his *Republic,* Plato devoted two books solely to education, in addition to including the cave allegory, representing the education of the philosopher; Aristotle wrote the *Nicomachean Ethics,* which details the significance of the early formation of good character; Rousseau used *Émile* to complement *The Social Contract;* Kant included a catechism at the end of the *Metaphysics of Morals* in addition to writing a short treatise called *On Education;* and Hegel, influenced by Rousseau, used *Bildung,* which provides a strong developmental focus to the *Phenomenology of Spirit.* This list simply names a few examples and they are all different in their ideas about the political and about education.[7] However, what they do share is an understanding that a subject *develops* in relationship to the larger society in which the subject is situated, and moral education is a fundamental component in this development. In most cases, this means the philosopher writes a political or ethical philosophy and then provides an educational philosophy to show how that end can be achieved.

When we approach the twentieth century, the conversation between political philosophy and educational theory essentially disappears. With few exceptions, e.g., the classical American philosophers, Western philosophers no longer engaged questions regarding educational theory. Indeed, with the rise of logical positivism and a rigid definition of what counted as "truth," and by implication, philosophy, finding philosophers interested in political theory was also a difficult task.[8] This lack of interest, in turn, affected how the philosophical canon has been taught with regard to which philosophical themes are considered relevant. Scanning the course offerings in most North American philosophy departments, one might never realize that the philosophy of education, intimately related to epistemology and metaphysics, not to mention ethics and political philosophy, was given considerable attention by most figures in the history of Western philosophy.

In addition to changes in the philosophical terrain, a multitude of other factors contributed to education's disappearance from the philosophical conversation, making it nearly impossible to hang the reason for its exile on one cause.

In the late nineteenth century, we see the emergence of Normal schools, which were colleges specifically charged with training teachers. Kindergartens came into existence and the primary role of the elementary school shifted from a knowledge-based environment (as we might find in the old Latin schools) to one that emphasized nurturing children.[9] This shift, in turn, altered the role of the teacher. "Pedagogy"—a science of teaching—became far more important than imparting information or cultivating minds. With the shift in emphasis away from knowledge acquisition, the field of education also shifted from men to women in the role of the teacher. Additionally, the development of psychology into its own research discipline offered the field of education theories of learning and behavior that appeared far more useful than theories of knowledge had been. Philosophy appeared obsolete with regard to what it could offer education and, more importantly, what it could offer schools.

The reasons for the changes in the educational landscape are numerous and complicated, and most likely over-determined; it would be both impossible and irresponsible to locate these changes in one single cause. More important for my discussion in this book is that the effect was for contemporary philosophy to wash its hands, and its curriculum, of any philosophical interest in educational theory, thus removing its critical and reflective voice not only from the development of our current educational models but also from the connection educational theory might have to the development of moral subjectivity.[10] Thus, with few exceptions, philosophical moral theory describes, or applies to, adults, not children.

My original aim in pursuing a project on the philosophy of education was to bring education back into conversation with not only political theory but also philosophy more broadly. By examining these complex relationships and divergences, I could then explore what this severed relationship means in the twenty-first century where news articles about our broken educational system appear almost daily. My initial concern was less the question, "Did the philosophers 'get it right'?" than it was underscoring that the philosophers recognized the significance of the relationship between politics and education, with philosophy always mediating this relationship even if it was not explicitly articulated.

Returning to the example with which I opened this introduction, we can identify two points about ethics and making moral decisions that became apparent in the general discussion and which help us see why Levinas redefines ethics as obligation or responsibility and shifts our attention away from ethics as simply decision theory or the development of a virtuous character. First, it was clearly important that these participants believed that there was one right choice and they had made *the* right decision. Having done this, they rendered the other choice not really an option. Indeed, it was striking how much faith, if you will, they invested in reason. There is a faith that reason will tell us *the* right thing to do. Several participants simply stated that studying philosophy makes us better people. They believed that studying philosophy will not only magically lead us to all the right answers in our moral life, but will also motivate us to act on those right answers, to do the right thing.

This particular view about philosophy is neither new nor unusual. The idea that the study of philosophy, or even the humanities more generally, would fashion better people certainly circulates widely in the academy.[11] I will say more about this view in chapter 1, but we need only look to Kant, or interpretations of Kant, to see how a view that studying philosophy, understanding what the right action is, and then choosing to do that action becomes equated with and reduced to mere decision procedures—and is wholly reliant on reason. Among other mistaken beliefs, this view assumes that there is *a* right thing to do, that our obligations are neatly defined, that ethics is not messy, and that my ethical obligations can be taken care of like a "to do" list.

Second, these conference participants had, mistakenly, but not uncommonly, conflated the obligation or responsibility for another, which Levinas describes as that which is precisely not chosen, with the ethical action that one takes. Thus, once the correct action is determined and enacted, the obligation—the *one* obligation—is fulfilled. Levinas's aim in his ethical project is to tease apart the obligation that persists from the view of ethics as "good" or "right" behavior or action. In several of his writings, obligation toward the Other is described as infinite and never fulfilled. Additionally, he refers to it as "an-archic," meaning that it is has no originating principle. The obligation toward the Other remains regardless of our capability to respond and independently of other competing obligations. There is no one right ethical act in any given situation, even if we could discern what that act was, that would then remove our obligation to that person or to any other. The obligation continues; indeed, it increases.

Returning to the role of reason in this instance, we can ask after the ethical warrant that will tell someone to choose funding national health care instead of keeping his own money. That is, why would an individual accept that another's life, read here as access to that health care, is more important than, or should be privileged over, the "right" to the money he earned?[12] Why would he turn away from what he perceives as his exclusive right to his money and toward a view that he is responsible for his neighbor? What would motivate him to view money as a good, mostly because of how it can help others? Why would he turn from his own interests to the suffering of the Other? In spite of claims to the contrary, it is not clear to me that reason will deliver the one correct answer. Through an appeal to economics, pragmatics, or familial obligations, reason could easily offer a justification for either claim: self-interest or care for the Other. The answer at which we arrive and the one we choose for ourselves is already conditioned by the things we value and how we understand ourselves as subjects who are rational and free. From a Levinasian standpoint, an individual will only part with her money in the service of others (without benefit to herself, e.g., a tax break) if she has first turned toward the Other—and reason does not necessarily motivate this turn to occur.

The example with which I opened this introduction reveals that there is an underlying obligation that informs both possible choices—my self-interest or the needs of the Other. The stronger point to be made, however, is that these two "obligations" are not really obligations. One is assumed to be a "right," e.g., my right to my money—and the other is a responsibility for the Other, to give up some of that money in order for others simply to have health care, simply to live. That is, there is nothing in a discussion of competing rights that will turn one away from one's own rights and to the Other. Philosophy can point out the error in our ways of thinking; it can indicate that there might be other economic systems that are more just than the one we currently embrace; but it is not clear to me that philosophy necessarily turns us toward the Other.

The discussion of rights is already at a level of discourse that has forgotten the ethical, the face-to-face responsibility that I have for another. There is no foolproof argument that will convince everyone, or even anyone. It is not a question of the right argument, for one does not exist. As long as one's own ego is central to any discussion of the self as subject, we will simply live out a contemporary version of Hegel's Lordship and Bondage dialectic, like a very sophisticated game of chicken. As long as I see my subjectivity defined in terms of my own freedom and with my own rights as central, then any engagement with the Other will simply be a test of wills.[13] As long as the sovereignty of the ego remains central, then neither philosophy in particular nor a humanities education in general will be sufficient to change the heart.[14]

Levinas seems clear in his early writings that ethics is not to be a punctuation mark in a life otherwise dominated by a self-centered ego. Rather, this ceding of the self will define the new subjectivity. He identifies this failure to turn toward the other, to put the other first, as a crisis in humanism.[15] The solution he offers in response is a new humanism based on a subjectivity defined by ceding the egocentric status for the Other. The writings that come under the category "philosophical" describe that subjectivity and one can look primarily to *Totality and Infinity* (1961), *Otherwise than Being* (1974), and the essays collected under the title *Humanism of the Other* (1972) for the strongest descriptions of this new humanism and his description of the subject and ethical responsibility. The argument that underlies Levinas's ethical project is that our obligation toward another person makes possible the very nature of an ethical dilemma and what often appears to us as a horrifying set of choices.[16] No matter how "rightly" we might act, even to the point of saving another's life at great risk to our own, our other obligations do not disappear. They are not canceled by the choice I make, no matter how right or complicated or even impossible that choice might appear to be. I cannot walk away self-satisfied, content that

I have fulfilled my responsibility. The Levinasian point is that the obligation to the Other remains even when our own life is threatened—this is what makes ethical obligation so radical.

The subjectivity Levinas describes is not simply that we are fundamentally intersubjective. In chapter 4, I demonstrate that the strict phenomenological reading of Levinas's account of subjectivity, which arrives at a view of intersubjectivity, is not sufficient to yield his version of ethical responsibility. The phenomenological argument alone is not enough to arrive at the normative claim made on me by the other. Levinas's ethical relation cannot, as others have argued, be captured by the argument that without the Other I would have no world or that the Other's value lies in making it possible for me to have a world at all. This position simply does not get us to the normative dimension; indeed, this language worries me.

The focus on "my having a world" sounds too much like Heideggerian ontology. To say that the Other has value because the Other makes it possible for me even to have a world is simply to argue for a phenomenological ontology that establishes intersubjectivity as a ground. I do not disagree with this claim. I disagree with the view that this intersubjectivity automatically yields the normative claim of responsibility. Levinas wants an ethical relation that is prior to my even having a world. To say that the Other has "value" for me is *not* equivalent to my having a responsibility for the Other. I can certainly acknowledge that without the Other I do not have a world, but there is nothing in this realization that necessarily assumes I must also have responsibility for the Other as Levinas understands that term. The view of subjectivity and ethical responsibility that Levinas describes is much stronger than this version. It is not simply a command not to kill the Other but to cede one's own ego to the Other—this is the move that would compel the master to give up the slave as such.[17] Levinas is less interested in a view of intersubjectivity that states: "I have a world because I am a person in relation with others," than he is in a view of asymmetrical responsibility such that the subject says: "I am responsible for you to the point of ceding my own rights."

Before all the other worries get announced, let's remember that this is the ethical, in Levinas's sense of the term, and *not* the political, which he also idiosyncratically characterizes more generally in terms of decision, deliberation, mediation, rationality, philosophy, ontology, and so forth. This ceding of my ego is a subjectivity that is prior to sexual difference, class, race, etc. It is not that we do not need to worry, nor that we should not worry about what this kind of ethics means if actually put into practice. Certainly, different people from different backgrounds, of different sexes and races and classes, will hear this obligation differently. To women and people of color, it will sound like the same old story, adding insult to injury. Yet, if Levinas's distinction between ethics and politics means anything, if his claim that the ethical Other comes before ontology is to mean anything, then we cannot invoke the problems involved in our current political practices to mitigate the radical obligation of the ethical that he intends.

* * *

If the question I posed earlier, "How does one develop ethically?" occupies much of moral education, the more specific question, "How does someone develop so that they turn toward the suffering of another?" haunts Levinas's ethical project. My work on the educational philosophy of several thinkers, including Rousseau, Dewey, and Nietzsche, prompted me to think about Levinas's own relationship to education. I recalled that Levinas's philosophical writing continually references teaching, creating images that often serve as moral examples, and he frequently deploys scriptural references, which serve a pedagogical function. I remembered that for thirty years following his release from the POW camp and his subsequent return to Paris, he served as the director of the Jewish day school run by the Alliance Israélite Universelle (AIU). During that time, he penned several essays on Jewish education in which we are given a bit more information than what we find in his philosophical writings. In these essays, he specifically identifies the new humanism as Jewish—biblical. He not only tells us that this subject can be achieved—that is, learned—but he also adds that the method by which this subject can and should be cultivated is through Jewish education, specifically learning Hebrew and a robust education in Talmud.[18]

I admit that even with my own abiding interest in education, I delayed reading these essays. I assumed that their focus was general curricular issues regarding the Jewish day school Levinas directed and therefore they would not have much philosophical significance or relevance to my questions. When I finally did read them, I realized that my initial assumption could not have been more incorrect. Throughout these essays, Levinas addresses a wide range of political themes: his concerns about assimilation, his critique of liberalism, and his call for a new humanism. He offers the return to a robust Jewish education—studying Talmud and learning Hebrew—as the relief from these concerns. I will discuss the specifics of this kind of education later in the book, but it is worth mentioning here that for Levinas, the Talmud, which includes the interpretations that the rabbis offer, and the Bible focus the reader's attention toward the Other. Additionally, this form of education is dependent on the community in several ways.

First, knowledge is produced in the smaller community of Jewish education, whether it is a yeshiva or Jewish study group. The view within Jewish education is that talmudic knowledge comes about through discussion with others, not as an insight that happens in solitary study. Second, the larger community of Judaism is the benefactor of the knowledge that is produced. Interpretations about talmudic law, for example, will have a direct bearing on the practices of the Jewish community. Finally, the talmudic commentaries and the midrashim demonstrate the complexity of both ethics and politics. Both are infinite tasks that require a subjectivity turned toward the Other and a sophisticated mind to engage the many possible ways to approach that responsibility.[19]

In these essays, he pleads with his Jewish audience to allow the Alliance and its school to shift their mandate from its original secular focus to one that is more overtly religious.[20] The political concerns he addresses, many of which are still relevant today, resonated with themes I had seen in much of his philosophical writing, most notably in the essays collected in *Humanism of the Other*. However, when I read these essays in tandem with his philosophical writings, I noticed they were profoundly similar with regard to his critique of modern humanism. The connection that Levinas drew between the political crises he identifies and the educational solution he offers brought me full circle to my original interest in that relationship found throughout the history of philosophy. Yet, where the other philosophers had failed in their attempts to uncover an adequate educational philosophy suitable to its complementary political theory, Levinas appeared to have succeeded.[21]

It is worth noting that in the past ten years the scholarship on Levinas's Jewish writings, especially by philosophers, has grown considerably. Yet, the uncertain status of the relationship of Levinas's Jewish texts to his larger philosophical project persists. Additionally, with a few notable exceptions, the scholarship that addresses his essays on Jewish education and his own time as an educator in a Jewish day school remains virtually non-existent.[22] Although Levinas's explicit references to education are numerous, they are scattered and brief. That is, they typically appear in his philosophical work without much development.

There are nonetheless several facts of his biography that attest to his deep and sustained commitment to education that are worth citing together: his dedicated attendance, from 1957 and for almost thirty years after, at the annual conferences on talmudic texts at the Colloquia of the French Jewish Intellectuals, where he presented his unique readings of select talmudic texts; his association, beginning in 1930, with the Alliance Israélite Universelle du Bassin Méditerranéen, an organization whose goal was to foster Jewish education in the Mediterranean and North African countries; and in 1946, his appointment as director of the École Normale Israélite Orientale, a branch of the Alliance, which trained teachers of Jewish education in France. Finally, he wrote several essays between the early 1950s and the mid-1970s devoted to the theme of education and the problems of assimilation, which were eventually published in a collection under the title *Difficult Freedom: Essays on Judaism*.

These essays on Jewish education were written not only during his thirty-three years as director of the École Normale Israélite Orientale, but also long after he left the ENIO and was a university professor. They mirror themes in Levinas's philosophical project from the 1960s, which we could argue he was developing at the same time that the majority of these essays were written. Additionally, the concerns expressed most explicitly in the essays on Jewish education parallel the concerns he expressed in several writings before the war, most notably the 1934 essay, "Reflections on the Philosophy of Hitlerism," and the one immediately following it in 1935, which was published in English as *On Escape*. That is, his essays on Jewish education mirror the same suspicion he has of Western or European man—even that which he calls the philosopher—found in his other writings, both Jewish and philosophical.

Writing these essays in France, only a few years after being released from a German labor camp, Levinas addresses similar concerns in his essays on Jewish education to those expressed by Franz Rosenzweig, writing forty years prior. However, Levinas's tone reflects an urgency that is absent from Rosenzweig's essays and it is not clear that his answer is the same. I will return to this point later in the book. Levinas entered France when the residue of the Dreyfus Affair still lingered.[23] He returned to France after the murderous years of World War II, and believed first and foremost that strengthening Jewish education in France was of the utmost concern. The original publication venue of the essays on Jewish education indicates that at times they were intended for an audience of Jewish educators and at other times they were directed at French Jewish intellectuals. Their purpose was, on the one hand, to convince their audience of the need to return to a traditional model of Jewish education, specifically, a model that includes instruction in Hebrew language and literature and, on the other, to reassure this audience that "returning" to Jewish education did not mean turning away from French culture and modern life—the original mandate of the Alliance.

These essays are written contemporaneously with several essays in which Levinas argues for Judaism's universalism. Read together, they ask us to consider both the peculiar nature of Judaism and its potential for a universal application. There is a dimension of Judaism, Levinas argues, that is universal and this dimension is also what makes Judaism uniquely Jewish.[24] Thus, while Jewish education hopes to succeed in maintaining that which makes Judaism unique, it is clear from Levinas's writings on Judaism in general that he believes the ethical impulse that is fundamentally and uniquely expressed in Judaism applies to everyone. These essays on Jewish education also indicate that he sees something unique in the way that Jewish education works—with regard to both content and method—and that the cultivation of those who would be a light unto the nations (Isaiah) had been neglected. More significantly, we find many of Levinas's strongest political statements in these essays. He laments the loss of Jewish education not simply because this might signal the loss of Judaism, but because the loss of Judaism would be a loss for the world. The loss of Judaism and Jewish education puts both Judaism and the world at risk in their confrontation with evil.

Yet, in spite of Levinas's dedication to Jewish education—e.g., as principal of the ENIO, publishing numerous articles on the role of Jewish education as a response to the crisis he has identified, and presenting his talmudic lectures—

scholars have paid scant attention to this chapter of his biography and the implications his interest in education might have for his larger philosophical project. This book returns to Levinas's relationship to education first expressed in these very early essays, which were published only a few years after his release from the German POW camp and his return to France. I argue that Levinas's diagnosis of the problem is a "crisis of humanism," which finds its seeds in modernity but comes to fruition in the inhumanities of the twentieth century. These inhumanities, Levinas would say, signify a violence toward the Other that is of a wholly different order from those that preceded them.

Like his predecessors, Levinas offers an educational model as a solution, but here the model—Jewish education—is significantly different from those offered by, for example, Rousseau and Nietzsche. It is crucial to understand what distinguishes Levinas from these other philosophers of education. Simultaneous with his turn to Jewish education, Levinas also identifies the need for a different subjectivity than has been cultivated through modernity. In his writings on Jewish education, he tethers the development of this subjectivity to the return to Jewish education, which includes a sustained relationship with the Hebrew language and the Talmud. Levinas's proposed solution, which he develops in these essays, is not only original, but it also allows his readers a glimpse of the fundamental role that education plays in his larger philosophical project—one that I would argue is indispensable to its coherence and its success.

Levinas's essays pressed me to reflect on the following question: What is the significance of these essays on Jewish education for his larger philosophical project in which he transforms the traditional conception of subjectivity? If this question motivates the present book, the following line of reasoning guides it: Levinas identifies a crisis of humanism in both his philosophical writings and his writings on Judaism. He describes the crisis in the same way. In both sets of writings he believes that the humanism modernity produced, one which leads us to believe we are each free, autonomous, and hold a privileged place in the sun, led to the cascade of inhumanities we experienced in the twentieth century. Reading against the conventional interpretations of his work, I make two claims: first, that Levinas indeed wants to secure ethical obligation; and, second, that a particular form of education will prepare one to be open to the face of the Other *and* respond to it, even if, as I acknowledge, he intentionally leaves open or unanswered *how* one is to respond.[25]

Levinas locates ethics—indeed, he locates the originary moment of humanism—in the Jewish tradition and thus argues that Jewish education is the source for producing this humanism. He argues for a new subjectivity—or rather a return to an old subjectivity whose roots are found in the ancient biblical tradition. The subjectivity he has in mind is the one that characterizes the group of people who accept the Torah at Sinai, the one willing to give up the sovereignty of the ego who will take on those commandments, which he reads simply as different iterations of turning toward the Other. If the formation of subjectivity is found in how we raise and educate our children, then only a new way of educating them will deliver this new subjectivity.

Why would Levinas emphasize a new humanism that is based on Judaism and why would he promote Jewish education as the mechanism to develop this humanism? We could reply that he is speaking to a Jewish audience, so of course he would do that. But in fact his audience comprised secular Jews. In advocating a more religiously motivated Jewish education he risked alienating himself from the secular Jewish community. He took a chance when he pressed his new view of humanism, which he not only argued is "old" insofar as he locates its origins in the Torah, but also that it is cultivated through a talmudic education. We can disagree about the accuracy of his conception of Jewish humanism and we can question both the necessity and the sufficiency of Jewish education as the means to achieve this humanism, but that he holds these views seems clear.

Levinas's writings on Jewish education, in which he makes his case for his Jewish readers to return to a deeper relationship to Jewish education, provide substantial support for my argument. We will see that the problems that he identifies in these essays on Jewish education are the same problems he identifies in his philosophical writings—he is searching for and describing a new subjectivity, a radical subject that complements his hyperbolic ethics. The asymmetrical ethical relationship is such because the subject always already puts the Other before himself. The ego is subordinated to the Other. In the essays on Jewish education, he clearly identifies this kind of subjectivity with Judaism—Judaism's aim is to produce this subject and he sees this point pervading the biblical narratives and the talmudic commentary. If we follow his line of reasoning found throughout his writings, that "being Jewish" is to be contrasted to "being Western" (European, which can also be read as philosophical, rational, etc.), then the educational system that yields that Western subject—defined as rational, solitary, independent, and virile—must be changed. If the solution to the "crisis" that Levinas proposes for his Jewish audience is a return to Jewish education, which will include learning Hebrew and studying Talmud, what then is the solution for the "Western" individual? What is his aim in his philosophical essays? How do we distinguish between philosophical reason and ethical wisdom?

* * *

If returning to a deeper relationship to Judaism and renewed Jewish subjectivity, which Levinas identifies as a self which puts the Other before it, is the solution to the crisis of humanism that he offers in the writings on Jewish education and if this same subject is the one described in his philosophical project, then how are we to read his continued references to teaching, his midrashic use of scriptural references, and the general rhetorical thrust of his overall philosophical project? Might we need to take them more seriously—read here as "normatively"—than we have up to this point? Nearly all scholars who have looked through any of Levinas's writings notice that he uses a trope, metaphor, or analogy of teaching throughout his work. Building on my first claim that the educational writings offer a solution to the crisis of humanism that he develops in his writings on Judaism, I argue that this emphasis on education is not confined to the Jewish writings. To the contrary, his repeated references to teaching and his emphasis on education provide coherence for the philosophical project itself and the questions that project raises.

Even a cursory reading of Levinas's writings reveals how they enact or perform a kind of pedagogical function. For example, his reading of Cain generates several questions regarding the nature of education. We can begin with Cain's own moral education. What could or should he have known? Is this something he should have known regardless of what he was taught? Is he capable of learning something otherwise? There is also the layer of our education as readers of Levinas's work: what do *we* learn when we read Levinas reading Cain? What are we asked to consider? How does Levinas's description of ethical subjectivity bear on us as readers? What conclusions do we draw and how do we arrive at them? We can see, then, why he turns to the biblical narratives as illustrations of his philosophical argument. In any number of places Levinas refers to midrash as an example of what he calls the Saying, that which remains unthematized. The Talmud emphasizes the numerous voices and interpretations that *necessarily* emerge from the text. The questions that Levinas's reference raises mimic the same questions that the rabbis raised in the midrashim. In this approach, Levinas engages his readers in a multi-dimensional educational journey.[26]

At the intersection of his writings on Jewish education and his philosophical work, we find a series of questions: What is the significance of this pervasive reference to teaching in his philosophical work? If the philosophical writings rely on an educational method to cultivate this new subjectivity, and if this educational method is not specifically Jewish, then how might this educational model look? If Levinas believes in this kind of power for an educational model, what might his ethical project and his insights with regard to education offer our contemporary methods of schooling, if, as I contend, one contributing factor to the problems that our schools currently face is precisely the subject that is produced by those schools? If it needs to accomplish something similar to what Jewish education, as Levinas conceives it, accomplishes, then might this educational model offer something of value to public schools in the United States?[27]

Levinas's ethical subjectivity would call for a new, or at least a radically different educational model from those currently deployed in the West. The intersection between childhood education and the creation of the subject who is independent, rational, and free is the focus on the self and one's own ego first. This subject is formed through education. Levinas believes that the subject can be formed differently, for it is not reason and introspection that will lead an ego, centered on itself, to the Other. If his claims about education are correct, then his argument suggests that we must look to our own failures as a nation in our attempts to educate our children. We must consider the roots of democratic education, child-centered education, and most importantly the so-called secular humanism that informs most schooling, but in particular, public schooling.[28]

In Levinas's view, the humanism of modernity has its roots in ancient Judaism. In a sense, then, we are all—or, rather, we all have the potential to be—Jewish. That is, for Levinas, Judaism has a universal dimension and it takes the form of an ethical subjectivity that is turned toward the other—a subjectivity that he believes is in stark contrast to the subject produced by modern European thought. Thus, his philosophical project describes an ethical responsibility and a human subjectivity that are also essentially Jewish in Judaism's universal expression. By making this claim, Levinas pulls out the roots of a philosophical prejudice that reserves universality for a certain type of Christianity while relegating Judaism to the realm of the purely particular.[29] Judaism maintains the tension—or balance—between particularity and universality. What Levinas seems to be searching for is a way to educate, a way to return to this old subjectivity so that ethics can live with politics, the particular can live with the universal, and that this tension will be productive. For Levinas it is not enough that the Jews deepen their relationship to their religion and reclaim the ethical impulse that he sees as uniquely Jewish, although this is his position in the essays on Jewish education. The world must eventually change. If it is the case, then, that we are all to "become 'Jewish,'" the next logical question to ask is "How is this to happen?" The answer, again, lies in considering Jewish education in relationship to Levinas's philosophical project.

I am not arguing that we should all attend Jewish schools. Rather, I argue that the role of teaching, pedagogy, and education plays a role in his project on multiple levels and in multiple registers. My claim, however, is stronger than simply acknowledging that teaching plays a role in his philosophical project. My aim in this book is to demonstrate that at the same time that Levinas's philosophy is descriptive, *the ethical subject that he describes assumes being educated or taught* in a manner that is wholly otherwise to how children are reared in the Western tradition and that the ethics he describes is dependent on a new way of educating our children (which in this context includes intellectual development). If the different parts of Levinas's corpus are read and thought of together, his project offers us not only a new way to think about subjectivity and ethics, but also a new way to think about education in light of the political tension between the universal and particular to which he attends.

The question, then, that guides me in this present work is "Why does Levinas turn specifically to Jewish education?" which includes the Jewish sacred texts? Is it not the case, in light of certain beliefs about a humanities education exerting a humanizing influence, that it can accomplish the task of cultivating humanity in the way that Levinas hopes?[30] Is it not the case that Shakespeare's writings could just as easily replace the Jewish sacred texts? Conversely, what does it mean that Levinas makes this case to the Jewish audience but does not offer a comparable discussion in his philosophical writing? That is, if this humanism is learned or cultivated, and if this cultivation is best done through Jewish education, what does it mean that it is offered only to Jews? Is the implication that Jews need this education and non-Jews do not?

If we follow the contours of Levinas's critique of liberalism and his promotion of the Jewish sources, then it would be odd, to say the least, that he thinks Jewish children were in *more* need than non-Jews of attaining this humanism. That is, it would be odd if he thought Jewish children were somehow more morally deficient than non-Jewish children. If that is not the reason he does not provide a comparable education for non-Jews, then what is? Why have any education at all? If it is the case that in *Totality and Infinity* he is only describing how we already are but in the practice of our daily lives we are simply mistaken about who we are, having covered over our responsibility for the Other—we are intersubjective but we just think we are isolated atoms—then what purpose would *Jewish* education serve? Would Jews be somehow less willing or able to believe this philosophical point about themselves than someone simply reading *Totality and Infinity*? Why the call for talmudic education? Why compel a community of young people to slog through years of studying Talmud and learning Hebrew when they could just read Hegel to learn this particular lesson?

His reasons for turning to Jewish education as that which will deliver the ethical subject reveal a similar suspicion to the ones which Rousseau admits: an abiding concern regarding intellectual reasoning unbounded by an ethical character. As much as he admired Shakespeare's literary genius, and even though he frequently references other literary works that resonate with the ethical subject he describes, Levinas does not appear to believe that Shakespeare's texts, for example, can do the work that is accomplished by the Jewish sacred texts, in part because he positions the Jewish sacred texts *within the larger context of a Jewish education,* which includes not only reading a certain set of texts but also a particular pedagogical style. Levinas believes that a humanities education "works" if one can assume that it is hitched to an education in which a particular kind of subjectivity has already developed. As a result, haunting all these discussions about the humanities and humanistic education, like the vulgar uncle no one wants to invite to Thanksgiving but who nonetheless always shows up, is the dispute between religion and secularity in the development of either ethical behavior or political citizenship.

Levinas turns to Jewish education not only because he is cultivating a different subjectivity from one he believes is delivered by a non-Jewish education, but also because this subjectivity is a more radical ethics than other scholars acknowledge. I argue that the philosophical work provides a phenomenological description of the adult subject who has gone through an educational process—Jewish or not—that cultivated this kind of humanism.[31] If he turns to Jewish education to cultivate this ethical obligation and if the philosophical writings appear in a philosophical register directed at a secular audience, or at least an audience that is not necessarily Jewish, then does his argument imply that everyone needs this form of education, a model of education comparable to what he believes Jewish education provides? My quick answer to this is yes, a new education is needed, but for particular, indeed, Jewish reasons, he will not prescribe it for anyone outside the Jewish community.[32] In his view, those who are part of the Jewish community accept a set of social or community values and practices based on certain shared views about its history. One of these practices is Jewish education. Levinas can appeal to the Jewish community to return to Jewish education because its members share a belief in its significance to that community. And, as we will see in chapter 4, he can appeal to the covenant at Sinai as the ground or source of this new humanism, because acceptance of that covenant, whether "real" or not, lies in the background of and guides the Jewish community.

If my interpretation of Levinas's philosophical project is correct, then he has provided us with a new way to think about not only ethics, but also education. This book, then, asks its readers to consider three points. The first is to consider the relationship of Levinas's essays on Jewish education, written while he was the director of the École Normale Israélite Orientale, to his ethical-philosophical project as a whole. The second is to consider the role of the scriptural references throughout his philosophical project and the pedagogical function these references play. In light of the first two points, the third point asks the readers to move beyond the boundaries of his project and to consider our own educational process, the political context in which this educational process occurs, and the young people whose cultivation is determined by how we understand the intersection of education and the political.

This book demonstrates that the function of Levinas's philosophical project is in part to persuade his readers, to persuade those outside of the community of Israel, that this subjectivity, this new humanism, is for everyone. He believes that this humanism is Jewish in origin, that it is the unique gift to humanity for which Judaism was created, and he believes that Jewish education is the means by which this humanism is cultivated.[33] My goal in this book is to reinvigorate questions about the relationship between education and the political. Can—or should—any line be drawn to connect education to the political? If not, then we need to rethink the relationship education has to the polis. If so, then we must ask if this role compromises the other aims of education. Can we educate for the ethical subjectivity that Levinas describes? And if so, can we achieve this end while also liberating and enflaming the mind? That is, his turn to Jewish education reflects his view that our ethical relation to the Other is at once cultivated while also *not* an anti-intellectual view. My aim is to draw out the connection that Levinas himself makes—the liberation and cultivation of the mind as intellectually acute is deeply connected not only to being open to the suffering of the Other but also to doing something about that suffering.

Insofar as one adopts this view of subjectivity, that person participates in the universal dimension of Judaism. Identifying several distinct features of talmudic study, he promotes a certain kind of Jewish education as the best way to achieve this humanism. In the last part of this book, I offer some examples of what might resemble parts of talmudic study, but none of these models are exactly parallel to it, leaving each deficient in some way. Like Levinas, I do not believe that it is my place to prescribe a particular kind of education that would, in theory, replace the models that are currently in practice. Yet it is clear that if his readers are persuaded by his view of subjectivity, then we have an obligation to change the educational models that persist in cultivating a subjectivity that runs counter to the one that he describes. In the end, we must each decide if we agree with his position and then we must figure out what comes next.

* * *

Before beginning the book, let me put some cards on the table. In my previous book I brought into conversation Levinas's philosophical writings and his writings on Judaism in order to explore the meaning and function of his use of the "feminine." I have heard the many arguments offered in support of maintaining the segregation of these bodies of writings. However, I view this segregation as not only unproductive but also as a contributing factor in the misunderstandings of and frequently hostile responses to readings that are radically different from one's own. In my own experience, it is the scholars who stand firmly against bringing the two bodies of writing into conversation with each other who have been the least receptive to and most dismissive of these alternative interpretations.

Contrary to a position that many Levinas scholars would hold, I maintain that not only is there a productive conversation to be had when these bodies of writings are engaged, but also that the Jewish writings are misnamed as a body of writing. Many of the ideas Levinas expresses in these essays are written in a secular register—and that would make sense since many in his audience are non-religious Jews. That said, I wish to be forthcoming and acknowledge that I take the writings on Judaism seriously. I do not think they are simply ancillary to his philosophical project; I believe instead that they lie at the center of and disclose what he believes most firmly. After reading Levinas's writings for nearly twenty years, I have arrived at a point in my thinking where I believe that Levinas wants something stronger than what many other Levinas scholars interpret him to want with regard to his ethical project. I believe this difference in interpretation emerges not only from reading texts differently, but also from reading different texts.

1 The Limits of the Humanities

The school is the essential distributing agency for whatever values and
purposes any social group cherishes. It is not the only means, but it is
the first means, the primary means and the most deliberate means by
which the values that any social group cherishes, the purposes that it
wishes to realize, are distributed and brought home to the thought, the
observation, judgment and choice of the individual.

—John Dewey, *Philosophy of Education*

No sane citizenry measures its public elementary schools by whether
they pay for themselves immediately and in dollars. We shouldn't
have to make a balance-sheet argument for the humanities, either,
at least not until the balance-sheet includes the value, to the student
and to the state, of expanded powers of personal empathy and cross-
cultural respect, improved communication through language and
other symbolic systems, and increased ability to tolerate and interpret
complexity, contemplate morality, appreciate the many forms of
artistic beauty, and generate creative, independent thought.

—Robert Watson

In his book *The Last Professors: The Corporate University and the Fate of the
Humanities,* Frank Donoghue, an English professor at The Ohio State University, traces the roots of the corporate model of education back to the turn of the
twentieth century, the rise of industrialization, and the increased power attained
by those with wealth. It was not long before the newly moneyed were exerting
power and influence over university education, while simultaneously expressing
their suspicion of the very education they were funding. As Donoghue's analysis shows, education that did not aim to produce anything—that is, humanities
education—was rejected in favor of something—anything—utilitarian. Stanley
Fish, Donoghue's former teacher, comments on the book's argument, and his
comments are worth citing at length:

> In previous columns and in a recent book I have argued that higher education,
> properly understood, is distinguished by the absence of a direct and designed
> relationship between its activities and measurable effects in the world.
> This is a very old idea that has received periodic re-formulations. Here is
> a statement by the philosopher Michael Oakeshott that may stand as a repre-

sentative example: "There is an important difference between learning which is concerned with the degree of understanding necessary to practice a skill, and learning which is expressly focused upon an enterprise of understanding and explaining."

Understanding and explaining what? The answer is understanding and explaining anything as long as the exercise is not performed with the purpose of intervening in the social and political crises of the moment, as long, that is, as the activity is not regarded as instrumental—valued for its contribution to something more important than itself.

This view of higher education as an enterprise characterized by a determined inutility has often been challenged, and the debates between its proponents and those who argue for a more engaged university experience are lively and apparently perennial. The question such debates avoid is whether the Oakeshottian ideal (celebrated before him by Aristotle, Kant and Max Weber, among others) can really flourish in today's educational landscape. It may be fun to argue its merits (as I have done), but that argument may be merely academic—in the pejorative sense of the word—if it has no support in the real world from which it rhetorically distances itself. In today's climate, does it have a chance?

In a new book, "The Last Professors: The Corporate University and the Fate of the Humanities," Frank Donoghue (as it happens, a former student of mine) asks that question and answers "No."[1]

If we recall the question I posed in the Introduction, "How does one develop ethically?" we can see how Fish's commentary on the humanities assumes a new relevance. This question remains central in education circles and in discussions about moral psychology. Questions about moral development, particularly with regard to formal education, are in turn often conflated with questions about the development of the citizen. As a result, the role of the intellect, and in particular, political judgment, comes into play and frequently muddies the discussion.

With the most recent attacks on the humanities at universities around the world, faculty members who teach in these disciplines search for ways to defend these fields in higher education. Although one can look back through history, to as far back as Plato, and see that there has never been a time when the humanities enjoyed an unchallenged existence, each time period reads as if the crisis of the humanities in that time is the worst yet. The response to the attacks on the humanities in the last few years pressed faculty and scholars once again to defend the humanities; this time, however, faculty invoked the very language used to attack the humanities and that now permeates the academy: value. Where the humanities were once viewed suspiciously because of what people realized it did, now the public demands its ouster from the university because it does not believe the humanities do anything—or rather, anything of use. In response, many of those who come to its defense argue vehemently that the humanities are central to moral and civic education.

When we think about education and the role that it plays in the formation of a self, the education to which we refer is some form of humanities education, even if it comprises a less sophisticated set of materials than those we imagine in a college curriculum. The raging battle over the soul of education is often motivated by the fears people have precisely because of what they imagine the humanities do. Those who believe the humanities are "useless" and lack any value at the same time reveal their fears regarding the dangers of the humanities, and in so doing, they attribute a power—whether real or imagined—to the humanities. The humanities cannot be both wholly useless, even if it is valueless to a particular group of people, and also capable of, for example, brainwashing. I would argue then that at the root of all this debate is actually a fear of what the humanities do accomplish—founded or not—rather than a belief that the humanities do not do anything. These critics often accuse the professoriate for politicizing the university and seemingly brainwashing students into its left-wing ideologies. These Philistine critics thus believe the humanities to be valueless because they do not do what they believe education should be doing: i.e., training students for a particular job.[2] They believe the humanities to be dangerous because in addition to being useless they can lead intelligent young people to ask questions that these critics do not want them to ask. In the end, they want the university education on the cheap in two senses of this term: they do not want to have to pay for it and they do not want students to have to learn anything that shakes their deepest convictions. Thus, we might reframe the question to be asked conversely: why should the public support a humanities education especially when its effects are perceived so negatively?

The fundamental question regarding humanities education can be stated in this way: Does humanities education have any value outside of the intellectual pleasure it gives to those who engage in it? How this question is answered yields a series of other questions. Ultimately, these questions ask after the fate of the university and those who teach the humanities in it.[3] This question has political implications for many reasons, not the least of which is that many colleges and universities are publicly funded and have a responsibility to answer to the constituency that supports them. Why should the public, or anyone, support the liberal arts in higher education if only those engaged in the liberal arts feel its effects?

Within the first six months of 2010, a flurry of books on education—addressing both primary and higher education—emerged with the goal of telling us precisely where in fact we have gone wrong and what we should do now. A survey of these books appeared in Stanley Fish's blog entry on June 10th, 2010, titled, "A Classical Education: Back to the Future."[4] Fish begins his piece by reminiscing about his high school ring, which he had worn for nearly forty years. His reminiscence was, in part, tied to attending his fifty-fifth high school reunion a few weekends before writing this entry. In this piece, Fish recalls the curriculum of the high school he attended, appropriately named Classical High School. As the name suggests, its curriculum was based on a classical education. And lest anyone protest that such an education was only for rich, privileged white males, Fish quickly contests this point with his statement that his classmates comprised all walks of life—including children of non-English-speaking immigrants.

The three books that Fish surveys are Martha Nussbaum's *Not for Profit: Why Democracy Needs the Humanities,* Diane Ravitch's *The Death and Life of the Great American School System,* and Leigh Bortins's *The Core: Teaching Your Child Foundations of Classical Education.* To their credit, all three books are thoughtful, and Ravitch in particular is to be commended for publicly admitting that her previous views on education were mistaken. Where Bortins and Ravitch focus on the primary grades, Nussbaum's book complements them by focusing on the connection that higher education, specifically one focused on the humanities, has to pre-college schooling. Most importantly, as Fish points out, what they all share is a focus on teaching and learning, and not testing and assessment, and all those other words that have become the vocabulary of administrators at all levels of education.[5]

I recognize that for the most part, education in the primary grades has a different set of goals than those viewed as part of higher education and I realize that the conversation can quickly become confused if we conflate these very different kinds of education. Yet, it is worth considering education theoretically, regardless of its level. It is worth noting that while the aims of pre-college education might differ from its higher education counterpart, the two are nonetheless intimately related. Often that which drives higher education influences how pre-college curricula are structured.

The questions I address in this chapter also trace the edges of this entire book: What do the humanities do? Do the humanities have the power attributed to them? If so, is this an effect that can or should be controlled and manipulated?[6] If humanities education does have value outside of its self-enclosed idiosyncratic pleasure, the question becomes even more pressing. What is its value? How do we identify it? And what do we do about those who fear it, where the object of the fear is simply the opening and developing of the mind? These questions, as Fish suggests, are indeed perennial, and he echoes Donoghue's observation that our current discussions imply a false sense of history about the relative health of the humanities across universities in the United States.[7]

Recalling Rousseau's distrust of community, we are reminded that these more contemporary suspicions of community and education did not begin in the nineteenth century.[8] Yet Rousseau was careful to separate the education of the citizen from the education of the "man" qua male, the latter of which included moral development. Indeed, for Rousseau, the development of the ethical person was central to the proper development of the political citizen, even if he saw the two tasks as separate. I will return to this point in more detail in the next chapter, yet it is worth noting that taken together, these two questions about moral and civic development lie at the heart of debates about the role, purpose, aim, and value of education.[9]

Additionally, while inherently significant, these questions point to a more basic question about the aim of education: What is the role education plays in the cultivation of a self, and more specifically, in the cultivation of a moral self? This question about the humanities guides Levinas in his essays on Jewish education. If the humanities are indeed successful at cultivating a virtuous self, then why turn to Jewish education? Is Jewish education just one kind of humanities education or does Levinas see it as a difference of kind? The aim of this chapter is to examine the limits of the humanities and humanistic education in order to examine Levinas's emphasis on Jewish education within that context. This chapter explores two prominent models of education whose impact can still be seen in the United States at both the university and pre-college level: the conservative model described by Hannah Arendt, which is positioned against the progressive model originally advanced by John Dewey.

Thus with regard to the question of humanities education and its relationship to the cultivation of character and the development of civic responsibility, we find, on one side of the debate, Hannah Arendt, who argues that education is not political and is not intended to effect change. Rather, its aim is to introduce the child into the world in which he or she is born, thus enabling that child to participate in the public sphere when she is an adult. The role of a classical education then is to introduce the child to those traditions and ideas that inform the world in which the child now lives. Although Arendt's political philosophy is often viewed as unclassifiable by conventional categories in political theory, having positioned herself against progressive education, her own view of education is decidedly conservative.

On the other side of this debate, we find another extreme put forth by Martha Nussbaum in her recent book *Not for Profit*. Where Arendt believed that education was not intended to mold in any particular fashion, Nussbaum takes up the mantle of progressive education and deploys it to promote an educational project that she believes will create more people who are better suited to participate as democratic citizens. For her, this means creating more people who will live with each other in mutual respect and fewer who will seek comfort in domination. Ironically, both turn to a classical education in the humanities to serve their respective ends. It is worth considering these two extremes in order to see where the flaws in these views lie.[10] My discussion is not meant to be an exhaustive analysis of moral education or civic engagement, nor do I intend to review the enormous body of literature that examines the possible role of humanities education in the cultivation of either.[11] Rather, my aim is to highlight and examine the claims that are prevalent in these discussions in order to consider how these views have shaped the complex relationship we have to and the expectations we have of our educational system at all its levels.[12] In particular, these questions point specifically to the humanities and humanities education of which philosophy is typically emblematic.[13]

Instead of providing an exhaustive account of American education, which would include its ambivalent relationship to the humanities and humanistic education, I highlight the tensions in these two opposing models of education.[14] In both of these models, the respective proponents argue that each is necessary for the creation of an active, productive, politically engaged citizenry. In Nussbaum's account, the humanities are offered as the savior to democracies around the world. This account of the humanities and its relationship to a democratic society carries its own set of questions. More importantly for this book, it relies on an assumption about the role of the humanities in the creation of a virtuous or morally upright self that Levinas finds questionable on multiple levels. The role of the humanities in the development of an ethical person is significant for my present discussion since Levinas turns to Jewish education and decidedly not to a classical humanities education to develop the ethical subjectivity he describes. My claim is that even if the humanities can cultivate a certain kind of character, this would not be the same as the ethical subjectivity he describes. And it is this ethical subjectivity in turn that provides a solution to what he identifies as the crisis of humanism in his philosophical writings and his writings on Judaism.

Education and the Public Space

In her 1956 essay, "The Crisis in Education," Hannah Arendt offers a challenging critique of progressive education and in so doing she explores this fundamental question: Is education political?[15] Focusing on primary education, Arendt believes progressive education is founded on several confusions, each resulting in succession from the previous one. Although progressive education's child-centered approach is a response to a previous confusion whereby children were thought to be little adults, the pedagogy that progressive education offers is just as pernicious. Arendt's critique of progressive education emerges from the way she answers the question, "Is education political?"

It would not only be impossible, but also an injustice, to sum up John Dewey's philosophy of education, and in particular his magnum opus, *Democracy and Education,* in only a few pages.[16] It would nonetheless be helpful to consider several prominent themes that run throughout his work in education before exploring Arendt's critique. In particular, Dewey focuses on the respective roles of the teacher and the student's peers, the creation of habit and moral education, and the relationship between past and present. Dewey's *Democracy and Education,* first published in 1916, contains the details of his educational project.

In the last section of *Democracy and Education,* Dewey sums up his theory of morals thus: "Discipline, culture, social efficiency, personal refinement, improvement of character are but phases of the growth of capacity nobly to share in such a balanced experience. And education is not a mere means to such a life. Education is such a life. To maintain capacity of such education is the essence of morals."[17] This view of education, which repeatedly characterizes education not in terms of the content learned but rather in terms of the processes by which it is learned, permeates his work in the philosophy of education. For Dewey, habit, which is the key to education, does not mean that our activities simply become rote and thoughtless. Rather, they become the means by which we form certain predispositions, which then enable us to act more easily in the future.[18] The wider the group of experiences and the greater the context and connections in which to have these experiences, the more habit can be interrupted by the novel, and the more able one might be to see the significance of something new as something new.[19]

Dewey's conception of how habits are formed, while being the most significant part of his educational philosophy, is also the part that is either ignored or misinterpreted. In spite of these problems of application, Dewey's focus on practice is the most compelling part of his educational theory. Contrary even to current models of teaching morals, ethics, and character, Dewey argues that one must practice these behaviors if one is going to cultivate them. Moral behavior is not learned through catechism; nor is it learned by reading posters on the school walls that have the words "honesty," "patriotism," and "fidelity" emblazoned on them.[20] Not unlike the educators who preceded him, leading all the way back to Aristotle, Dewey believes that the character we develop is the character that is practiced.

We see, then, how he arrives at his view that democracy and education have a reciprocal and mutual relationship—democracy is dependent on an educated populous if it is to function effectively; conversely, if democracy is not *practiced* within the context of schooling, all the "education" or knowledge learned in and out of schools will not enable an individual to become a participating citizen in a democracy.[21] For Dewey, democracy is not a structure that exists outside of the individual. Rather, it is an attitude or a disposition that one inhabits. More importantly, as stated above, education is not a means to moral development, or rather a means to moral behavior; it *is* moral. The very act of engaging with others, the social dimension of education, necessarily makes the process of education moral. This is why, for Dewey, to disengage education from its social dimension is to undermine the very nature of education. Lining up chairs, one behind the other, rather than in an arrangement that would encourage children to engage with each other is not in itself problematic just as simply putting chairs in a circle is not sufficient to encourage the social dimension of a classroom. If, however, the physical arrangement intends to limit the social interaction that is natural to the school environment and necessary to the educational process itself, then Dewey would signal this as a cause for concern.

Long hailed as the "father of progressive education," Dewey lived long enough to see a complete perversion of these ideas in their implementation. Most of the criticisms of progressive education, including those put forth by Arendt, are more relevant to the implementation of progressive education than to Dewey's vast writings on it. This faulty implementation encouraged critics of progressive education, who continue to have no shortage of complaints, including an accusation that the curriculum lacks any content and is morally bankrupt. For example, twenty-two years after *Democracy and Education,* Dewey published *Experience and Education,* which provides a detailed but succinct description of progressive education. His response in this book addresses not only the critics of progressive education, but also the progressive educators who have misinterpreted and inaccurately implemented his philosophy. Additionally, this concise book reads like it anticipated the criticisms advanced by Arendt and thus provides direct responses to the array of criticisms Arendt offered.[22]

Within these pages, Dewey takes up the question of "the old and the new" with regard to the question of tradition and content, one of Arendt's main targets. He states very clearly, and logically, that tradition has a place in progressive education. He never held the position that his curriculum should ignore tradition, the past, or "books." Specifically, he never intended for teachers not to know anything, which by definition would mean they have no authority in the classroom, and certainly no authority with regard to matters of the intellect or creativity. Rather, Dewey's focus was on *how* material is taught. His view was not an Either/Or philosophy of education: either we have tradition, and books, and a knowledge base, which requires students to sit in their seats and read books in order to accomplish this task; or, we let children roam around the room not really learning anything, but developing the desire to learn and dabbling in an interest here and interest there. The first view insists that to know anything, to be an expert, is to read books. The implication is that while students might know more facts, they will not have really learned anything. The second view argues that while students might be experiencing more, we are developing nothing more than a generation of dilettantes. The war between theory and practice being played out on the educational battlefield appears to arrive at an impasse. Dewey's view quite simply put, but more difficult to implement, as the history of the contemporary public school has shown, is that it is not enough that children learn a certain body of material; rather, they need to have their whole disposition toward learning habituated to want to learn more, to see how learning one thing naturally leads to learning something else, and those connections should be encouraged and pursued.

Contrary to how he has been viewed by his critics, Dewey's philosophy of education is not anti-intellectual. Rather than being empty of content, Dewey's philosophy of education emphasized even more content—seeing an allusion in a poem should prompt a student not only to look up the word in a dictionary but explore its origins, for example the mythological tale from which it was taken. Teachers need to be trained not only to encourage more learning, to keep students' interests alive, but also in a discipline, if not many disciplines—teachers need to be able to see these connections, have intellectual material available to them, and be thoughtful, reasonable thinkers. They need to be able to encourage their students to pursue their interests and insights. Their authority needs to be grounded precisely in knowing something. To counter the conservative claim that just as roaming around a classroom does not mean children are developing habits to learn freely, neither does sitting still in a chair with mouths closed mean children are learning any more facts, reading any more efficiently, or becoming more thoughtful.

In spite of my brief defense of Dewey's philosophy of education against its detractors, there remain significant concerns that need to be addressed and here Arendt's criticisms are helpful. Returning to the 1956 essay, Arendt's principal criticism of progressive education develops from her position that children are born into a world and it is the responsibility of both the parents and the teachers (read as the educational system) to educate these children about *this* world, not the world it might be in the future. We have a responsibility to the children and to the future world not to imagine for these children what the world might be but rather to let the world unfold. Contrary to the view that education is political—and progressive—Arendt believes education is conservative, in the most literal sense of this term. Her argument for this position lies in her view of natality and action.[23]

Education, according to Arendt, lies in the gap between past and future; its goal is to enable the future by teaching about the present (which includes the past). Without knowledge of the world in which they live and the past that influenced the coming about of this world, children and then adults are in no position to effect change. We, as parents and teachers, must take responsibility for this world, even if it is not the world that we created and even if we wish it were different from what it is. Children are new, but they are born into an old world. To educate them about the possible new world, and not this old world, is ironically to close off their possibilities—for it is already to imagine the new world and educate them in this limited way, for this one possible world. Thus, Arendt argues, in spite of being motivated by change and inspired to make the world a better place, progressive education, ironically, promotes a fascist educational system, one directed by a particular ideology for a particular future.[24] For Arendt, then, education is not about action, nor is it about the creation of the novel—the new. These are reserved for the public space, which for her does not characterize the classroom.

Arendt's view of the relationship between education and the political is counter-intuitive, but compelling nonetheless. Although she sees politics as progressive, education for her is conservative, since it preserves the past and teaches about the present. Without knowledge of the world in which they live and the past that influenced the coming about of this world, children and then adults are in no position to effect change. In Arendt's analysis, although progressive education delineates between a child's world and an adult's world, this separation nonetheless has the dangerous effect of essentially leaving children to their own devices. Teachers, she concludes, are no longer the authority in the classroom. Worse, she observes, the tyranny of the "child" majority can often be more tyrannical than the absolute authority of the adult teacher.[25] This confusion over "who's in charge" led to a similar confusion in the public and private spheres, where education, by virtue of the state mandate surrounding it, pushed schools, education, and childhood into a political realm. She argues that the privacy needed for children to grow and mature, relatively undisturbed, has been compromised by this thrust into the public arena.[26]

Arendt's definition of the public space reveals that we are required simultaneously to take risks and to engage in self-restraint. She observes that the latter has the potential to stymie growth. Education should remain a private space in which this self-restraint is not required. One can see the insight in Arendt's claim, even if one might disagree with the extreme position. As Arendt sees it, in order for the public space to work, the participants must be willing to allow their honest opinions to come to the fore and be assessed openly by everyone participating in that space. Those who are involved in intimate relationships with others with whom they also participate politically must be willing to set aside the intimate relationship and engage the other person with the kind of respect that would allow the other to share his/her political position. This entails a continued negotiation of the self that occupies both a personal or private space and a public space.

Arendt fears that this kind of negotiation is too complex and potentially too dangerous for school-age children who would need to negotiate the selves they are as friends with the selves they might be if engaged politically. The light of the "public eye" on a self that is still developing as a personal self might be too much to bear for a young child or even a young adult. A brief look at the history of the child star, or the children of famous people, supports Arendt's point. Continually placed in the public's view, many of these children never develop into flourishing adults. Even an unscientific poll would confirm that children often keep very honest opinions to themselves if they fear those opinions might set them apart from their peers or open them (personally or intellectually) to ridicule, thus validating Arendt's twofold view that children recognize that their peers can be more tyrannical than the adults and that in turn, the classroom does not provide the safe space needed for children to exercise their political views.

As a result of her observation, Arendt's view of education is paradoxically both optimistic and pessimistic. On the one hand, her optimistic view that self-restraint is *not* required in education contradicts not only many of our personal experiences with education but also her own goal of education as a kind of cultivation.[27] She argues in her account of freedom that it is in the public space that an individual often discovers what one is capable of, acting in ways that were not predicted. Is this not the case in education also? Do we not discover who we are and what we believe when we participate in discussions that require us to take intellectual risks? On the other hand, her pessimistic view that making education a public space would stymie growth runs counter to the progressive view that specifically endorses individual growth and development, via the pursuit of one's own interests, ideas, and activities. It also runs counter to the progressive view that the "public" is learned or practiced.[28] Instead, we might note that education provides an opportunity for a diverse set of equal individuals, not between the student and teacher, but among the students themselves to be given a voice.

It is not clear that Dewey would entirely disagree with Arendt's concerns. However, he would probably ask Arendt the following question: how can we expect adults to have the capacity to think creatively, to solve problems, to relate to their peers respectfully and forcefully, if we do not allow them to create these practices through the educational process beginning in childhood?[29] In other words, if freedom is defined as spontaneity and unpredictability, it is then positioned against a view of freedom that would emerge because the agent acts from a self that has been cultivated with certain habits and a set of choices. What then does it mean to be a self who is free, if at the end of the day, the way we act is not within our control? The kind of freedom that Arendt presses recalls the radical freedom of existentialism, one that is paradoxically so free that it is "unfree" insofar as it no longer seems willed by the agent. We find evidence for this claim when Dewey ends the first chapter of *Experience and Education* with the following problem: "We may reject knowledge of the past as the *end* of education and thereby only emphasize its importance as a *means*. When we do that we have a problem that is new in the story of education: How shall the young become acquainted with the past in such a way that the acquaintance is a potent agent in appreciation of the living present?"[30]

The question "Is education political?" not only depends on how we define "political" and how we understand the aims of education, but also how we understand the subject of education: the child who is cultivated into the adult.[31] What "political" means for Arendt is very different from what it means for Dewey or another philosopher following traditional categorizations of this term. What is most interesting about "child-centered" education, which emerged out of Rousseau's philosophy—(see the legacy in Dewey, Montessori, et al.)—and of which Arendt is so critical, is that very few if any of the schools who boast its pedagogy are aware that both Dewey and Montessori trace their ideas to Rousseau. Even if these schools could name Dewey or Montessori as the inspiration for their child-centered educational approach, few, if any, know anything about its origins, its connection to political philosophy, and the development of the political citizen, which in light of Rousseau's concerns may or may not be the kind of political citizenry we want to develop.[32]

Most educators who have adopted a child-centered approach like Montessori's method or Dewey's progressive education have simply divorced the educational process from the political philosophy that inspired that educational model. This separation continues today where public schooling has become a patchwork quilt of mixed messages and subtexts, and where the lessons that are most effective with regard to sending a message have very little to do with the content introduced in a classroom.[33] For example, do those who adopt this approach also subscribe to the suspicion of community that motivated Rousseau? For Dewey, such a suspicion would tragically undermine the very community of learning that he promotes. Yet, given his emphasis on moral philosophy and evidence of his own moral courage as a professor in the academy, Dewey might have agreed with Rousseau's political concerns and thus his motivation for developing the educational treatise as he did. Montessori's emphasis on individual learning picks up on the streak of independence that runs through *Émile,* but Rousseau reveals both at the end of *Émile* and in its sequel that cultivating independence at the expense of not seeing ourselves as dependent and vulnerable is a flawed project through and through. I will return to this point in the next chapter.

The significance of Arendt's analysis of the crisis in (American) K–12 education lies in how her critique of progressive education necessarily reinvigorates the age-old question of the respective roles that theory and practice play in education. This question, in some form or other, lies at the heart of every debate about education: the return to the basics, core education, vocational training, critical thinking, applied science, service learning, and the role of the humanities. In many cases, but certainly not all, we can see the theory-practice dispute as an undercurrent in these debates. Although they are presented as mutually exclusive, they need not be. Indeed, one might argue that the political dimension of education is precisely where theory and practice intersect.

Arendt's position is not without merit. However, when pushed to its end, one wonders what she sees as the purpose, function, or even value of education. Certainly one can argue that it is only through a foundational education that one is then able to participate creatively in the public space and if this kind of creativity is encouraged too early, the creative experience could be undermined. Additionally, if all those who participate in this kind of public space are not able to participate as equals, then the children run the risk of the tyranny of their peers—in spite of the democratic approach being instituted precisely to mitigate the tyranny of the school experience itself. Arendt defines the political as diverse equals coming together to create something spontaneous. For her, the political is precisely that which is not *practiced* and not *learned;* it is that which is spontaneous, unexpected, and unpredictable. Many of the examples of political action that she provides even indicate that those who acted had personal histories that would not have predicted or anticipated their future political activity. That is, although education is thought to enable the future, it is not clear that

Arendt sees any connection between the education one receives and the possibility of political action that will affect the future. If this is the case, then one wonders why any educational system could be recommended over any other.

Saving Democracy

Nussbaum opens *Not for Profit* with the following line: "We are in the midst of a crisis of massive proportions and grave global significance . . . a worldwide crisis in education."[34] Nussbaum attributes this crisis to radical changes at all levels of education, namely, cuts in the humanities and the arts.[35] For Nussbaum this crisis signals the fragile future of democracy, which hangs in the balance. Economic growth sought by so many nations has led people to go for the bottom line at all costs and at the expense of educating for abilities that are fundamental to a secure democracy. She writes: "These abilities are associated with the humanities and the arts: the ability to think critically; the ability to transcend local loyalties and to approach world problems as a 'citizen of the world'; and, finally, to imagine sympathetically the predicament of another person."[36] She links the future of democracy with humanities education and thus explicitly links education with the political development of the individual.

Where Arendt does not see the possibility for education effecting change at all, much less counting on it for positive change, Martha Nussbaum, professor of philosophy and law at the University of Chicago, believes that the future of democracy hangs in the balance and the humanities are both necessary and sufficient to save it. Variations on this theme can be found in all the books I mentioned earlier in this chapter, giving me cause for concern even as I admire many of the points each makes. Nussbaum's book in particular, in its zeal to defend the humanities, overreaches and may promise a feat that the humanities cannot achieve, nor should they be expected to do so. By making this promise, she may actually render the humanities and humanities education more vulnerable, rather than less, to its critics.

In the chapter "Educating Citizens," Nussbaum explores the cultivation of citizens with moral courage, those who would have stood strong in Milgram's experiment with authority and would have been immune to the position they were assigned in the Zimbardo prison experiment. She tells us in this chapter that "[w]e need to understand how to produce more citizens [who are prepared to live with others on terms of mutual respect and reciprocity] and fewer of [those who seek the comfort of domination]."[37] How do we achieve this goal? Her answer—through an education in the humanities. In the chapter immediately following this one she outlines an educational process that is at once child-centered (Rousseau, Dewey, et al.) and based on a Socratic pedagogy, i.e., one that takes critical questioning as its point of departure. She cites progressive education as a means to accomplish this task and praises, for example, the Philosophy for Children program, developed by Matthew Lipman, which is based on Dewey's philosophy of education with an emphasis on developing critical thinking and reasoning skills. With this focus, Nussbaum's view of education is put in direct opposition to Arendt's.

We could approach Nussbaum's claim from several different angles, but the first one that comes to mind is to ask what it means to educate for a democracy when one of the values that a democracy holds dear is precisely the plurality of voices within it. Taking up the mantle of progressive education, Nussbaum seems to consider democracy in only one form—that we are all like-minded with a similar set of values. But this is not true of either a democracy or of humanities education. Indeed, we must consider that when we teach the humanities, all of humanity—the good side and the dark side—is explored. Additionally, we must consider that when we teach our students, who they are as individuals will influence how they filter both what they read and what we, their teachers, say.

Nussbaum advances her argument by deploying both Rousseau's *Émile* and an education founded on a Socratic pedagogy. These two models do not fit together neatly. Rousseau needs the kind of education he describes in *Émile* to mitigate the ability reason can have either to corrupt or empower an already corrupt soul. Rousseau needs to cultivate a man who will be immune to the corrupting forces of reason exemplified in particular by philosophical reason, which too frequently looks like sophistry. Reason at an early age is precisely the problem, and "child-centered" for Rousseau would not mean the Philosophy for Children program, which Nussbaum mentions as an example of a promising educational model.[38] I would argue that it is more than a promising educational model, but not for the reasons Nussbaum wants.[39] And as we will see in the next chapter, Rousseau's educational project spectacularly fails.

In the end, in this particular chapter, Nussbaum attempts to draw an easy line between Socratic questioning and democracy while also trying to draw a line between humanities education and the morally cultivated to create an argument that is remarkably deficient. If we know anything about Socratic questioning it is the presumed integrity it displays in the pursuit of truth. Socratic questioning requires the participants to question everything including the future—or value—of an idea for which Nussbaum wants to install Socratic education to defend, namely, democracy. True to its own mission, the Socratic gadfly pokes and prods everything, including those values that we might now believe to be true and right. And we must expect and allow our students at any age to do the same.[40] The humanities education that Nussbaum promotes, which includes critical reasoning, not only runs the risk of creating people who are not concerned about others but also people whose greed and selfishness are now backed by reason to justify those actions.

As was pointed out by the political theorist Ryan Belot, if Nussbaum is arguing that a humanities education is superior for achieving moral wisdom, then those of us with PhDs in the humanities are super superior, leading us down the path of the philosopher king, which is decidedly not democratic.[41] Of course, the irony that Belot so astutely identifies is then betrayed by the fact that many with PhDs in the humanities are not morally superior at all and too frequently they act in ways that realize Rousseau's worst fears about reason providing the moral justification for bad behavior. Nussbaum could argue in return that those who are using reason to justify greed or other forms of bad behavior could be shown through reason the error of their ways. But then we could find ourselves in a game of intellectual chicken with recourse to nothing that could tip the argument one way or the other. On this model, there is nothing that could be referenced as the final arbiter of the dispute.

I believe that Nussbaum's intuition is correct but her solution to the problem is not. Let me return briefly to Arendt and Dewey. Hannah Arendt warns us in her essay that children can often be much more tyrannical toward their own peers than adults are toward children and this peer pressure could turn from healthy encouragement to bullying. We know even as adults how hard it is to go against our peers. Although Dewey recognizes that there can be a fine line between the leader and the tyrant, he believes that children are capable of identifying the difference. One could argue in response that to act in either of these ways—either by being tyrannical or by absenting oneself—is the behavior of someone who is not truly a member of the democratic community in the classroom, but to say that is to admit that the citizens would have already been cultivated rather than to say that it is education that does the cultivating. Dewey may be correct that children know the difference between the one who is "too bossy" and the "real" leader. However, children are not often capable of standing up to such people. And my point here is simply that even Dewey's model of education *already assumes* another layer or level of cultivation in order for the political dimension of this community to be effective. That is, in order for the social community to work as such, in order for it to be effective, which by implication means to be ethical, the children and participating subjects might already need to be cultivated as such. I believe this is Nussbaum's error also. Nussbaum wants character formed in a very particular way. The education that Nussbaum believes the humanities deliver cannot be achieved by the humanities, especially if the humanities are taught in a way that liberates the mind.

Humanities Education Redux

Where does this leave us? My intention is not to undermine the humanities, discount progressive education, or dismiss wholesale a conservative approach to education. The complexity of education—what it does or should do—cannot be captured by any single position. My point is that with the humanities placed in the crosshairs, those who have come to their defense may have overstepped the boundaries in their claims about what the humanities can do and unwittingly focused the target for those taking aim.[42]

Returning to the question at hand, certainly, one can be compelled by those who, like Stanley Fish, argue that humanities education has no value outside of the pleasure it gives to those who study it—becoming like the ultimate Aristotelian Prime Mover of thought thinking itself.[43] We can concede that humanities education does not *aim* at "production" in the same way that engineering or computer science, or any other applied fields do.[44] Nor does humanities education promise that, by receiving such an education, one is more likely to be able to solve any current political crises or be more likely to be moral, even if there are claims made that one might become a more creative or nuanced thinker. In this regard, humanities education differs from its polytechnic counterpart, which simply promises the cultivation of or training in a set of skills.[45] I would like to reconsider this question but in a different context. I take this approach because although Levinas does not utilize the humanities to develop the ethical subject, his educational model has an intellectual ground that is comparable to the role of the humanities in secular education.

As I mentioned previously, the view that as a result of this non-utilitarian approach humanities education becomes completely dispensable is challenged by those who claim that the humanities make us more human, which is frequently read as, "make us better people." Ironically, the very defense becomes the weapon of attack by those who oppose it. That the humanities have an influence precisely on how we think, especially with regard to matters that concern us as human beings, is the concern that lies behind the accusations that the university is filled with liberal-minded professors, where here "liberal" does not mean "free"—as in open-minded and liberating, unconstrained by prejudice in the literal meaning of that word—but rather left-leaning and holding certain (here read as unacceptable) political views that are being foisted on unsuspecting or vulnerable students.[46] Those who teach and do research in the humanities are left damned if they do (have value) and damned if they do not. If they do not contribute anything, why have them? If they do, well then, we need to worry about that. Additionally, humanities professors are left torn between wanting to argue that the humanities are good for something—in order to maintain some kind of respected position in an academy that is increasingly turning its attention to that which not only can produce something for society, but can also produce something that is profitable to the university—and wanting to maintain an elite position that the humanities, the pinnacle of education, are a good in themselves, and in fact it is precisely because they are not utilitarian that their presence distinguishes a college education from the training one might receive in a trade school.[47]

Certainly one could argue that humanities education is both/and and neither/nor. That is, humanities education is not as strikingly narcissistic as Fish would portray it but neither is it the salve for all of humankind, as Nussbaum would have us believe. It neither has no effect on students who read it, simply taking it in as a hodgepodge of ideas, nor is it so persuasive that all students will emerge as left-leaning graduating seniors. These positions woefully neglect the fact that there is an active mind and a situated body engaged in the learning process—these students will indeed be transformed, in some form or other, but as someone who filters what he or she hears and reads, that is, presumably as a person who is able to think for herself. Thus, the student is not left unaffected by the education he or she receives but neither is it the case that all students are alike. Each will interpret and relate to the material differently than do his or her peers. And this interpretation may be contingent on what kind of character this person has already developed, not to mention other variables such as the individual experiences of the student. More importantly, the good that humanities education offers is not something that can be quantified or seen—like a widget. As a result, the effects of this education often remain invisible, even to the student, until several years after having studied in a university. Both positions, then, are inaccurate in their assessment of what a humanities education does and does not do. Their inaccuracy notwithstanding both positions feed into the current crisis that we see in education today: one need only note the culture wars that are fueling the Texas State Board of Education, which is making national headlines at the very moments that I am writing these sentences.[48]

The debate, then, is structured as a false dilemma and we must ask if these are our only two options. Is it the case that humanities education—or any education—should be directed at solving the *present* political crises and producing moral perfection (if not making widgets or life-saving machines) *or* if it does not accomplish this, should it be banished to its elite ivory tower home of useless, but pleasurable, navel-gazing? It is just as inaccurate to say that education is not political (in the bad sense of this term) as it is to say that humanities education will deliver us from fascism. More likely, the truth lies somewhere in between these two extremes.

In his *New York Times* opinion piece, "The 'Learning Knights' of Bell Telephone," Wes Davis transports us back in time fifty years when the humanities were seen as good "training" for leadership.[49] In the early 1950s, Bell Telephone initiated the Institute of Humanistic Studies for Executives. Davis provides an interesting background note when he writes: "The sociologist E. Digby Baltzell explained the Bell leaders' concerns in an article published in Harper's magazine in 1955: 'A well-trained man knows how to answer questions, they reasoned; an educated man knows what questions are worth asking.' Bell, then one of the largest industrial concerns in the country, needed more employees capable of guiding the company rather than simply following instructions or responding to obvious crises."

The brief experiment in 1955 with the Bell Telephone company employees supports a view that the humanities humanize within a certain context of what that means. A group of smart technicians were given the opportunity to participate in a yearlong seminar on the humanities coordinated by the Bell Telephone Company and the University of Pennsylvania. By the end of the year they were reading difficult texts, most significantly, James Joyce's *Ulysses*. Although they noticed that they had enjoyed this year of reading together, most notable about the year was how their decision-making process had changed. They had become more sensitive to the impact their decisions had on the communities, families, and themselves and found themselves no longer able simply to go for the "bottom line." In fact, Bell Telephone had to shut the program down precisely because the participants had lost their cold-hearted edge in their decision-making. They now wanted jobs that were meaningful to them. The program had ironically become too successful.

Nonetheless, the view that the humanities can make one a "better" person is easily challenged by turning to those who participated in the Nazi regime. For every Bell Telephone employee who becomes more sensitive to the community in which he lives, more aware of the full effects of his decisions, and thus less able simply to go for the bottom line in business, there is also the Eichmann who read his Kant—correctly—and did his duty to his nation by working to exterminate the "traitors" or "poison" infecting that nation. It is not clear that any amount of philosophy, classics, literature, or languages would have changed Eichmann's mind, much less his heart. It is a cruel irony that reading Kant, a philosopher who is emblematic of the Enlightenment, did not make a Nazi's soul any more sympathetic or his conscience any more burdened by the job he had to fulfill during the day.

Clearly, a classical education, while it might push one to ask more questions and even become a more astute reader of texts, is not sufficient to make someone a better person nor does it guarantee that one will use good judgment—even if we assume that one has good judgment. The point I wish to emphasize is that education cultivates the mind, but how it is formed cannot be predetermined: it can be opened up or shut down or it falls somewhere in between the two. Students change as a result of their education. They might hold their convictions more steadfastly than they did previously, now having good reasons to do so, or they might question them, modify them, or jettison them completely. Even if we say that the change is only about being able to ask more penetrating questions of a text or contemplate the question of beauty, either way students who enter our classrooms are changed by that experience. If a student was unable to do that prior to entering a classroom or unable to do this more profoundly, that student has changed—and that change will reverberate throughout that student's life—just as those did who participated in the Bell Telephone seminar. If students are not changed by our classes, we really do need to ask ourselves as educators what we are doing.

Rather than say that the participants in the Bell Telephone experiment became "better" people, I might frame the discussion differently in a way that more accurately represents what the humanities do and why those of us who engage in the study of the humanities, including our students, love doing so. These participants engaged their minds in a way that they had not experienced previously. They interrogated questions that are fundamental to the human condition and they did so in a learning community with others pursuing the same questions. Their explorations led them to consider their own lives, what is important to them, and who they want to be. They became more thoughtful people. Not necessarily nicer people, more generous people, or even more honest. They might have already been this kind of person. Rather, their minds were ignited by perennial questions about humanity, and like nearly everyone who studies these questions, they could not help but think about them in relationship to their own lives. It has been said that studying the humanities trains us to consider different perspectives, and these men did just that.

When we say the humanities humanize, I think we are better positioned as defenders of humanities education if we say they humanize in the way that Aristotle meant—that we come close to fulfilling our potential as rational beings with creative minds. It is not that there is no effect, no change, or no transformation. Indeed, there is. This is why those who engage the humanities continue to do so—it is something we know from the inside. It is not something that one can typically see from the outside. The humanities bring us face to face with perennial questions that still pertain to human existence. They bring forward a wealth of wisdom, of human experience, emotion, action, judgment, and relationships. They ask us to imagine, think, reflect, and question. They expand our minds even if we cannot control how the mind will develop. And most importantly, what many fail to or will not admit, there is great joy, great pleasure in reading these texts with others.

We grow as human beings when we participate in a humanities education. Having read *King Lear,* I have a much deeper understanding of my relationship with my parents and how complicated love is in a family. But this is not the same thing as becoming "better" in either an ethical or political sense of that term. The men who participated in the Bell Telephone experiment derived such joy from thinking that they could not help but ask themselves if they wanted to return to jobs that no longer delivered that kind of challenge or that kind of pleasure. If there is something more to human existence than the exchange value of the economy, can one still make business decisions based on money as the bottom line? Contrary to Nussbaum's view, we cannot say that all of them will ask these questions, nor can we say that even those who do ask these questions will answer them in a way that would reflect an ethically cultivated person. But some of them will.[50]

Theory and Practice

It would seem that we have come to an impasse with progressive education at one end and an Arendtian version of conservative education at the other. Arendt is positioned at the far end of the spectrum from Nussbaum and for similar reasons is just as incorrect. In a manner of speaking, both of these poles are not accurate. The battle over the soul of education—what it can, cannot, should, and should not do—seems as old as the concept of education itself. Should education be about teaching a skill; should it cultivate the mind; should it do both; does it have an inherent moral dimension? These questions find their roots in the ancient debate between Plato and Aristotle, and how each understood the knowledge—skill/techné, practical knowledge, theoretical wisdom. Pierre Hadot takes up this distinction in his book *Philosophy as a Way of Life* when he returns to the question of what it means to do philosophy today.[51]

In the final chapter, which carries the name of the book, Hadot opens with a quote from Philo of Alexandria. In its emphasis on individual transformation and resistance to that which causes grief, the quote betrays more of the Greek influence on Philo than any Jewish influence that might remain. Hadot continues this line and reminds his readers that philosophy was not simply the love of wisdom, enacted by reading books written by the great thinkers; instead, it was a love of wisdom that transformed how an individual "is": "it makes us 'be' in a different way."[52] Hadot observes, "Wisdom, then, was a way of life which brought peace of mind (ataraxia), inner freedom (autarkeia), and a cosmic consciousness. First and foremost, philosophy presented itself as a therapeutic, intended to cure mankind's anguish."[53] He locates the roots of the move away from this kind of relationship to philosophy in the distinction between *discourse about philosophy* and *philosophy itself*, that is, when we segregated theory from practice.[54]

In spite of this segregation and the conflict that emerges in discussions about education between the focus on the theoretical and the focus on the practical, we can see then how the roots of our idea of virtue as self-development became tethered to our conception of education. It is worth noting that what the Greeks meant by practical is vastly different from how we understand that term today within the context of education. A more apt description of what this conflict resembles would be the distinction that Aristotle draws out and which includes the third category of techné. For Aristotle practical wisdom was still theoretical knowledge, though it led to action. For Aristotle, techné was the kind of knowledge concerned with the production of things. Putting techné to the side, we can see how the study of the humanities became blended with a way of being— to study the humanities was, or is, to engage in a life that separates one from the everyday worries that plague the average person. It puts one "above" those petty worldly concerns and turns one's thoughts to the cosmos, such that one can live a life that is unaffected by the many daily pains and struggles.

The return to the way of Greek being that Hadot describes is tempting and on the surface it sounds like precisely what many of us wish for in the pursuit of education, that is, that theoretical knowledge would be intimately tied to practical wisdom, that studying Kant would mean something other than a philosophical exercise to see who can make the best argument and that students would realize that ideas matter. Yet, a closer examination reveals exactly that which worries Levinas; indeed, it worries a great number of modern Jewish philosophers, including, as we will see later in the book, Abraham Joshua Heschel. The idea that the study of philosophy would enable us, or even encourage us to live a life divorced from human pain and suffering lies at the heart of Levinas's worries about how philosophy covers over the ethical. His analysis in *Otherwise than Being* is not intended to be anti-intellectual; rather, he demonstrates that philosophy can verge on sophistry, that in the pursuit of the best argument, reason can justify many horrifying actions and one never has to take a stand. One can remain indifferent.

If the focus is on the development of the self, if humanism is about the centrality of the human—a particular human as an independent, rational creature—how then do we turn to the Other in a way that puts that Other first, before ourselves? That is, fundamental to modernity's view of humanism is not simply that the human is central, but also that the human is a Self who is free, rational, choice-making, and autonomous. The self is not initially thought in terms of intersubjectivity, much less as a subject that is fundamentally responsible for the Other. To live a life that removes one from daily struggle is precisely to see the transformation as self-transformation, as a transformation that is independent of any responsibility for another person.

The focus of the Stoic philosophy, which was carried into modernity, was a focus on the individual. The humanism that emerged from this view was a humanism that defined the human in terms of a single, independent, rational, and free individual—free from anguish, free from constraints (self-imposed or not), free from dependence. For Levinas, this distinction between a self that is central but independent and a subject who becomes a subject through the response to the Other is what distinguishes the Western (and this includes the United States and Europe) and the Jewish conceptions of humanism. This distinction sets Jewish education apart from other models of education that are informed by modernity.

If it is philosophy that directs our minds toward the cosmos, it is religion—as Levinas understands this term—that directs us back to earth and everything it means to be a creature who needs, desires, and suffers.[55] If modernity delivered a certain philosophical view of humanism, it was modernity's educational models and political systems that reproduced this view and its values. The Enlightenment—in the broadest use of this term—allowed for philosophy, along with the other liberal arts, to refocus itself, making "the human" central to its study.[56] With the Protestant influence on this period, modernity's humanism took on the appearance of a universality that was independent of any particular set of religious beliefs.[57] The philosophy that dominated modernity—and which still informs the central texts of the modern canon—was mediated through modernity's Protestant values, enabling the production of a "secular" humanism, which packaged itself as a-religious, universal, and moral. The respective educational model that was developed to cultivate the citizenry, particularly in the early thirteen colonies and then the United States, did not acknowledge this humanism's original roots in the Hebrew Bible.

In a more interesting way, the relationship that moral development has both to the intellect and to habits lies at the center of this discussion. Does one become a "better" person by reading widely in the humanities? By reading the Hebrew or Christian Bible? By reading other sacred books, for example, the Qur'an? Or, does one become a "better" person by practicing ethics, by creating habits? In a sense, both of these questions miss the mark with regard to the question that concerns Levinas. The humanities offer more than narcissistic pleasure but they are far from a magical salve. Nor is he concerned with whether or not we are patriotic. He is not concerned with whether we develop the democratic principles that are encouraged by studying the humanities. Nor is he concerned with simply teaching good behavior. His concern is at once much more basic and much more complicated: how do we become a subject who puts the Other before our own self-interests? How do we become a subject who can put centrality of our own self-interest into question? This question lies at the center of Levinas's essays on Jewish education.

In all the discussions of the humanities, and there are many, the humanities are presented differently with regard to what they can accomplish—for some it is critical thinking, for others it is leadership, and still others, like Nussbaum, it is the cultivation of democratic principles and ethical behavior. Yet, what I argue, and what I believe Levinas also sees, is that the myriad views of the humanities hang on another moral and intellectual education, a pre-humanities education (in the classical sense) that is not articulated but which is also presupposed. The presumption of this education allows the views offered by both Nussbaum and Fish. On the one hand, Fish can make his claims because he does not see the humanities as necessary for moral cultivation; that happens elsewhere. On the other, Nussbaum can make the claims that she makes because she presumes the foundations of a moral education that have already taken root. Nussbaum and Fish are simultaneously right and wrong. They assume that moral education must happen elsewhere, but as we will see Levinas locates the roots of the problem in traditional models of education that are in turn based on a particular conceptions of the human: one that is solitary, rational, and independent. This is why the question that guides the rest of this book is "Why Jewish education?" Is it not the case that humanities education in general could be just as effective at developing this subject? This book argues that the answer to this question *for Levinas* is no, a humanities education is not as effective, or at the very least, it does not accomplish what some attribute to it. For this reason, Levinas identified a vision of education that is necessarily distinct from what we understand as humanities education, or "liberal education." For, if a humanities education is going to come close to delivering what Nussbaum claims, there is another education that must precede it. This book explores why that is the case and what that education looks like.

2 Solitary Men

> No man is an island, entire of itself . . . any man's death diminishes me,
> because I am involved in mankind; and therefore never send to know
> for whom the bell tolls; it tolls for thee.
>
> —John Donne, *Meditation XVII*

"No one is more self-sufficient than Rousseau," Levinas proclaims in his 1935 book, *On Escape,* a statement that could be easily dismissed as a passing swipe at the eighteenth-century thinker.[1] No doubt, Levinas would have ambivalent feelings about Rousseau, whose philosophy is often cited as influential in the French Revolution and the development of the French Republic. Yet, Levinas's stab at Rousseau's emphasis on self-sufficiency is not simply a throwaway line; self-sufficiency lies at the heart of a humanism that would develop out of modernity and to which Levinas offers a sustained response. In short, "self-sufficiency" sums up everything that Levinas believed went wrong with modernity.

Thirty years later, Levinas opens his 1968 essay, "Humanism and An-Archy," with the following assertion:

> The crisis of humanism in our times undoubtedly originates in an experience
> of human inefficacy accentuated by the very abundance of our means of ac-
> tion and the scope of our ambitions . . . The unburied dead of wars and death
> camps accredit the idea of a death with no future, making tragic-comic the care
> for one's self and illusory the pretensions of the rational animal to a privileged
> place in the cosmos, capable of dominating and integrating the totality of being
> into a consciousness of self.[2]

Put simply, the death camps and all that they signified, e.g., not being able to do the most banal of tasks like burying the dead, put to rest any illusion we had that we are in control, masters of our own destiny. This counter to self-sufficiency appears in Levinas's writing as early as the mid-1930s before he could have understood the full impact of Hitler's reign, the death camps, and the relationship they have to a particular view of the human. Nonetheless, it is a concern that pervades his thought from beginning to end. This chapter focuses on the educational philosophy of Jean-Jacques Rousseau and Friedrich Nietzsche in light of their respective models of education, both of which emphasize a form of self-sufficiency. Chapter 3 will then trace Levinas's response to this view of self-sufficiency, beginning with his 1934 essay on Hitlerism and ending with three important essays from the 1960s that were collected under the title *Humanism of the Other*.

I realize it is certainly odd to pair Rousseau with Nietzsche. The former is a late Enlightenment figure often held up as the influence for the French Revolution and the development of the Universal Rights of Man, what Levinas frequently refers to as "the Principles of 1789." The latter is often characterized as precisely hostile to universal rights, indeed, he promotes a philosophy that is not only antagonistic to a liberal democracy but which is also fundamentally elitist. I pair them because they are both astonishingly acute in their diagnosis of what ails political life, yet in spite of their brilliance, they are both unable to deliver a satisfactory cure for the disease they each detect.

The Solitary Child

Influenced directly by Montaigne, and Aristotle indirectly, Rousseau inaugurates two major trends in contemporary education—the Montessori movement and Deweyan pragmatism. Both are considered "child-centered" approaches to education, but each method comes with its own philosophical foundation and respective concerns about what is real, what is truth, and how learning best occurs. Although both find their origins in Rousseau's child-centered approach, Montessori emphasizes individual learning while Dewey's pragmatism, though it fosters individual flourishing, also encourages that learning happen within a community. In spite of this difference in emphasis, both focus on the individual growth of the child through the child's expression of his or her own interests.

Although both philosophers can trace their roots back to Rousseau, the political concerns that motivated Rousseau's thinking with regard to education have long been forgotten. Additionally, both educational models developed in the wake of the Enlightenment and are part of liberalism's legacy, which focuses on the growth of the individual. In particular, Dewey's pragmatism emphasized the child as a growing and dynamic individual. He championed an educational model that would complement this view. However, his emphasis on democracy in education and experiential learning, which were both grossly misinterpreted, led to an unfortunate view that the goal of education is homogenization. Equality of opportunity and equal rights gave way to treating everyone the same. As a result, we can, in part, locate the origins of Levinas's concern in the philosophies of education that characterize the work of these thinkers.

It is this brand of liberalism—the autonomy and self-sufficiency of the individual—that encourages Levinas's anxiety. If we are to understand why these educational methods have failed, why they assume so much, and why Levinas would be deeply concerned about them, we need to understand and respect that they are indebted to other models of education that developed within particular political contexts. As a result, both Nietzsche and Rousseau provide the perfect educational models to examine, precisely because their diagnoses are accurate and their solutions are natural extensions of these diagnoses that nonetheless fail. They are both unable to provide a sustainable cure. What then are we to do if their solutions are not viable?

Rousseau opens his 1762 treatise on political philosophy, *The Social Contract*, with his famous statement, "Man is born free; and everywhere he is in chains."[3] An Enlightenment thinker, Rousseau understands himself to be responding to the two dominant traditions of political thought at this time: the voluntarist tradition of Hobbes, Pufendorf, and Grotius; and the liberal tradition of Locke and Montesquieu.[4] The former group supports an absolute monarchy (benevolent or not), with the famous statement by Hobbes, as its signature: in the State of Nature, "life is *solitary,* poor, nasty, brutish, and short."[5] The only solution is to surrender one's freedom to the sovereign and thus escape the brutality and depravity of life in the state of nature. The latter group argues that civil society exists to protect certain natural rights, one of which is liberty.[6]

Rousseau's philosophical thought draws ideas from both traditions, while also demonstrating that he disagrees with both in significant ways. His goal in *The Social Contract* is to explain how humankind might accentuate its freedom through the institutions that form civil society. However, Rousseau realizes that the most formidable threat to this kind of freedom might not be another person *per se.* Instead, we are threatened by our dependency on others, which is cultivated through *amour-propre,* a form of self-love exemplified by greed, vanity, and selfish desire.[7] This dependency then contributes to political decisions and political alliances that are not based on justice, but rather on our fear that we might lose those tangibles or, worse, the flattery, that we believe we now need. In turn, these social institutions, rather than enhancing our freedom, as Rousseau believes they should, contribute to what makes us appear un-free. This threat thus accounts for our reluctance to enter willingly into the social contract; we are reluctant to exchange our so-called "natural" freedom for the civil freedom that would justify the chains that we construct for ourselves in any event. As Rousseau describes it, the social contract is a human artifice that is meant not to remove our chains but rather to justify them. Dependence on others becomes voluntary.

Rousseau's legacy can be seen in his significant influence on modern education. On the one hand, his political philosophy, rooted in an abiding suspicion of community—or more precisely, the political community—yields a corresponding educational treatise, that like Nietzsche's, appears to reject dependence and vulnerability in his male student, Émile, by explicitly confining those traits to the feminine sphere. Rousseau's influence on contemporary American education, even if mediated by other educational methods (e.g., Montessori, Dewey, etc.), also cannot be underestimated. The political fears that motivated Rousseau's political and educational philosophy have been long forgotten, thus severing the educational model he produced from the politics that originally informed it. On the other hand, Rousseau's political philosophy is often credited with influencing the French Revolution, the development of the Universal Rights of Man, and French Republicanism. These developments enabled Jews, for the first time, to enjoy the same human rights as other social groups in certain parts of Europe.[8] Yet, this very move that recognized them as citizens nonetheless came with a price tag.[9] We can locate Levinas's ambivalence regarding liberalism in this tension between the universal and the particular. To enjoy these rights offered by universality, the Jews had to renounce their public participation in and identification with Judaism. Thus, if we think back to the opening line of this chapter, we can see how Levinas would be drawn to but also deeply suspicious of the eighteenth-century philosopher's view that promotes the "solitary man."

Rousseau's *Émile* (1762), the educational treatise that was meant to complement his political thought, is by his own admission not a textbook on education; nor did he intend it to be put into practice as described.[10] However, it does follow the development of the child, Émile, who Rousseau hopes will be the exemplar of an individual raised to be self-sufficient, that is, not dependent on others for things that might lead him to make decisions that will violate his integrity.[11] Instead, Rousseau wishes to complete his political thinking by providing its educational supplement. To this end, Rousseau's *Émile* places an extraordinary emphasis on gender, one that is frequently overlooked in the literature. Gender is not incidental to Émile's upbringing; rather it is central. Rousseau states outright that he is concerned with raising a man qua man and will not stand for Émile developing any qualities that he perceives as effeminate. For Rousseau, there are two distinct genders and they should not be confused. It is in light of this point that examining Émile through Rousseau's discussion of Sophie—the woman—and Émile's relationship to Sophie is fundamental to understanding why Rousseau places such a premium on self-sufficiency. We will see later that the role gender plays in defining subjectivity will provide an interesting point of intersection between Levinas and Rousseau.[12]

This rigid division of genders eventually breaks down, and Rousseau reveals that among other things, Émile is not the master at all. Rather, the master is Sophie. Moreover, the ambiguous conclusion of this book and the short sequel that followed *Émile* lead us to wonder if such an education, even in this fictional account, is possible or even desirable. In his efforts to ensure that Émile is educated in order to avoid becoming a victim of *amour-propre*, Rousseau risks educating Émile to be incapable of having or sustaining any relationships at all. In other words, Rousseau is so concerned that Émile not become a victim of dependency such that he might sell his soul for vanity, that Émile seems unable to sustain any healthy elements of being dependent on others. Rousseau thus implies that there are no healthy attendants of dependency.

The most interesting subtext of *Émile* is that we can see the flaws only when we understand how much of this book is about controlling gendered behavior. It is not only that Rousseau wants Émile to be self-sufficient; it is that self-sufficiency is identified with being male—being a man. Dependency—all forms of it—is identified with femininity and thus must be rejected wholesale. This bad faith leads him to believe that he can reject, or undo, the most obvious and necessary example of dependency—our original relationship to our mothers. In order to understand how the education of Émile is really the education of a boy developing into a man, it is necessary to turn our attention to Rousseau's comparatively brief discussion of the woman.[13]

At the beginning of book 1 of *Émile,* Rousseau addresses his audience by saying, "Tender, anxious mother, I appeal to you." The author's footnote to this address begins as follows:

> The earliest education is most important and it undoubtedly is woman's work. If the author of nature had meant to assign it to men he would have given them milk to feed the child. Address your treatises on education to the women, for not only are they able to watch over it more closely than men, not only is their influence always predominant in education, its success concerns them more nearly, for most widows are at the mercy of their children . . .[14]

This statement is noteworthy for several reasons. First, we begin book 1 of *Émile* immediately with the question of the identity of Rousseau's audience. In the body of the text he directly addresses women, or more specifically, mothers; but the footnote, referring to both men and women in the third person, makes the audience for this text less clear.[15]

Second, even if we grant that he is addressing his comments to mothers, their role is limited and instrumental, since they are to hand Émile (the child) over to the tutor who will complete his education. The original influence and importance of the nursing mother is subordinated to the significance of Émile's "real" education, which begins when the child is handed over to the tutor to be educated in near isolation. These originary intersubjective relations that reveal humanity as dependent and vulnerable, Rousseau either overlooks or forgets when he moves Émile to his new life with the tutor, a relationship in which Émile is supposed to be kept ignorant of the dependency that is nonetheless cultivated.

Similar to other models of education and other views of women, Rousseau's discussion in book 1 of *Émile* leads us to believe that the role of women in this contrived environment is to bear and nurse the child only to turn that child over to the tutor. And again, similar to other models of education, the educational model described by Rousseau implies that women—or at least, mothers—are not fit to be tutors. The tutor needs to be someone who will not stand in the way of the student by projecting onto the student his or her own interests, desires, and needs. It would seem that a distant observer, a disinterested tutor, is the ideal candidate. Where the mother would fail in the endeavor to raise Émile with immunity to the corrupting forces of society, Rousseau believes the tutor will succeed.[16]

Rousseau acknowledges that some dependency is non-negotiable. As we see at the end of the book, Émile does become dependent on the tutor; the significant point is that Émile developed unaware of this dependency. Thus, for all his concern about dependency, Rousseau's educational model relies on a relationship of dependency. In light of the corruption that Rousseau fears dependent relationships will yield, ought he not fear that this child is at the complete mercy of the tutor? What is to prevent the tutor from taking advantage of the child? Rousseau presupposes that the tutor is in fact a "mensch," without providing any explanation for his origin. Additionally, he invests all of this dependency in one relationship—that between the child and his tutor. The goodhearted tutor whom Rousseau conjures up is not only over-determined, he is nothing short of magical.[17] I will return to the "problem of origins" later in this chapter.

Having abandoned the female influence early in *Émile*, Rousseau reintroduces it to us in book 5, when we meet Sophie, the woman to whom Émile is romantically matched. Book 5 tells the story of Sophie's education, a discussion that complicates the status of the woman in this educational project. In fact, although Émile is the one who is "formally" educated and ostensibly educated away from the corrupting forces of society—including the mother—his encounter with Sophie indicates that his entire education has been intended to culminate in this one event: how to be a man in a relationship with a woman. Additionally, Sophie is charged with the responsibility to oversee Émile's behavior. Émile is educated by a man to be a man; Sophie's education "must be planned in relation to man" for she is the one who tends to him as a parent tends to a child.[18] Her teaching efforts model the tutor's. But there is an important difference: Sophie must speak and act such that she *leads* Émile to do what is expected of him:

> Thus the different constitution of the two sexes leads us to a third conclusion, that the stronger party seems to be master, but is as a matter of fact dependent on the weaker, and that, not by any foolish custom of gallantry, nor yet by the magnanimity of the protector, but by an inexorable law of nature. For nature has endowed woman with a power of stimulating man's passions in excess of man's power of satisfying those passions, and has thus made him dependent on her goodwill, and compelled him in his turn to endeavor to please her, so that she may be willing to yield to his superior strength.[19]

Sophie is "educated" to win Émile's affections, and ultimately to have mastery over him by keeping his affections; it is a dependency that Rousseau applauds. Thus, it is Sophie who knows much more about *who* Émile is than he knows about himself. The layers of knowledge and self-knowledge that go without comment or discussion are remarkable in light of this book's focus on education. Rousseau subscribes to the classic, and old-fashioned, view that it is women who *really* have the power in the home, even if that power is both implicit and ephemeral. Yet, here I wish to note that the law supports and enforces Émile's power.[20]

Nonetheless, Rousseau leads his readers to believe that through her wily ways Sophie is in control.

It is worth noting that the role Sophie plays in this book is parallel to the one played by the feminine in Levinas's larger ethical project.[21] Both Sophie and Levinas's "feminine" are ultimately the figures with epistemic privilege and ultimately ethical privilege, even if that is not how either philosopher would characterize this point. Although Rousseau has Sophie in a subordinate educational position, Sophie is nonetheless the one who knows more than Émile knows. Sophie replaces the tutor and is in charge of managing Émile. Her responsibility is to persuade Émile to do what is right, but he needs to act with the belief that he has made his own decision. This careful manipulation requires Sophie to know herself and Émile in a manner similar to that described by Hegel in the Lordship and Bondage section of the *Phenomenology*. Just as the slave drives the dialectic, Sophie drives this relationship.

Insofar as Émile is dependent on Sophie, his dependency is unknown to him, and Rousseau believes that this lack of knowledge regarding his dependency is crucial. In fact, this dependency is denied by all parties in order to maintain the noble illusion of male independence. Sophie must continue to win his affections and have Émile believe his actions issue from his own choice, rather than because she has tricked him, for whatever reason, into acting according to her own wishes. Émile's love for Sophie is the result of a careful manipulation, and Sophie successfully "pleases" him. In spite of Rousseau's display of contempt for the coquettishness and manipulations of French women, it is clear that he needs Sophie to be manipulative since Émile cannot know that he is in fact dependent on her. So just as Émile finds himself "falling" for her—potentially hopelessly devoted to her—the tutor arranges for Émile to travel abroad so that he can return to Sophie "worthy" of her—i.e., as the autonomous male he was educated to be, one who believes he can live without her. In the end, it is Sophie to whom the tutor transfers his guardianship of Émile even though this dependency is kept secret, thus undermining any "fact" that Émile is truly independent of her.[22]

The layered complexity of dependency is underscored by the very last few lines of the book, in which Émile embraces his tutor and tells him that he is more dependent on the tutor than ever before, now that he, Émile, is on the verge of becoming a father.

> My master, congratulate your son; he hopes soon to have the honor of being a father. What a responsibility will be ours, how much we shall need you! Yet God forbid that I should let you educate the son as you educated the father. God forbid that so sweet and holy a task should be fulfilled by any but myself, even though I should make as good a choice for my child as was made for me! But continue to be the teacher of the young teachers. Advise and control us; we shall be easily led; as long as I live I shall need you. I need you more than ever now that I am taking up the duties of manhood.[23]

Here, however, Émile is aware of his dependency on the tutor, in part because the tutor confessed the truth of how he raised him. This dependency appears more profound than the tutor anticipated. In the end, as revealed in the sequel to Émile—*Émile et Sophie, ou Les Solitaires*—Émile turns out to be far more dependent on the tutor than he might have been in any "normal" relationship between a parent and child.[24] There is a strange sense in which Rousseau has both inverted and perverted the originary parent-child relationship and then later the relationship between lovers. The unhealthy dependency that develops between the tutor and Émile ultimately prevents Émile from developing a healthy relationship of dependency on Sophie.

Central to this educational model is Rousseau's reliance on the magical, goodhearted tutor, who enters into the relationship with Émile prepared to help him flourish and always with Émile's best interests in mind. Rousseau delivers an educational model that while accentuating the independent male, relies on at least a minimal dependency; Émile is serially and "monogamously" dependent, one person at a time with a limited number of people on whom he can form this type of relationship. If we follow the gender analysis through to its end then we see how Rousseau identifies the limits of the original relationship of dependency on the mother in order to emphasize Émile's dependency on the tutor, and then ultimately on Sophie. Rousseau's wish to avoid all unhealthy dependent relationships in order to be immune to forces of corrupt institutions leads to an educational system precisely as he describes it—one which continues the suspicion of community and sends the mixed message where dependence is simultaneously encouraged and shunned.

According to Rousseau, we somehow need to develop the psychological and emotional maturity that will advance us to the stage of accepting a commitment without knowing what the commitment will yield, and we need to do this voluntarily. For example, those of us who are married know what it means to be married; we know that the rhetoric of those who are single and believe themselves to be "more free" is in one sense simply rhetoric; in another sense it is accurate. Although unmarried people are able to act in ways that a married person cannot (or maybe should not), this kind of freedom is not the kind of freedom promised or delivered by the institution of marriage. The same can be said of having children or going to school. From the outside, the people on the "inside" appear constrained, in "chains." Indeed, the outsiders are not mistaken; the insiders are in chains. Rousseau never promised to remove the chains, only to justify them. We choose them because we understand them to be the conditions of something more fulfilling than natural freedom. We know something that the outsiders can know only by first taking that leap and entering the institution. And they can get there only if there is an institution to help them along. What does this mean for an educational project?[25] While Rousseau brilliantly diagnosed the problem, and while he also brilliantly recognized that a complementary educational method is necessary to achieve the ideal subject, he could not deliver the educational component to deliver the kind of man he wanted—one able to sustain a healthy dependency while also able to eschew all the unhealthy ones.

Overcoming the Myth of the Overman

A seminal nineteenth-century existentialist, Nietzsche, in his educational philosophy expressed primarily in *Thus Spoke Zarathustra,* repeats themes found earlier in the ancient Greeks, yet with a more sophisticated commentary. However, what distinguishes both Socrates and Zarathustra from other teachers is that the former believe they have seen the problem with education. To their credit, they are able diagnosticians, and I admire them precisely because they tried to remake themselves into a different kind of teacher—Socrates refusing money from his students, for example. My question is the following: are they different enough, and if so, are they different in ways that matter? The effects that Socrates has on his interlocutors and that the dialogues frequently have on our own students indicate that he might not have been as successful as he wished.[26] The common response of both teachers—Socrates and Zarthustra—is to blame the students and then rework the pedagogy so that it fits this new, and frequently patronizing, conception of them. While I grant that responsibility on the part of the student needs to be taken more often than it typically is, this approach to pedagogy is not effective. Socrates falls short of his own goal not only to provide a critical account of the problem with education, but also to become one of the "new" teachers. In the end he reveals how closed he actually is and how patronizing he is to his students who, in some instances, are also identified as his friends.

My examination of Zarathustra reveals the mythology that there exist rigid boundaries between those who are teachers and students. This is not to say that teachers have nothing to teach and students have nothing to learn. Rather, my point is that this process is dynamic, not static, and that the inability to see this relationship as such stems from a more basic view of the self as solitary or self-sufficient. Additionally, it contributes to a view of education as one that is also solitary, in spite of the presence of the teacher. Teachers, if they are attentive, continue to learn; they continue to be self-reflective; and they realize that self-knowledge must always undergo a change in perception about oneself. Students must also be attentive to what a teacher is attempting to convey and the message that is actually being sent. They must realize that in their responses to their teachers, they convey things back to the teacher about him/herself.

Zarathustra also presents a particular image of himself, and yet he believes his disciples grossly misunderstand him. The textual evidence reveals that this misinterpretation of him is due largely to his own presentation and his own language, all of which is the result of his, in fact, not knowing who he is. In spite of the underlying philosophical message to "know thyself," both Socrates and Zarathustra reveal their respective lack of self-knowledge.[27] In light of Nietzsche's aim to provide a critique of traditional philosophy, Zarathustra's lack of insight is ironic. Zarathustra needs more self-knowledge and more philosophy, not less. In the end, Nietzsche knows this and his critique is less about philosophy as self-knowledge than it is about the hypocrisy of philosophers who claim to want that self-knowledge but whose own pedagogical style reveals that they neither have this knowledge nor have any real interest in obtaining it. Additionally, we find in *Zarathustra* Nietzsche's critique of modernity and precisely those values that are glorified, namely, self-sufficiency and autonomy. Contrary to how Nietzsche is often presented, the epigraph that Levinas cleverly uses to introduce the second essay in *Humanism of the Other,* which I turn to in the next chapter, points to a Nietzsche, or a Zarathustra, that has a different view of humanity as an end. The question is whether Nietzsche, or Zarathustra, has achieved this end and, if not, to consider the reasons for the failure.

Whatever his flaws, we cannot underestimate Nietzsche's influence on the future of German philosophy and in particular French and German existentialism, nor should we ignore the fleeting negative comments that Levinas directs toward Nietzsche, in spite of whatever commonality Nietzsche and Levinas might share.[28] My aim in this chapter is not to decide if this reading of Nietzsche is correct. Similar to my point about the depiction of Socrates, for the purposes of my argument in this chapter, the question is not whether the reception of Nietzsche has remained faithful to what Nietzsche intended, but rather that this is the model that was adopted and has influenced several generations of thinkers. Indeed, this pedestrian but all too common reading of Nietzsche misses his original insights. That these appropriations of his thought have not remained faithful simply reaffirms my claims in this chapter that there is frequently, and maybe even necessarily, a discrepancy between the message the teacher hopes to convey and the message the student receives. As a result, the myth of self-sufficiency, perpetuated by our models of education, needs to be addressed.

In his 1954 essay, "Who is Nietzsche's Zarathustra?" the German philosopher Martin Heidegger examines the relationship between two of Zarathustra's teachings: the overman and the doctrine of the eternal return. The question however is not so easily answered.[29] Heidegger presents a persuasive case that while Nietzsche thought he was bringing an end to metaphysics, *Zarathustra* reveals a fundamental reliance on metaphysics. Heidegger offers a compelling reading of these two teachings and their link to each other. However, my interest lies not in the unity of the teachings, but in the project as a whole. What is the link between these teachings and Zarathustra's pedagogy? In the end it does not matter what the teachings prove if Zarathustra is not equal to the task of trying to teach them. Put more simply, I am interested in the unity of Zarathustra himself, a problem that is revealed in the representation of Zarathustra's identity to others.

In Book II of *Thus Spoke Zarathustra,* Zarathustra says, "My friends I do not want to be mixed up and confused with others."[30] Although Zarathustra implores his disciples not to confuse him with others, his demand is too late. Throughout part 2 we continually see that Zarathustra is trying to distinguish himself, even if unsuccessfully, from how others identify him which then requires us to ask after the source of this confusion. Zarathustra's question, "Who am I?" at the end of part 2, indicates that Zarathustra himself is confused about his own identity. The confusion then can be seen from two perspectives: (1) who he is as seen from the point of view of his disciples and (2) who he is as someone whose identity remains obscure even to himself. It is not clear that these two perspectives are mutually exclusive, and they might even be necessarily intertwined. The disciples' "confusion" might not be a confusion at all but rather an identification of the Zarathustra that is presented to others even if unwittingly so by Zarathustra himself.

Later in the text, the experience of revenge plays a role in Zarathustra's confusion.[31] At the end of part 2, Zarathustra's ressentiment evolves into bad conscience—"I am ashamed." According to Gilles Deleuze, each of these reactive types is made bearable, as well as possible, by an ascetic ideal.[32] These "moments" of revenge parallel Zarathustra's movement toward self-realization. During the time when Zarathustra is caught in the spirit of revenge—ressentiment or bad conscience—he is confused about who he is. Deleuze's observation that "our knowledge of the will to power will remain limited if we do not grasp its manifestation in ressentiment, bad conscience, the ascetic ideal and the nihilism which forces us to know it" reveals the necessity of moving through revenge.[33] The spirit of revenge gives us insight into spirit itself, and thus gives us insight into the will to power. As part 2 progresses, Zarathustra begins to move out of revenge toward self-discovery.

The final source of his disciples' confusion can be found in the later speeches of this second part in which we see emerging from this confusion Zarathustra's initial awareness regarding his own confusion. Revenge, then, is embodied in two ways: ressentiment, which is revenge externalized, and bad conscience, which is revenge internalized and thus turns into guilt. The key to redemption is to overcome the spirit of revenge through an affirmation of the past. To will the past and to will it again does away with blame and guilt. Without suffering, the cycle of guilt and punishment is broken. This moment of linking the will to power to the eternal return is the key to Zarathustra's own identity, to his own discovery about who he is. His confusion regarding his own identity is more apparent in light of his moments of self-discovery. As the hunchback notices (in "On Redemption"), Zarathustra speaks differently to others, to his disciples, and to himself. Yet, this could be an indication that Zarathustra is not only misunderstood by his disciples, if indeed he is misunderstood, but that Zarathustra misunderstood them. By the end of the soothsayer speech, he sees that they are not who he took them to be, and by the end of the speech "On Redemption" he begins to realize that it may be he, and he alone, who is the redeemer. At the end of part 2, Zarathustra believes that he must make a complete split from his disciples; he must make the journey to the overman alone. He misunderstood his disciples when he believed that the way of the overman was for them. It was not; it was for him alone.

The confusion about Zarathustra's identity is significant since it is upon Zarathustra's discovery about who he is that he also recognizes his mistaken assumption about whose task it is to go on the journey to the overman. Upon realizing who he is, Zarathustra also sees his disciples for who they are, and more importantly, who they cannot be. At the end of part 2, Zarathustra realizes that it is he alone who must assume this task. I use the term "realizes" with hesitation, since it is not clear his realization is accurate or even authentic. This belief, however, grounds what we see as a standard model of education, and more specifically, teaching. The teacher must go the distance alone without the students. The teacher's intended message is not always the message the students receive. In spite of Zarathustra's insistence that he will not return from his journey to the overman, he in fact does return.

I do not dispute that Zarathustra is searching; his frustration with his students, which leads him to rethink his teaching methods, is a sign of this searching. However, his search lacks inward reflection; he does not search himself. His focus on his students as the location of the flaw in the teaching leads to the second level of the pedagogical problem. In order to correct the teaching, Zarathustra journeys alone in the search. The reciprocity necessarily inherent in an effective and sophisticated model of education is disregarded. Like Rousseau's, this model assumes that education is static for the teacher. The teacher is oblivious to the other person, the student, and therefore remains untouched and unchanged by him or her—or, at least, is unable to acknowledge these changes as a result of contact with the other person.

We find a similar return in Plato's cave allegory in book 7 of his *Republic*. The allegory poses the possibility of the "return" as hypothetical—what *would* happen if the escapee who now has seen the light were to return to the cave? However, Socrates can certainly be viewed as the most famous escapee, who not only returns to the masses repeatedly but whose return eventually did motivate others to kill him. Like Zarathustra, Socrates cannot help himself. We see his return in Plato's *Republic, Euthyphro, Meno,* and *Apology* to name only a few: Plato's *Republic* begins with Socrates' announcement that he went down to Piraeus; the *Euthyphro* shows him engaged with a young man who, returning from the courthouse, tells Socrates that he has just charged his father with impiety; *Meno* elucidates the problem with teaching virtue; and the *Apology* recounts Socrates' final act of the return—that of trying to convince a jury of his peers that he is innocent of the charges against him.

Plato's dialogues are carefully, and artfully, crafted, and we are led to believe that Socrates is the hero. He is more frequently than not referenced as the ideal teacher, and many of us secretly wish we could choreograph our classroom discussions so that we too could gently lead our students to see the error of their own arguments and unsupported beliefs. For me, that wish is often tempered by an accompanying discomfort with the model. What if we were to consider that Socrates simply upholds a model of teaching that is not only ineffective but also dishonest? Is Socrates who he presents himself to be? And similar to the problems encountered by Zarathustra, what does this mistaken identity mean for Socrates? What does it mean for the teacher in general? Additionally, and not unrelated to these other questions, we can ask what role listening plays in teaching. In what ways do students have something to teach teachers, not simply about the material at hand but about who the teachers are as individuals? How might student responses reveal that identity? What if the image we think we convey about ourselves is not the one that our students see, and what if our students can give us a more accurate accounting? How might we understand the relationship between teacher and student differently? How might we understand the model of education differently? My point in raising these questions is to acknowledge, on the one hand, that both Socrates and Zarathustra are pivotal figures not only in philosophical education but also in philosophical theories about education. Socrates is offered as the model teacher, the exemplar of teaching; Zarathustra is presented as a radical critique of philosophy and education. Yet, on the other hand, both reveal that they subscribe to a model of education that is conventional and frequently ineffective.

What is common to both Socrates, as represented by the Platonic model of teaching, and Nietzsche's Zarathustra is an emphasis on the privileged position of the teacher of virtue who, as a result of this position, stands above his students.[34] As Daniel Conway notes, "[the teacher of virtue] views the construction of his position as neither contingent nor arbitrary. He consequently exempts himself from his own teaching on the grounds that [in Zarathustra's case] he has already renounced his belief in God."[35] But as Conway also notes, Zarathustra has "invented" the conditions of his success as a teacher. The same could be said of Socrates.

Good Diagnoses; Bad Cure

In spite of what might appear to be radical differences between them, *Émile* and *Zarathustra* share a view of education that explicitly advocates autonomy and independence as the goal of education, while implicitly relying on dependence and vulnerability for education to occur at all. That is, both texts overlook or discount the role of the community in the educational process, and for good reason. As we saw in the Socratic/Platonic model, community equals mass-thinking, and this is a corruption of creative, independent thinking. Additionally, as Rousseau demonstrates, the community is often something to fear. However, this valorization of the individual allows, in particular, Socrates, Zarathustra, and the magical tutor in *Émile* to disregard any learning on their own part. They are listeners, but only of the contemptuous and sophomoric comments of their students.

Like Rousseau, Nietzsche represents someone who almost gets it right. Like Rousseau, he can identify the problem, but he cannot solve it on his own. Nietzsche's *Zarathustra* clarifies, more than any other book in the history of philosophy, the flaws in the standard model of teaching and philosophical education; it seems that this is precisely Nietzsche's intention. Nietzsche's description of and admiration for the *agon* might have led him to admire the talmudic approach to education, which is often criticized for its competitiveness.[36] Similar to Rousseau, Nietzsche also identifies what is wrong with philosophy and philosophical education. However, if I am right that the radical critique of this model of education could only come from wholly outside of it, then the solution is one that Nietzsche could only have glimpsed. He might never have been able to find it on his own. In fact, one might even say that this is precisely the moment where Nietzsche's ambivalence with regard to Judaism betrays him. Nietzsche's diagnosis of the problems in philosophy and philosophical education is correct, but he needed the help of the Jewish "doctors," whom he dismissed as part of the problem, to help him cure the disease.

The primary problem with Nietzsche's analysis is his apparent conflation of Christianity and Judaism. No doubt, Christians have their own complaints about how Nietzsche has characterized Christianity; but we cannot ignore how he characterized Judaism. We can begin with Nietzsche's own ambivalence toward Judaism, some of which is probably the result of his lack of knowledge about Judaism. Most readers of Nietzsche recognize that his admiration for Judaism is the Judaism of the Torah—the kingly Jews, the Jews who were warriors, and Yahweh, a God whose wrath was feared. It is the post-Diaspora Jews, the Jews represented by the prophetic and priestly periods, whom Nietzsche does not completely respect.[37] For Nietzsche, the rabbinic period is simply more of the same.[38] To his unschooled eyes, these later stages of Judaism simply look like Christianity. Yet, it is precisely in these periods that we find the radical distinction between Judaism and Christianity, for it is in the rabbinic period which gave rise to the Midrash and then later, the Talmud, that we find Jewish wisdom, a love of life, and a unique educational model. Nietzsche's disdain for this Jewish period and his naïve view that it resembled Christianity precluded him from seeing precisely how Judaism was different in one of the most significant ways. Judaism does not begin with an ascetic ideal.[39] As a result, problems like ressentiment are simply pseudo-problems.

Nietzsche's fondness for the God of the Hebrew Bible, which he viewed as a God of vengeance, a God who "took no crap," so to speak, reveals his own limited understanding of the Hebrew Bible. The God of the Hebrew Bible is viewed in terms of both justice and mercy—this duality is not simply a later addition. To be fair to Nietzsche, it probably did not help matters that most of the Jews in Nietzsche's midst—late nineteenth-century Germany—were in the habit of converting to Christianity, thus making Judaism, at least contemporary Judaism, seem interchangeable with Christianity, or worse, giving way to it. One can also ask after the resemblance that contemporary Reform Judaism has to Protestant Christianity, an unfortunate comparison that Reform Judaism continually battles. Even if one takes this comparison seriously, it is not the Orthodox Judaism of today—a striking contrast to Christianity—that Nietzsche would praise. Rather, I suspect he would valorize the secular Judaism of Israel that finds itself continually standing to defend itself in a literally warlike posture.

Nietzsche's lack of knowledge about Judaism prevented him from seeing what this Jewish tradition could offer for his diagnosis of what is wrong with philosophy and philosophical education. Regardless, no matter what perspective we take when we look at Nietzsche's work, we see that he is indispensable for philosophical analysis even if insufficient to provide us with answers. In order to correct this deficiency, I argue that we need to turn to a different model of education.

Although this chapter focuses on Rousseau and Nietzsche, we find similar models of education and their respective flaws throughout the history of philosophy. In light of the little attention philosophy of education is given by philosophers today, one might be led to believe that education, either in theory or practice, was not important to philosophers. Yet, the history of philosophy is in fact a history of the philosophy of education—the single question that we see dealt with repeatedly in some form or other is the question of education. We see this question addressed when a philosopher offers a method for the best way to achieve the ideal polis. But we also see it simply in the way that philosophy talks about itself. For example, in the pursuit of knowledge, someone has an insight, attains wisdom, or finds truth. The all-consuming question, then, becomes how to convey this experience to others. The paradox of this educational model lies in the manner in which one attained the wisdom and the pedagogical stance one now assumes. To put it simply, the educational model that persists in Western philosophy and how we apply this model in real schools begin in a flawed state.

We do not need to return to the ancient Greeks to find the flaw—nor is it clear that the flaw lies with the Greeks as much as it lies with those who appropriate and deploy the model. Regardless, we find this same model of education promoted by philosophers in the modern period. As we saw earlier in this chapter, Rousseau's *Émile* is characterized first and foremost by a magical tutor who has been charged with the responsibility to educate Émile in a manner that will at once prevent him from being vulnerable to the corrupting forces of society while also preparing him to find his place in that society. Additionally, like Zarathustra and Socrates, the tutor in *Émile* constructs an educational model that is built on deception.

Like Nietzsche, Rousseau has accurately, even if unfortunately, identified the primary problem of dependency—it can lead us to make decisions, serious decisions, based on greed, vanity, and fear rather than on justice and morality. Thus, Rousseau opts for an educational model that removes the student from society and educates him in near isolation, with only the tutor for company and social education. Without question there are many philosophical problems with this model, for example: who is the tutor; where does he come from; how does he become the person most able to accomplish this task; and why does he not represent some residual elements of the society from which he is also to protect the child? Most obviously, how does one learn to be a participant in a society when raised in near isolation? Similar to Zarathustra, the tutor is represented as static and unchanging; it is Émile who must learn. The pedagogical relationship that Rousseau depicts is not dynamic, where each participant is changed by his/her participation.

To repeat my claim at the beginning of this chapter, it is putting it mildly to say that the educational method that is founded on this model persists in a flawed state.[40] If we recall the discussion of Rousseau's *Émile,* the most pressing problem is how to start anew—from where does this magical tutor, who is not himself contaminated by culture, come? Rousseau's *Émile* exemplifies the problem of origins, a philosophical problem that can be traced back through the history of philosophy. The paradox appears most famously in Plato's *Republic* when the children are rounded up, separated from their parents, and placed in an educational environment that will help sort them according to their natural state. And it appears again in Aristotle's *Nicomachean Ethics* when the discussion of educating the young children emerges—who will teach them? How will a *phronemos* come into being? In all these instances, education promises a new and improved generation, but the question of who will do the educating, who has "magically" been able to become the kind of person that this education promises without this education, is never answered. It is a problem that plagues all political and educational models that must start anew and that assume a kind of person who is needed in order to produce these very citizens. Although it can certainly be chalked up to a thought-experiment, like the state of nature in political theory, it is nonetheless a real problem. If a new model of education is needed to produce a certain kind of person, then who will be the teacher? Yet, I would argue that from a particular perspective, the paradox is illusory and serves as a distraction. If we allow the paradox to take hold, we will be paralyzed and do nothing.

In her 2009 book *Emergency Politics,* political theorist Bonnie Honig frames this paradox in terms of law: We need good citizens to make good law and we need good laws to make good citizens.[41] Developing what she labels a Jewish political theory, Honig works through this paradox to offer an alternative theory to the dominant views regarding the state of exception. In emergency situations, when can a sovereign override the accepted rights of its citizens? The prevailing framework for the discussion traces its roots back to Carl Schmitt's political theology, which has reinvigorated contemporary discussions through such figures as Giorgio Agamben. Finding the contemporary debates inadequate and thinking that political theorists and philosophers are spinning their wheels by returning to the same originary ideas, Honig seeks a new possibility, one that might be more useful to democratic societies.

Honig's book provides a compelling argument for conceiving political theory in a radically new way. To accomplish this task, she turns to Jewish philosophy as her resource. Although she discusses the important role of pedagogy, she does so in the context of addressing an adult audience who would learn something new—e.g., how do these examples of resistance function pedagogically? The absence of a discussion of "pedagogy" that would be relevant to younger people nonetheless reminds me that much of the work that we need to do as a society should take place with the younger people who will assume responsibility in this democratic society. I do not mean to suggest that Honig should have written a different book. Indeed, Honig gestures toward education in her discussion of the paradox of politics, which although framed slightly differently, resembles the paradox, or problem, of origins.

Honig rightly rejects a view that directs its attention only to the adult and this understanding of the political. Yet, I would argue that the process needs to begin earlier than where Honig begins. If we need to cultivate citizens who can engage complex problems with creativity, imagination, and intellectual acumen, then starting as adults and doing this *through* law might not be the best approach. I concede that growing up in the shadow of the civil rights movement and attending schools that were desegregated shaped my life and my relationship to the world in ways that cannot be articulated. On reflection, I realize that it was not the law *per se* that accomplished this goal; it was the enactment of the law. It was going to school with and having friends who were of different backgrounds—racially, economically, and religiously—that shaped my world. Like the chicken-egg problem, the paradox of political origins is an interesting philosophical problem: we can wonder indefinitely about which comes first. Yet, the fact remains that we have both chickens and eggs, and our attention now is focused on how to keep producing both. We can do the same with education. In a move that parallels Levinas's, I argue that for Honig's political theory to be effective, we must begin with and radically change the education of the younger people in our communities.

My intention is not to chastise those philosophers who replicated this model. Rather, my interest lies in the striking similarity of all these models throughout the history of philosophy, in spite of even the most radical critiques of philosophy presented by the philosophers themselves. Nietzsche's *Zarathustra* does not escape a traditional pedagogical model, even though he launches one of the most insightful critiques of philosophy and religion of his time. In Nietzsche's defense, one might say that similar to Rousseau's discovery revealed in *Les Soli-*

taires, the sequel to *Émile,* Nietzsche has seen the error of this way. Yet, while both Rousseau and Nietzsche identify the problem with education, neither demonstrates the capability of finding the tools to fix it. I would argue that given the constraints of their own thinking neither of them could have seen how to fix it.

These models of education not only developed in humanism's wake but also carry forward both its promise and failure, promoting both the humanism and the anti-humanism against which Levinas argues. Our contemporary models of education are indebted to the Enlightenment, the development of French Republicanism and the promise of universal rights, and the implicit view that secular education shapes character—a fundamental premise of humanism. Although contemporary educational models vary widely, they can generally trace their basic tenets to Rousseau's *Émile,* which was put into practice most widely by his inheritors, Maria Montessori and John Dewey. It is significant that Rousseau's political and educational philosophy is frequently linked to the French Revolution, which gave rise to the development of French Republicanism and the principles of the Rights of Man. The apparent counter to Rousseau's model is seen in Nietzsche's character of Zarathustra. Returning to these formative models of education reveals the intimate relationship that education has to questions about the cultivation of the individual and the citizen—that is, its relationship to the political. The paradox Honig raises recalls my original questions: What is the relationship between political and educational theory? What is the relationship between politics and education? How does Levinas's turn to Jewish education fit into the answer?

If Levinas's project leads us to believe that radical critique of this model of education could only come from wholly outside of it, then the solution is one that Nietzsche and Rousseau could only have glimpsed. They might never have been able to find it on their own. In fact, one might even say that this is precisely the moment where Nietzsche's ambivalence with regard to Judaism betrays him. Nietzsche's diagnosis of the problems in philosophy and philosophical education is correct, but he needed the help of the Jewish "doctors," whom he dismissed as part of the problem, to help him cure the disease.[42] Yet, it was not only Nietzsche who dismissed the Jewish "doctors." As Levinas laments, so too did the Jews.

3   The Crisis of Humanism

> I love him whose soul is overfull so that he forgets himself, and all
> things are in him: thus all things become his downfall.
>
> —Nietzsche, *Thus Spoke Zarathustra*

In his 1933 essay "Biblical Humanism," Martin Buber outlines the distinction
between Western humanism and what he calls biblical humanism.[1] Similar to
the kind of argument that we will see Levinas make, Buber argues that just as
Western humanism has drawn from its respective literary sources, so too should
Judaism draw from the sources that inform it, thus leading to a humanism that
would be distinctly biblical. He maintains that there is a difference between a
Hebrew man and a biblical man where "only a man worthy of the Bible is a Hebrew man."[2] He continues, "Only that man is a Hebrew man who lets himself
be addressed by the voice that speaks to him in the Hebrew Bible and who responds to it with his life . . . This is the meaning of biblical humanism."[3]

Levinas offers a similar definition of humanism in 1946 when he returns to
the Alliance Israélite Universelle (AIU) in order to assume the Directorship of
the École Normale Israélite Orientale (ENIO), the branch of the AIU that provides Jewish education to French youth and trained the male students to become
teachers. Less than a year into his service in this position, Levinas pens a short
essay on the reopening of the ENIO, whose operation had been suspended for
the previous six years. He writes the following:

> Our martyrdom, since 1933, gives us a more acute awareness of our solidarity
> across space but also across time, the need to find in the sources of our being
> our reason for being and the mystery of our destiny, the meaning of our hard-
> ships. Whether as a return to the land of their ancestors, or in a more general
> and perhaps more profound form, the recovery of mystical experiences and
> ethics on which Judaism is based and from which it could never be banished—
> *there exists in Israel the need for a Jewish humanism. The ENIO must also take
> that into account.* There must be open access to this Jewish humanism . . . A
> long-term undertaking, certainly, and full of difficulties, but we must attempt
> a future worthy of the ENIO of the past, creating in the old building on Rue
> d'Auteuil[4] a center of Jewish Western spirituality [*spiritualité juive occidentale*]
> which will once again bring something new to the Judaism of the Orient.[5]

We can see from this citation that even as early as 1946, having just returned
from the war and barely having begun his time as director of the school, Levinas

already identifies the need for a Jewish humanism, which by implication is different from the humanism to which Western culture currently subscribes. Additionally, his reference to Israel, in 1946, is two years prior to the formation of Israel as an independent state. His reference to Israel signifies the community of Israel, those who identify as part of the Jewish community. Situated between Levinas's 1934 essay on the philosophy of Hitlerism and his three essays collected in *Humanism of the Other,* the philosophical writings in which he identifies the crisis of humanism, this essay calls for a new humanism, a Jewish humanism.[6]

This humanism will provide the solution to the problem he describes in those essays from the 1930s. The essays written in the 1960s describe how that new humanism will look, and his essays on Jewish education tell us how to achieve it. Using these two points as bookends, this chapter examines how Levinas ties the classical philosophical views we explored in the previous chapter to the "philosophy" of Hitlerism presented in his astonishingly prescient 1934 essay, "Reflections on the Philosophy of Hitlerism." I first trace Levinas's concerns motivated by the trajectory of ideas in the history of Western philosophy that he believes leads to a philosophical discourse that justified Hitlerism. I then turn to his essay "On Escape," published just one year later, in which he continues his exploration of the bodily needs and the myth of solitude as deployed in Western philosophy. In this 1934 essay, Levinas diagnoses a crisis in intellectual thought that emerges from an inability to negotiate the tension between transcendence and immanence.[7] As a result of this crisis, he predicts, our humanity hangs in the balance. In his 1935 essay, he inaugurates a search for a remedy to this crisis.

In 1990, more than fifty years after the essay first appeared in French, an English translation of the essay was published in *Critical Inquiry.* In his prefatory note, written expressly for the translation and republication of the essay, Levinas asks: "Does the subject arrive at the human condition prior to assuming responsibility for the other man in the act of election that raises him up to this height?" The prefatory note appears anachronistic because of his references to "election" and "responsibility to the other man," themes believed to emerge only later in his writings.[8] This 1934 essay tackles the dual problems of classical transcendence and immanence.[9] How then could this essay be about ethics, a term not only absent in this early work, but also not mentioned until 1961 in *Totality and Infinity*?[10] The claim that this prefatory note is anachronistic assumes that Levinas's interest in transcendence and immanence is simply philosophical—the result of a conceptual problem or puzzle in the history of philosophy that he needed to address. Further, this concern with transcendence might also suggest that Levinas's interest in ethics was not a primary concern; rather, it was a secondary concern, the result of seeing the ethical relation as the solution to the philosophical problem of immanence and transcendence. Is the relationship between Levinas's early work and his later work simply the relationship between the posing of a philosophical question and finding its answer?

In contrast to the view sketched above, this chapter argues that Levinas's philosophical work follows a continuity of thought from his early concerns in the 1930s expressed in his essay on Hitlerism to his final works in the 1970s and '80s. My claim is that although we can mark changes in his use of vocabulary and the emphasis he places on different themes, his concern for and interest in ethics, religion, and social justice all based on a reconceived subjectivity not only underly all of his work, but also motivate it. I argue that from his very earliest writings in the 1930s, Levinas saw the question of immanence and transcendence *as* an ethical question, one that speaks to "the very humanity of man." Levinas's sustained discussion in his essays on Jewish education support this point. He identifies the crisis of humanism early in his philosophical writings, and his plea to the Jewish community to return to Jewish education in response to this crisis spans the duration of his philosophical career.

A Cassandrian Prediction

Levinas opens his 1934 essay on Hitlerism by observing that the dangerous elementary feelings—the "secret nostalgia"—that Hitlerism awakens harbor a philosophy. He warns us of precisely what others were unable to see, much less admit: Hitlerism was not simply an accident of evil, the acts of a "sick" man.[11] Rather, its underlying logic permeates a type of thinking that puts into jeopardy "the very humanity of man."[12] In this essay, Levinas reveals the two poles of thinking that provide the context for the tension between immanence and transcendence when both are traditionally understood.[13]

His own words indicate that he also saw the dangerous ethical implications of Hitlerism, even if he could not imagine the real horrors it was still to produce. "Ethics," therefore, while not mentioned explicitly in this essay, was a concern motivating Levinas from the beginning. He ends his 1934 essay alerted to the problem, issuing a warning to his readers, but not yet aware of the solution.[14] As this essay reveals, as early as 1934 he had glimpsed the fundamental difference between Judaism and other modes of religion—the former's emphasis on a relationship to others and the latter's emphasis on self-sufficiency (paganism) or the saving of individual souls (Christianity). If Levinas's concern emerges from his view that the pagan is "sufficient unto himself," then it should not surprise us that his ethical model, which emerges directly out of his reading of Judaism, not only assumes but also privileges a dependent relationship.

Levinas sees that the "elementary feelings" Hitlerism awakens in us "express a soul's principal attitude toward the whole of reality and its own destiny. They predetermine or prefigure the meaning of the adventure that the soul will face in the world . . . It questions the very principles of a civilization" ("Hitlerism," 64). That is to say, if the story of Western civilization is narrated through the tension created by the relationship between immanence and transcendence, then how one orients oneself, how we understand our relationship to the world in terms of immanence or transcendence, determines the future of that world. As Levinas indicates early on, and then reminds us in his concluding paragraph, this is not a conflict played out only between Hitlerism and Liberalism; the fate of Christianity also hangs in the balance.[15] Additionally, reason—read in this context as philosophy and liberalism—is put into question. Is reason, is liberalism, enough to protect against Hitlerism? And while we can call this relationship a logical contradiction, that alone cannot judge the event. To find the meaning of this logical contradiction, he traces the path back to the origin that made this contradiction possible.

Levinas traces the path of religious and philosophical thought that made possible not only Hitlerism but also its accompanying contradictions, such as Christianity's alliance with it. He begins with the following statement:

> Political freedoms do not exhaust the content of the spirit of freedom, a spirit that, in Western civilization, signifies a conception of human destiny. This conception is a feeling that man is absolutely free in his relations with the world and the possibilities that solicit action from him. Man is renewed eternally in the face of the Universe. Speaking absolutely he has no history. ("Hitlerism," 64)

As Kant disclosed, time is a condition of human existence and as such places a profound limitation on us. In spite of Heraclitus's claim that we cannot step into the same river twice, since the waters change as they move, the changing present that Heraclitus describes is illusory. Underneath the eternal flow of things lies "the tragedy" of a past that cannot be undone ("Hitlerism," 65). And so Levinas claims, "true freedom, the true beginning would require a true present," which implies a destiny that is always able to begin anew ("Hitlerism," 65).

On Levinas's reading, Judaism responds to this tragic view and it bears the following message: "Remorse—the painful expression of a radical powerlessness to redeem the irreparable—heralds the repentance that generates the pardon that redeems. Man finds something in the present with which he can modify or efface the past. Time loses its very irreversibility" ("Hitlerism," 65). More simply, one makes mistakes, but then one can repent, one can be forgiven, and the past can be modified, or even more strongly, it can be effaced. This "changing of the past" is accomplished through a human act. Although Judaism bears this message, and although this message informs the view of humanity that follows, it is not this particular message that is carried through. Rather, our current views of time, freedom, and destiny are found in the drama that is played out between the Greek view of destiny—namely, fate—and the Christian response to it.

Set in contrast to Greek destiny, which can be seen vividly in the drama—and ultimately the tragedy—of the House of Atreus, Christianity offers the "mystical drama" of the Cross, which opens up the possibility to be set free from one's past. The Eucharist—the communion with Christ—"triumphs over time and this emancipation takes place every day" ("Hitlerism," 65). Through this act, Christianity makes freedom fully possible and it absolutely changes the idea of a past that is subordinate to the present ("Hitlerism," 65). Thus, Christianity allows for one's destiny to be chosen; the choice is not only itself free but also one that at any moment can be changed. In response to the strength of Greek destiny Levinas nonetheless observes that it is not easy to recover one's freedom. Christianity promises a new order, and its break is complete and definitive. In Levinas's words, "freedom has an austere purity that comes from a transcendent inspiration." Christianity promises the equality of all souls. Based on the power given to the soul to free itself from the past, to be "born again" each day, "to regain its first virginity," this equality is independent of the material or social conditions of people ("Hitlerism," 66).

In response to such a mystical drama, liberalism offers the sovereign freedom of reason ("Hitlerism," 66). In so doing it alters the terms of the game. One can now participate in this equality without having to accept a particular set of metaphysical beliefs, such as the virgin birth, resurrection, or the trinity:

> The whole philosophical and political thought of modern times tends to place the human spirit on a plane that is superior to reality, and so creates a gulf between man and the world. It makes it impossible to apply the categories of the physical world to the spirituality of reason, and so locates the ultimate foundation of the spirit outside the brutal world and the implacable history of concrete existence. It replaces the blind world of common sense with the world rebuilt by idealist philosophy, one that is steeped in reason and subject to reason. In place of liberation through grace there is autonomy, but the Judeo-Christian leitmotif of freedom pervades this autonomy. ("Hitlerism," 66)

Political liberalism promotes a self that is unencumbered by history. Its secular alternative to what Christianity promised provides a useful antidote to the religious view of the soul. Yet, in spite of the simplicity of this exchange, it is not complete. Even the French writers of the eighteenth century, "the precursors of a democratic ideology and the Declaration of the Rights of Man, in spite of their own materialism, confessed to being aware of a reason that exorcises physical, psychological, and social matter." In response to that insight, Levinas asks, "*what remains of materialism when matter has been completely pervaded by reason?*" ("Hitlerism," 66, emphasis added). Unlike Judaism or Christianity, liberalism claims freedom from one's history and thereby opens up possibilities for choosing one's destiny: logical choices are presented and a dispassionate subject makes those choices ("Hitlerism," 66). That is, history and thus destiny play into the present in Christianity, thus making the Eucharist necessary. By contrast, for liberalism and the modern subject there is no history; there is only reason and the possibilities that reason produces.

Continuing his historical narrative (in fewer than ten pages), Levinas turns to Marxism's critique of liberalism, which he claims places limits on the human spirit. Contrary to what was previously thought, human spirit, which is prey to material needs, does not enjoy pure freedom. Rather than suggest that the human spirit transcend these material needs, Marx presents a reversal in the relationship. Responding to Hegel, Marx argues that matter is no longer at the mercy of reason—"reason is impotent and the material needs carry more weight and significance" ("Hitlerism," 67). For Marx, this struggle preexists intelligence and thus "being determines consciousness" ("Hitlerism," 67). By limiting the human spirit's absolute freedom, Marxism opposes not only Christianity but also the whole of idealist liberalism. Levinas credits Marxism with disrupting "the harmonious curve [*courbe*] of [European culture's] development" ("Hitlerism," 67). Marxism's break with this development and with liberalism is nonetheless not complete insofar as it consciously continues the traditions of 1789. Significantly, Marxism retains within it the power of the human to change its destiny. Insofar as individual consciousness retains, at least in principle, the power to "shake off the social bewitchment that then appears foreign to its essence, that is to become conscious of one's social situation," one is able to free oneself from the fatalism entailed by that situation ("Hitlerism," 67).

Thus far, Levinas has taken us through a narrative of intellectual development that delivers the reason of liberalism as a simple exchange for the Eucharist. This exchange frees man completely from the chains of history; there are no links that cannot be undone and there is no history to determine one's destiny. There is only reason. And what we also see is that it is not Marxism that is the opposition to this view. Levinas contends that a more radical view of materialism is needed—one that is not simply an add-on to liberalism, or a development of liberalism, where the power of reason, even if made impotent from its power in liberalism, is nonetheless retained.[16] The link made to the past and that determines the future is not a radical link; it can be broken or modified. To confront the power of reason to change the past and create a new destiny, we must have a new view of European man.

This task can be accomplished only if the situation to which the European subject was bound was not added to him but formed at the very *foundation of his being*. This paradoxical requirement is one that the experience of our bodies seems to fulfill ("Hitlerism," 67). Thus, to begin to respond to this question, Levinas returns to the Greeks to examine what having a body means to these traditional interpretations of the self. He notes that on the one hand "it means tolerating [the body] as an object of the external world. It weighs [*pèse*] on Socrates like the chains [*chaînes*] that way him down in the prison at Athens" ("Hitlerism," 67). In this description, the body is an obstacle to be overcome—and we see this view taken up by and informing Christianity. The body drags the spirit back down to the earthly conditions spirit had hoped to escape. This feeling of eternal strangeness fueled not only the dualism of Christianity but also that of modern liberalism: "It is this feeling that has persisted through every variation in ethics and in spite of the decline suffered by the ascetic ideal since the Renaissance. If the materialists confused the self with the body, it was at the price of a pure and simple negation of the spirit. They placed the body in nature, and accorded it no exceptional standing in the universe" ("Hitlerism," 67–68).[17] The body, then, is not only something eternally foreign, but also that which some thinkers relegated to an inferior level.

On the other hand, from a phenomenological perspective, we identify with our bodies and in so doing, we also create the need to separate from them. Levinas identifies several examples of how we experience our bodies that contribute to our identification with them. For example, we feel a unity with our bodies before the development of the self that claims to be separate; certain activities are performed in such a way that erases any distinction between mind and body. And when someone is ill and turns over to find some peace in a position of comfort, she experiences the "indivisible simplicity of [her] being" ("Hitlerism," 68). For Levinas, this move reveals the spirit's opposition to the pain, a rebellion of sorts not to be reduced to it or remain within it, to go beyond it. But he wonders if this very rebellion undoes the power of spirit to escape: Does the failure to go beyond the pain reveal despair as that which "constitutes the very foundation of pain?" ("Hitlerism," 68).

In spite of how Western thought approaches these "facts" of our existence, which are perceived as crude and diminished, this physical pain can nonetheless "reveal an absolute position" ("Hitlerism," 68). The body is not simply viewed as an accident—happy or not. Rather, "*its adherence to the Self is of value in itself. It is an adherence that one does not escape and that no metaphor can confuse with the presence of an external object; it is a union that does not in any way alter the tragic character of finality*" ("Hitlerism," 68). This adherence prevents any discovery of a spirit that struggles against this enchainment to the body. To struggle against this chain is to betray the originality of the feeling from which one began—thus creating its own paradox and thus its own self-enclosed lock. The feeling gave rise to a view of the self and thus that very feeling cannot be questioned. Unlike modern liberalism, which relegated the body to a mere obstacle to be overcome, this view gives the body a new importance:

> The biological, with the notion of inevitability it entails, becomes more than an *object* of spiritual life. It becomes its heart. The mysterious urgings of the blood, the appeals of heredity and the past for which the body serves as an enigmatic vehicle, lose the character of being problems that are subject to a solution put forward by a sovereignly free Self. Not only does the Self bring in the unknown elements of these problems in order to resolve them; the Self is also constituted by these elements. Man's essence no longer lies in freedom but in a kind of bondage [*enchaînement*]. To be truly oneself does not mean taking flight once more above contingent events that always remain foreign to the Self's freedom; on the contrary, it means becoming aware of the ineluctable original chain that is unique to our bodies, and above all accepting this chaining [*d'enchaînement*]. ("Hitlerism," 69)

Any view of society or a social structure that allows for emancipation with respect to the body is viewed as a betrayal. Thus, any view that promotes this emancipation is viewed as false and deceitful; it leads to society based on blood kinship "and then, if race does not exist, one has to invent it!" ("Hitlerism," 69).

In his return to liberalism and the view of reason that it produces, Levinas reminds us that in liberalism the freedom of spirit is characterized by the distance reason has from its material needs, from the body and the world in which it lives. It is distant and passionless; it can choose anything. The individual is also free not to make a choice, thus making skepticism possible. That is, the responsibility to make a choice, to act, that accompanied both Judaism and Christianity is absent from liberalism. One can reside in a state of perpetually not choosing. Regardless, even when one does choose, freedom is retained and thus the choice can be undone, the choice can be unmade. Within the choice resides its own negation. For Levinas, this freedom constitutes the whole of thought's dignity, but it also harbors its danger: "In the gap that separates man from the world of ideas, deceit insinuates itself" ("Hitlerism," 69). Thought becomes a game. The person does not commit to any truth and the power to doubt is transformed into a lack of conviction. Recalling philosophical nihilism, Levinas observes that an individual's unwillingness "to chain himself to a truth becomes for him not wishing to commit his own self to the creation of spiritual values. Sincerity becomes impossible and puts an end to all heroism. Civilization is invaded by everything that is not authentic, by a substitute that is put at the service of fashion and of various interests" ("Hitlerism," 69–70). It is in this philosophical view of the body that we find the roots of Hitlerism, a society based on and motivated by its views of blood kinship.[18]

We see in Levinas's critique of both immanence and transcendence his own struggle to maintain some aspect of each. A view of transcendence that looks to another place and time allows us to ignore the ills that plague humanity on a daily basis. Pure transcendence takes us away from this world, away from the banal, and quite simply, it denies the reality that we are riveted to our bodies, that our bodies suffer, and that this suffering demands attention. The turn to materiality does not "fix" the problem; instead, it simply adds to it. Materiality acknowledges our connection to daily life and to our material needs and therefore the material needs of others. However, it leads to a view of the body that enchains us to it without any hope for escape from it. Thus, it leads to a dangerous view of humanity that is defined by blood and kinship.

This enchainment in turn precludes "man" from seeing his own ability to escape himself. In other words, to believe that we are enchained simply leads to self-deception regarding the choices that we do make, but more importantly, that we can make. What follows from this kind of thinking is a view of the body that becomes a universality that then gives way to expansion. As Levinas remarks, "the expansion of a force presents a structure that is completely different from the propagation of an idea" and this is how universality gives rise to, or allows for, racism ("Hitlerism," 70). The very way in which this power is wielded allows some to be part of it while others are necessarily excluded. This power yields the world of masters and slaves determined by blood and body, in short, the world of Nazi Germany. Levinas's task henceforth is to reconcile a view of transcendence with a view of being chained to one's body. How can we give an account of transcendence that does not dispense with this world, the world of suffering? How can we give an account of the body that does not leave us enchained?[19]

When Levinas ends this essay with the claim that "it is not a particular dogma concerning democracy, parliamentary government, dictatorial regime, or religious politics that is in question. It is the very humanity of man," he implies that what is at stake is not simply a philosophical or academic question. It is not a question that simply engages the mind; it is not a question on which nothing of significance rides; it is not a question up for debate. It is not simply a philosophical conundrum. Rather, everything rides on it. Everything is at stake. The question is the very question of what it means to live and it is not a question that has more than one possible answer. To answer this question incorrectly might mean the very destruction of humanity. Thus, from the beginning, Levinas is concerned with the ethical, even if he has not named his concern as such.

Levinas continues his exploration of the problematic outlined in this early essay in *On Escape*.[20] Published one year after his essay on Hitlerism, this essay describes the phenomenological structures that demonstrate the interplay between immanence and transcendence in our expressions of existence. The experiences of malaise, suffering, and nausea reveal both our enchainment and our need to escape. That is, these experiences reveal that neither immanence nor transcendence, the latter as classically understood, can offer a satisfactory account of our own being. Levinas's account of nausea is particularly compelling. In his description of this experience, Levinas uncovers the root of the experience— nausea reveals our own vulnerability and complete possibility of nudity before the Other. Nausea functions as a leveling experience in its reminder that we all have bodies; to have the experience of nausea is to be reminded that no matter who we are our bodies can still betray us and reveal us to the Other as nude and vulnerable. The structures that Levinas describes in *On Escape* reveal our identification with our bodies; they remind us of our enchainment, of our being riveted to our bodies, while also revealing our need to escape, even though any escape will not be complete. The "escape" from the "self" still maintains a foothold in being.

Judaism contra Paganism

In this early work, Levinas identifies the philosophical problem that occupied his thought for the next five decades: How can one articulate an answer to the question produced by the history of philosophy? This early work does not identify, at least not explicitly, the solution. We can return to the view posed at the beginning of this chapter, which claims the prefatory note to the 1990 English translation of the Hitlerism essay as anachronistic. The argument for this position might be summarized in the following way: Levinas's project, although ostensibly about ethics, is really about transcendence, a theme that runs through his project from beginning to end. I do not dispute this point. However, to claim that Levinas's focus on ethics is only the result of seeing it as the solution to a philosophical problem overlooks the fundamental relationship between the two, and it ignores the intimacy of this relationship as understood in the Jewish tradition.[21] It seems that from the beginning, Levinas was concerned with a view of humanity that included an acknowledgment of the material needs that we have.[22] His concern with transcendence and immanence in this early work is directly tied to the dangers involved with these conceptions generally, but also specifically insofar as he sees them lead to the philosophical logic that underpins Hitlerism, a violent structure that he then sees replicated in all violence toward the Other.[23]

An alternative reading to the one sketched above suggests that this early essay is not simply a critique of Kantian enlightenment, Marxist emancipation, or Paganism. Let me state clearly that Levinas is not an anti-Enlightenment thinker. Indeed, his writings—all of them—struggle with the relationship between the universal and the particular, and he is very aware of the value of universal rights, in particular human rights. It is precisely because of this awareness and the tension that emerges from his attempts to work through this relationship that his work is so interesting and so complex. That said, Levinas also cleverly traces how the Enlightenment project, with its rejection of religious transcendence, was able to morph into, indeed ironically return to, Paganism, which he finds particularly dangerous.[24]

Levinas not only registers these concerns about Paganism most explicitly in "L'actualité de Maïmonide," published in the same year as On Escape, he also positions Paganism in opposition to Judaism. Repeating the views he expressed in the Hitlerism essay, he confides that he is deeply troubled by the implications of Paganism, one of which is the intimate identification between self and body—or blood kinship:

> Paganism is not the negation of the spirit, nor the ignorance of a unique God. The mission of Judaism would be quite trivial if it limited itself to teaching monotheism to the earth's peoples. This would be to instruct those who already know. *Paganism is a radical powerlessness to get out of the world*. It consists not in denying spirits and gods, but in situating them in the world . . . Pagan morality is only the consequence of this basic incapacity to transgress the limits of the world. The pagan is shut up in this world, *sufficient unto himself* and closed upon himself. He finds it solid and firmly established. He finds it eternal (second emphasis added).[25]

Forty years later, in his 1971 essay, "Hegel and the Jews," Levinas defends the Jews against a similar attack. In this brief essay, he considers a few of Hegel's writings that were presented by Bernard Bourgeois and that were intended to be incorporated into the Hegelian system.[26] As is familiar to most of us, neither Christianity nor Judaism is the end of the Hegelian system; they are both steps along the way, being superseded by something else. Levinas observes, however, that while it is true that both are superseded, each is represented quite differently from the other. Christianity, though not necessarily recognizable to some Christians, is also not represented in such a way as to be offensive to them. In contrast to the representation of Christianity, the critical discourse surrounding Judaism, Levinas notes, has "nurtured anti-Semitism."[27]

Levinas's primary concern with Hegel's presentation of Judaism as the negation of spirit is that it leads to a type of anti-Semitism that "is based within the System" (*DF,* 236). As a result of this characterization, the most common charge against Judaism is that it is "particular" as opposed to "universal." It is tribal and exclusive. But the more damning comments from these Hegelian meditations are the ones that refer to Judaism, and in particular Abraham, as material and bestial, focused only on self-preservation and animal needs. This view of Judaism is then cast in opposition to freedom. Contrary to the claim that Hegel makes, as cited in the earlier discussion, the Jew is not animal-like, material, and un-free. Rather, this is a description better suited to the pagan. For the Jew, however, the world contains the trace of the temporary and the created. This tension between immanence and transcendence, played in the tension between Paganism and Judaism (even with its many Christian permutations) and in the Greek and the Jew as seen respectively in the journeys of Odysseus and Abraham, is the narrative of Western civilization, but it is a narrative that for Levinas has serious consequences.

The Hegelian rendering of Judaism sets the stage for Judaism to be viewed as particular, while Christianity is viewed as universal, able to accommodate or include anyone. "Hegel and the Jews" was first published in 1971, but as we can see from the above discussion, Levinas had already begun to counter these simplistic critiques of both Judaism and materiality in the mid-1930s. Yet what is at stake for Levinas at this point is not simply the critique of Hegel's view of Judaism but his own interest in putting forth a positive position that argues for a universal dimension of Judaism. Indeed, Levinas's interest in returning to and promoting a Jewish humanism rests on his view, contrary to Hegel's reading, that fundamental elements of Judaism are in fact universal.[28]

Levinas's most immediate charge that the pagan is "sufficient unto himself" appears to be his central concern. We can see then how his announcement that "there is no one more self-sufficient than Rousseau," at the beginning of *On Escape,* accurately and succinctly characterizes Rousseau, especially if we recall the eighteenth-century French philosopher's thoughts on education.[29] Levinas's comment directs our attention to the fundamental problem with that philosophical position sponsoring an approach to education. Among other themes explored in this 1935 work, the most noteworthy is Levinas's emphasis on the body and the role that embodiment plays in the formation of our identities. This early writing continues Levinas's exploration of our enchainment to the body and our simultaneous need to escape that enchainment that he first identified in the essay on Hitlerism. His phenomenological description reveals that our embodiment requires our vulnerability and dependence.[30] Our bodies demand our attention, and thus our first responsibility is to feed them, clothe them, and protect them. Our primary needs betray our belief that we are free in the sense that Rousseau celebrates.

One can also see that Levinas would be drawn to Rousseau, whose writings are considered influential to the French Revolution and the development of the French Republic, in part because out of Rousseau's writings emerges a radical polity that granted civil rights to Jews, though admittedly the history of France in the Enlightenment period (and certainly previously) is a history that continues to raise the "Jewish question"—in this case, should the Jews received full emancipation? Should the Jews receive full civil rights? Regardless, that the Jews were indeed emancipated in law is a fact of history that is not lost on Levinas—indeed he embraces it even as he also expresses his ambivalence about this kind of universalism. Yet, just as Levinas is drawn to Rousseau's influence, he is also able to see what is fundamentally flawed in Rousseau's political project. Wittingly or not, Levinas is able to counter this flaw precisely by turning away from a Western conception of subjectivity and looking to Jewish sources for his answer.[31]

Levinas's writings follow the trajectory that begins with these early essays. In striking contrast to Rousseau's philosophical position, they advance the view that we are essentially dependent on others and this dependence is part of what it means to be human. As we see in his later philosophical writings, especially *Totality and Infinity* and then *Otherwise than Being,* subjectivity is defined by one's ethical response to the Other, not by one's freedom or ability to make autonomous decisions. Interestingly, this thread entwines with another, that of his treatment of the feminine. In his early formulation of the ethical relation, the feminine inaugurated the experience of alterity and then developed into a transcendental condition for the possibility of the ethical; that is, it provided the means for the subject to transcend to the level of the ethical, while not participating directly in the relation.[32]

Levinas ultimately names the feminine, defined as the maternal body, as the paradigm for the ethical relationship itself.[33] However, he does not expect that it is only women who either are or should be capable of ethical response. His use of the maternal as a simile—"the psyche is *like* the maternal body"—assures us of that.[34] Rather, it is the feminine, in this case, the maternal body that provides us with the best description of that which he cannot otherwise describe—an unwilled, irrecusable responsibility. He uses the feminine to define the ethical, but it is the ethical that defines us, all of us—men and women—as human. Again, in contrast to Rousseau, his view of subjectivity simultaneously endorses and rejects a rigid emphasis on sexual difference. His philosophical project exploits this originary dependency, revealed by our own primary needs and our original relationship to the maternal body. In contrast to Rousseau's aversion to dependence, dependence forms the ground for Levinas's radical subjectivity and the ethical project based on that subjectivity.

We see this point made as early as 1949 in "The Transcendence of Words," a commentary on Michel Leiris's *Biffures*.[35] Levinas affirms that teaching is not simply about the transmission of truth, the search for the forms, or the knowledge of true beauty; teaching is about assuming responsibility for the Other. It is also worth noting that this statement comes after Levinas's discussion of *Robinson Crusoe,* which presents a rather different interpretation of this story than the one we find emphasized by Rousseau in *Émile.* If we recall, the only book that Émile is allowed to read is *Robinson Crusoe,* since it apparently emphasizes the solitary, self-sufficient man. Levinas, however, reads this story differently. Not only does he notice, as do most of us, that Crusoe is not alone, but in fact has the company of Friday, he also emphasizes the significance of speaking.

> Contemporary philosophy and sociology have accustomed us to undervalue the direct social relations between persons speaking, and to prefer the silence or the complex relations determined by the framework of civilization, mores, law, culture. A disdain for the word, derived no doubt from the degeneration that menaces language, forms the possibility of its becoming idle chatter or empty formalities. But it is a disdain that cannot gainsay a situation whose privileged nature is revealed to Robinson Crusoe when, in the tropical splendor of nature, though he has maintained his ties with civilization through his use of utensils, his morality, and his calendar, he experiences in meeting Man Friday the greatest event of his insular life—in which a man who speaks replaces the ineffable sadness of echoes.[36]

He continues, "The presence of the Other is a presence that teaches; that is why the word as teaching is more than the experience of the real, and the Master more than a midwife of minds," a reference to Socrates, no doubt.[37] In an illuminating discussion of this particular essay, Seán Hand writes, ". . . Levinas stresses how the notion of an original bifurcation prohibits the reduction of multiple meanings to a single origin. An original bifurcation means that any static identity or representation overflows from the beginning. The primary *space* which this creates is one filled with infinite anxiety for Levinas, unless it includes a relation with someone, that is the necessity of critique."[38] The presence of the Other makes communication necessary; but this communication indicates that sound comes into being with the word—"sounds, or words produce a transcendence by breaking the world of self-sufficiency. Speech situates the self in relation to the other in a way that shows us how being for the other is the first fact of existence."[39] In contrast to the privileging of self-sufficiency, Levinas identifies teaching not only as fundamental to our lives in the very ways in which speech is part of what it means to be human, but also as an activity that fundamentally concerns the Other. Thus we see the early seeds of Levinas's project to dispel the myth of self-sufficiency as a defining feature of modernity's subject.

The Crisis of Humanism

In his 1992 interview, "The Awakening of the I," published in *Is it Righteous to Be?* the interviewer opens with this question: "You have had the occasion to say, 'Europe is the Bible and the Greeks.'" . . . Could you indicate first what 'the Bible' represents in this phrase 'the Bible'?" (*IR*, 182). And Levinas replies:

> The Bible, or, if you prefer, the Judeo-Christian source of our culture, consists in affirming a primordial responsibility "for the other," such that, in an apparent paradox, concern for another may precede concern for oneself. Holiness thus shows itself as an irreducible possibility of the human and God: being called by man. An original ethical event which would also be first theology.[40] Thus ethics is no longer a simple moralism of rules which decree what is virtuous. It is the original awakening of an I responsible for the other; the *accession of my person* to the uniqueness of *the I called and elected to responsibility for the other* (*IR*, 182, emphasis added).

The interviewer then replies, "The attitude you describe evokes holiness," to which Levinas replies,

> Holiness is nevertheless the supreme perfection, and I am not saying that all humans are saints! But it is enough that, at times, there are saints, and especially that holiness always be admired, even by those who seem the most distant from it. This holiness which cedes one's place to the other becomes possible in humanity (*IR*, 182–183).[41]

That is, while Levinas is perfectly aware that not all humans are saints, it is holiness and the very real existence of saints that make ethics possible for the rest of us. Moreover, for Levinas, there is something divine in the act of the everyday average human ceding to the Other. For Levinas, then, humanism is not simply placing the human at the center; it is specifically a focus on the Other. One might say that humanism for Levinas is actually two humans, one turning away from his own ego toward the needs of the Other.[42] Indeed, ten years earlier, in his essay "Demanding Judaism," he observes that while no religion explicitly excludes the ethical, some religions "place what is specifically religious above [the ethical], thus 'liberating' the religious from ethical obligation" (*BTV*, 5).[43] Referencing Isaiah 58, the prophet's powerful speech to a community that has lost its way by adhering strictly to ritual observance, in this case, fasting on Yom Kippur, but forgetting what the point of the fast is, namely to feed the hungry, clothe the naked, to care for those who are vulnerable in the community, Levinas concludes that this prophetic text advances a view of Judaism in which "the religious is at its zenith in the ethical movement toward the other man; that the very proximity of God is inseparable from ethical transformation of the social, and—notably and more specifically—that it coincides with the disappearance of servitude and domination in the very structure of the social" (*BTV,* 5). And lest we interpret this prophet's attack on the community as a call for simply a bureaucratic response, Levinas reminds us that Isaiah adds, "Is it not to share your bread with the hungry, and bring the homeless poor into your house; when you see the naked, to cover him, and not to hide yourself from your own flesh?" (*BTV,* 6). Although noticing that in one's midst there are those who are hungry, merely noticing this fact is not enough. The bread must be shared. From Isaiah forward, it is the ethical that accomplishes the religious. Thus, returning to Levinas's reference to the "holy" we can see that for Levinas, holiness, or religiousness, is in fact the accomplishment of the ethical—and the ethical described very specifically as the response to the Other.

We find evidence of this particular humanism in his philosophical writings as early as 1964 in his essay "Signification and Sense," where Levinas addresses the movement that the ego makes turning away from itself and toward the Other.[44] In section 7 of the essay he refers to the nakedness of the face as "destitution and already supplication" (*HO,* 32). More significantly, he notes that this "humility unites with elevation. And announces thereby the ethical dimension of visitation . . ." (*HO,* 32). A few pages later he observes,

> There, in the relation with the face—the ethical relation—the rectitude of an orientation or sense is traced. The *consciousness* of philosophers is essentially reflective. Or at least consciousness is grasped by philosophers in the moment of its return, *which is taken for its birth.* In its spontaneous pre-reflective movements it already casts a sidelong glance, they believe toward its origin, and measures the path covered . . . "Turn to the truth with all one's soul"—Plato's recommendation is not simply a lesson in common sense, preaching effort and sincerity. Is it not aimed at the ultimate, most underhand reticence of a soul that, in the face of the Good, would persist in reflecting on Self, thereby arresting the movement toward Others? Is not the force of that "resistance of the unreflected to reflection" the Will itself . . . [and is] the will not thorough humility rather than will to power? (*HO,* 34–35, emphasis added).

For Levinas, ethics is not simply that the Other is my concern; rather, we must give up the sovereignty of the ego and the self-certainty of introspection and reflection and turn toward the Other. His invocation of the "After you, sir!" is not merely a reference to a banal discrete event.[45] This turn—to put the Other first—needs to become the *guiding condition* of our lives. He describes this humility in terms of the one who has no time to turn back to self. It is not a question of "denying" the self—as in an asceticism, for the self is not yet of concern. It is not the choice between me and the Other, for that choice is not yet possible.[46] Rather, the self is turned toward the Other.[47]

Levinas's three essays collected in *Humanism of the Other* span the 1960s with the earliest, "Signification and Sense," published in 1963, to the third essay, "No Identity," published in 1970. All three are written and published in between the publication of his two major books: *Totality and Infinity* and *Otherwise than Being, or Beyond Essence* (1974). The second essay, "Humanism and An-Archy," published in 1968, is striking in its ability to see that Nietzsche was simultaneously aware of the accuracy of his diagnosis and the failure of his cure. Levinas links this insight to his own discussion of the crisis of humanism. If Levinas's essays from the 1930s direct our attention to the origins and dangers of the mythological self-sufficiency valorized by Rousseau, his essays from the 1960s collected in *Humanism of the Other* offer a powerful antidote in the form of a human subjectivity redefined as the responsibility for the Other.

Published nearly twenty years after "The Transcendence of Words," Levinas introduces this 1968 essay with the following epigraph taken from Nietzsche's *Thus Spoke Zarathustra*: "I love him whose soul is overfull so that he forgets himself, and all things are in him: thus all things become his downfall."[48] In this aphorism, which is part of his teaching, Zarathustra proclaims the need for overcoming the self but also laments the failure to accomplish this task. Levinas uses this epigraph to introduce an essay that opens with this claim: "The crisis of humanism in our times undoubtedly originates in an experience of human inefficacy accentuated by the very abundance of our means of action and the scope of our ambitions" (*HO*, 45). How should we understand Levinas's use of the epigraph? Does he agree with it or does he cite it for irony? What is the connection between the epigraph and the "crisis of humanism" that he announces at the beginning of this essay?

Rather than argue that Levinas is taking an opportunity for a gratuitous jab at Nietzsche, I would offer instead that Levinas is nodding at Nietzsche's own awareness of the failure of his project. Or, instead, that like Rousseau, Nietzsche displays the ability to identify a problem accurately but the constraints of his own thinking lead him to the natural, even if untenable solution. That is, both Nietzsche and Rousseau offer solutions to problems that on the surface seem correct and even compelling; but they in turn create even more problems. Additionally, "Humanism and An-Archy" connects a critique of Heidegger's humanism to Zarathustra's self-awareness regarding the ineffectiveness of his own teaching.

Although all three essays collected in *Humanism of the Other* are directed at Heidegger's philosophy, and indeed, the third essay has a section devoted to Heidegger by name, this second essay offers the most pointed critique.[49] Returning to the first sentence of the essay, Levinas announces that the crisis of humanism in our times originates in a belief that we have a certain element of control over our lives, and he links this belief to a view of technology that encourages it. We believe we have control over our lives, that as *rational animals* we are accorded a privileged position in the cosmos. Yet the unburied dead of wars and the death camps betray that view of ourselves and indeed even create an ambivalence, a tragio-comic response to the care of ourselves. We cannot control how or when we might die. We *must* care for ourselves and yet our life and death are beyond our control.

This essay develops out of Levinas's concern over the "thingification" of the human, which he links to the social sciences and the manner in which the human has become an object of study like any other natural object (*HO*, 46). Further, in this pursuit, the social sciences play games with subjectivity, which include simplifying, or reducing to simple explanations, the very complexity that is characteristic of the human. The worry that Levinas has could be called a worry about naturalism—the naturalizing of the human and that which one calls human.[50] That is, he links the development of anti-humanism to the reduction of everything to being.[51] The question then becomes if it is possible to reclaim both the human and its correlative reference to humanism such that it means something other than a reduction to the "Being of the being" (*HO*, 50). He replies that it is if we could come up with a new concept of passivity, one that is "more radical than that of effect in a causal series, *beneath* consciousness and knowledge, but also *beneath* the inertia of things reposing on itself as substances and opposing their nature, material cause to all activity . . . Pre-original anteriority that could of course be called religious, if the term didn't carry the risk of theology *impatient to recuperate 'spiritualism'*" (*HO*, 50, emphasis added).[52] The social scientists, in their study of the human and their claims to undo subjectivity, essentially *de*humanize. The point is made less obliquely in the first section of "No Identity," where he calls out those who proclaim "the death of the subject" (*HO*, 58).

Levinas is not unaware of the risk involved in this investigation. He realizes that it revives doubts about freedom as the origin, an investigation that seeks a subjectivity in radical passivity (*HO*, 50). However, if the alternative is to return to the *dichotomy* between free and not-free, then this is precisely the investigation and the subjectivity that he seeks. His goal is a return to the beyond, or the anterior, that which lies outside of this dichotomy. He redefines the relationship that a subject has to an Other. As a result, he redefines both subjectivity and humanism. In these next paragraphs he anticipates the themes that will permeate his 1974 text, *Otherwise than Being*. He writes:

> Absolute non-freedom absolutely could not show itself. But the ego can be put in question by Others in an exceptional way. Not as by an obstacle that it can always measure, or by death that it can also give to itself; the Ego can be accused despite its innocence, by violence of course, but also, despite the separa-

tion where it is left by the exclusivism and insularity of the psychic, by Others who as such nevertheless "obsess" it and who, near or distant, impute to it a responsibility, unimpugnable as a traumatism, a responsibility for which it made no decision but cannot escape, enclosed in self. (*HO*, 51)

The theme that guides the contours of this discussion is the "going beyond" of the traditional dichotomies of freedom/non-freedom, being/non-being. It is a pre-original that does not find an origin in matter, in freedom, in being. Herein lies the description of the "preoriginality of responsibility for others by a responsibility prior to all free engagement . . . Through this susceptibility the subject is responsible for his responsibility, unable to escape from it without keeping a trace of his desertion. It is responsibility before being intentionality" (*HO*, 52).

In the following section, Levinas opens the discussion by asking if this inability to escape responsibility is not servitude: "*Not being able* to get out of responsibility? How can this passivity place the subject 'beyond freedom and non-freedom'? How is the susceptibility of pre-originary responsibility prior to confrontation with the logos, to its presence, prior to the beginning that is represented (or presentified) to the agreement one grants or refuses to the logos, how is this not enslavement? Why does the subject, banished in self, held at bay by responsibility, brought back to its irreplaceable unicity by this irrefusable responsibility, exalt in the irrefusability of the One?" (*HO*, 52). He describes the servitude that he speaks of as being gripped or determined by the Good, which is not an object of choice. It seizes the subject before the subject has the time necessary for choice (*HO*, 53). Levinas readily admits that there is no enslavement more complete than being seized by the Good—"this election," this responsibility, "the enslaving character of responsibility that overflows choice—of obedience prior to the presentation or representation of the commandment that obliges to responsibility—is canceled by the bounty of the Good that commands" (*HO*, 53). And then Levinas makes this striking claim: "Here ethics makes its entry into the philosophic discourse—rigorously ontological at the start—as an extreme reversal of its possibilities" (*HO*, 53).

Briefly mentioning Plato's description of the cave and the divided line, where the person sees the sun, Levinas says, "The invisible of the Bible is the idea of the Good beyond being. To be obliged to responsibility has no beginning . . . Responsibility overflowing liberty, that is, responsibility for others. It is the trace of a past that refuses itself to the present and to representation, the trace of an immemorial past" (*HO*, 54). He ends this penultimate section with the following statement: "But the responsibility that owes nothing to my freedom is my responsibility for the freedom of others. There where I could have remained a spectator, I am responsible, that is to say again, speaking. Nothing is theater anymore, the drama is no longer a game. Everything is serious" (*HO*, 55).

He is clear in this discussion that the reference to God—"A value that is named God" (*HO*, 54)—is not simply a placeholder, as some wish it to be. Levinas deploys this term precisely because of what it connotes in Judaism. God in Judaism cannot be seen, has no gender, or has all genders, is amorphous and timeless. He contrasts this view of God to the incarnation, which precisely did thematize God, indeed it gave God a particular body. Anticipating the distinction between "the saying" and "the said," that will be significant in *Otherwise than Being*, in this essay, Levinas uses the term "God" to mark the saying, by which he means that which is unthematized. The term works for him because, as paradoxical as this sounds, it allows him to mark the saying in a way that as best he can retains the signification of that which is unthematized. That is, in a sense, "God" functions the same way in both Judaism and in Levinas's philosophy—to refer to the anarchic responsibility for others. In the concluding section of this essay, he writes:

> the Ego brought down to Self, responsible in spite of itself, abrogates the egoism of the *conatus* and introduces sense into being. There can be no sense in being except for sense that is not measured by being. Death renders senseless all care the Ego would like to have for its existence and destiny . . . Nothing is more comical than the care for itself taken by a being doomed to destruction, which is just as absurd as questioning, in view of faction, the stars whose verdict cannot be appealed. Nothing is more comical or nothing more tragic . . . But the pre-original responsibility for the Other is not measured by being, is not preceded by a decision, and cannot be reduced to absurdity by death . . . No one, not even the promisers of religion, is hypocritical enough to claim that he took away death's sting; but we may have responsibilities for which we must consent to death. The Other concerns me despite myself. (*HO*, 56–57)

In the above citation, Levinas draws on themes that were first explored almost ten years prior in *Totality and Infinity*. He contrasts the responsibility for another with the temptation of eros. He then describes the temptation as a temptation to play, to enjoy the freedom in being "not my brother's keeper" (*HO*, 55). Yet, while he contrasts the two, he also claims that responsibility needs this temptation. He concludes this essay by stating, "Modern anti-humanism may be wrong in not finding for man, lost in history and in order, the trace of this pre-historic an-archic saying" (*HO*, 57). One cannot help but think that in addition to responding to Heidegger he is also speaking directly to Rousseau and Nietzsche.

Contrary to how many of us would like to understand Levinas's ethics as being meaningful without "telling us what to do," his work frequently indicates that ethics requires one to do something. Response is not simply "seeing" the face of the Other; seeing the face of the Other means responding to it. How, then, are we to understand what "action" means for an ethics that is considered "pre-ontological," "pre-cognitive," "pre–decision making"? We can see Levinas's answer more clearly when we understand the way in which he transforms humanism. Levinas's humanism as he describes it in these essays is not the anti-humanism of Heidegger, where the human loses its central place. Rather, the central focus here is not on one human but two—one becomes a subject not by virtue of being a free ego, required to make choices. Rather, one becomes a subject in the face of the Other, in response to the ethical claim of the Other. This turn, to put the Other first, needs to become the *guiding condition* of our lives. He describes ethics as not simply that the Other is my concern; rather, we must give up the sovereignty of the ego and the self-certainty of introspection and reflection and turn toward the Other.

He continues this discussion in "No Identity," the last of the three essays included in *Humanism of the Other*. If there was any doubt that Heidegger was the target in the first two essays, the separate section treating Heidegger in this essay removes that doubt. Levinas concludes that section by stating that Heidegger had "led the triumph of mathematical intelligibility, sending the subject back into ideology, or else rooting man in being, making him its messenger and poet" (*HO*, 61). Yet, while Heidegger is indeed a target in this essay, the social sciences are more so. Continuing the discussion he began in "Humanism and An-Archy," Levinas argues that the social sciences have stripped the human of all that is human. Indeed what he wants to say here is that the social sciences are incapable of measuring or observing the very thing that makes the human: the opening of vulnerability where opening is represented by the stripping of the skin so that it is exposed, the uncovering or the passivity that he mentioned in the previous essay. Significantly, he uses an interesting biblical expression to make his point about the human as that which is vulnerable: that of "turning the cheek to the one who slaps him . . ." (*HO*, 63). For Levinas, to turn the cheek again, as we find in Matthew, is to make a choice, to deliberately seek suffering or humiliation. But receiving the initial slap reveals the fundamental vulnerability, the primary possibility of suffering, and the "impotence or humility 'to suffer' that is beneath the passivity of submission" (*HO*, 64). It is without choice.

In the penultimate section of this essay, he dares to ask questions of Heidegger—most significantly, he asks from where do we get our nourishment? Only from the pre-Socratics? Or maybe also from the Bible? Biblical verses, while not functioning as proof, do function as testimony of a tradition and an experience (*HO*, 66). Just as Buber asked in his essay on biblical humanism, Levinas demands, "Don't they have as much right as Holderlin and Trakl to be cited?" (*HO*, 66). Indeed, the question becomes how might humanism benefit from a different set of sources informing its development? He repeats here the same theme that responsibility is pre-original, before freedom, and prior to any choice.

If Levinas's 1934 essay on Hitlerism was prescient, it was so not only because of the violence and inhumanities that came to pass during World War II but also because it signaled a failure of modernity's ethics in its reliance on reason to save us. Levinas concludes that essay with the claim that the very humanity of man is at stake. One could argue that the very definition of the human and how intellectual thought would be influenced for most of the twentieth century were at stake in the 1929 Davos debate between Cassirer and Heidegger, where Levinas initially sided with Heidegger.[53] The question of how these two ideas are related is precisely what Levinas seems to work out in his essays on Jewish education—the humanity of man is contingent on that very definition of man and where and how "man" is positioned in the world.[54]

As novel and interesting, and indeed influential, as Heidegger's thinking is, it would be not only too easy to blame all of the problems of the twentieth century on him, but also inaccurate to do so. It would attribute way too much power to a thinker than is probably warranted. The danger lies not necessarily in the thinker but in the appeal a thinker has to sentiments that may have already emerged and gained traction. And yet, in spite of that influence on Heidegger's thought, Levinas views Heideggerian philosophy as fundamentally hostile to the message of the Hebrew Bible, thus allowing us to think that his critique of Heidegger is also a critique of that which runs counter to this biblical message.[55] That is, if Levinas's philosophy is viewed as a critique of Heidegger's philosophy, and certainly this is a prominent scholarly tack, then by Levinas's own account, indeed even his own words, his own positive philosophy is a formulation of Jewish ideas that are not only fundamentally amenable to the biblical message but also advance that biblical message.

Levinas closes this third essay with a section entitled "Youth." Here he offers a passing commentary on the events of 1968 and he observes that what appeared to be revolt against conformity did not take long to lapse into that very conformity. In spite of—and in the midst of—the pressure to conform, there emerged the youth that were defined by sincerity. That is, these youth were defined not by a brutality of the violence of the act, but rather by an approach to others and a taking charge of one's fellow man that comes from human vulnerability: "Youth that could find responsibilities under the thick layer of literature that releases from responsibility, youth—that can no longer be chided with if youth only knew—stopped being the age of transition and passage and showed itself as the humanity of man" (*HO*, 69). Here Levinas notices an authenticity that for the moment lacks cynicism. The youths' protests were motivated by beliefs. It was an approach toward the Other. Similar to Buber's expression of humanism cited at the beginning of this chapter, Levinas appreciates that realizing the humanity of man depends on how we educate our youth and thus he turns to Jewish education for his solution to the crisis. What the youth of 1968 had was not found in "secular" literature.

For Nietzsche, the turn to self-preservation is a function of the sickness that plagues humanity, not a natural current of the human species. When a being is healthy, that being can give up its grip on self-preservation. Levinas's discussion in "Humanism and An-Archy" takes this view one step further, asserting that those who cling to self-preservation have in fact been duped into believing the care of the self can overcome death. Returning to Nietzsche, the aphorism that serves as Levinas's epigraph lies at the heart of the teaching which

Zarathustra has been appointed to promulgate. Yet, Zarathustra is unable to teach it because he has not yet embraced it himself. Those who hear this teaching receive it as if it is presented with qualifications and hesitations—because it is presented this way. Nonetheless, this teaching comes fantastically close to Levinas's radically altered view of subjectivity, which has also loosened its grip on self-preservation.

We can see why Levinas comments on both Rousseau and Nietzsche, even if only to take a potshot at Rousseau's insistence on self-sufficiency or to reference Nietzsche's teaching of the overman, both of which are failed projects. Yet, it should also not surprise us that Levinas has at minimum an ambivalent relationship to both thinkers. He can see that both thinkers were able to offer brilliant diagnoses. Rousseau is correct that too much reliance on others might lead to greed and vanity, both of which will cloud our judgment and our decision making. His solution then emphasizes self-reliance, independence, and reason, which provides the seeds for the French Republic and the Universal Rights of Man, but also fosters a deep suspicion of community and an allergy to the Other. Nietzsche is correct that one must let go of self-preservation, and yet our anger and resentment can be productive. But even as both Nietzsche and Rousseau diagnosed the problem correctly, they were each unable to offer an adequate cure. Their failure reveals not only the commonality between them, but also reveals how radically separated they are from the subjectivity that Levinas puts forth, in spite of any apparent similarity.

Returning to the epigraph Levinas borrowed from Nietzsche, if Zarathustra is successful in teaching the overman, the overman will be he whose soul is so full that he is open to all others, that self-preservation is no longer his highest priority. This capacity to open himself to the world is both superlative and self-destructive. He allows all influences to touch him—thus, he lets everything come into him. This view, like Levinas's, runs counter to the prevailing themes promoted by the social Darwinists, who believed that self-preservation is the highest priority. Continuing themes from the previous chapter's discussion, this chapter explored Levinas's view that the self as masterful is illusory—and the care of the self is tragic-comic. However, in the twenty years since he first addressed this theme, Levinas developed an account of subjectivity that is directed toward the Other, thus paving the way for a new humanism.

4   Before Phenomenology

To adore the Lord God is not to shy away from humanity, a humanity
that is unique and united, a humanity toward which eternal thought
leans [se penche] and to which it pours out its heart [s'épanche].

—Emmanuel Levinas, *Difficult Freedom*

... and since it is true that study, even when done properly, can only
teach us what wisdom, right conduct and determination consist
in, they wanted to put their children directly in touch with actual
cases, teaching them not by hearsay but by actively assaying them,
vigorously molding and forming them not merely by word and
precept but chiefly by deeds and examples, so that wisdom should not
be something which the soul knows but the soul's very essence and
temperament, not something acquired but a natural property.

—Michel de Montaigne, "On schoolmasters' learning"

"How does one become the kind of ethical subject Levinas describes?" This
question typically emerges in response to discussions about Levinas's ethical
project. In other words, the discussion frequently shifts from the description
of the ethical subject to the question of origin: Is Levinas simply describing an
ethical subjectivity that already exists or is he describing a subjectivity that is
"not yet"? Implicit in these questions is an underlying concern that there is a
normative dimension to this ethical subject. And of course, one response to this
type of question is simply to say that it is the wrong question to ask. Levinas
is describing a subjectivity that we already are and that we have simply covered over.

On the one hand, Levinas refers to ethical obligation as anarchic—without a
fundamental or grounding principle. On the other hand, responses to Levinas's
project include statements like, "I just do not *feel* compelled by the Other," or
"I am not persuaded by his phenomenology." How is one to respond to these
comments? If Levinas's project simply describes ethical obligation phenomenologically, indicating that his aim is not to establish ethical obligation in the first
place, but to demonstrate that this obligation is already present, then how do
we respond to an opposing claim that appears to undermine this description?
What does it mean to ask after the warrant for Levinas's ethical responsibility?
If Levinas claims simply to describe the ethical obligation for the Other, then

the warrant for ethics is not required. Yet, these questions nonetheless persist. Even if Levinas is simply describing the ethical relationship, an obligation to the Other that is present even if we do not experience it as such, we are pulled into a discussion that asks how this relationship toward the Other arises.

The frequent questions posed in response to Levinas's ethical project reflect an underlying theme that is rarely articulated: How does one become an ethical subject in the sense that Levinas defines subjectivity? This is to say, is it learned? Is it innate? I do not mean to pose the questions so simplistically, but the question of how one becomes an ethical subject is not addressed in the many discussions of his ethical project and yet the question lingers. In other words, simply offering a phenomenological description of the ethical relationship does not explain its origin.[1] Since the claim not to experience the obligation as described is a frequent objection to Levinas's ethics, simply stating that the obligation is always already there might not persuade those who raise the doubts in the first place.

Additionally, this particular puzzle speaks to a more controversial question: "What is the ground of this ethical obligation?" This question, I argue, is for Levinas intimately related to the origin of the ethical subject. I recognize that if one readily accepts the phenomenological account, the question about "ground" becomes meaningless—indeed, it may even become a violation of the very discussion. I also realize that by framing the question in this way I imply that Levinas is conjuring up an ethical ideal and foisting that ideal on us—what gives him the right to do this? Those who are skeptical of my approach might be inclined to say: it is one thing that Levinas describes ethical subjectivity as such; it is quite another if his version of ethical subjectivity requires development. As I mentioned above, the common response to a discussion of Levinas's ethics is typically, "But I don't feel compelled by the Other. I am not aware of any claim." These responses indicate that on the one hand our everyday experience points to an unethical world in which even if the claim is made, it is easily unacknowledged. On the other hand, there is the more typical response of those who recognize the claim but willfully violate it. Somehow making the case that the claim of the Other is there but no one does anything about it has become a common way to talk about the failure of Levinasian responsibility in the world we inhabit. This either/or opens a space for the nihilist to claim there is no such thing as ethical responsibility. And we are then back where we started. Responding to the opposition might take more effort and require explanations that are different from those that have been recently provided. I suggest that we not read Levinas's project as an either/or but rather as a both/and. The description of the ethical subject in *Totality and Infinity* is indeed a phenomenological description of an ethical subject, but an adult subject.

One way to consider the relationship between Levinas's philosophical writings and his writings on Jewish education is to juxtapose them with other philosophical works that have a static account of the subject, one typically referred to as ontological, and a complementary genetic account that describes the development of that subject. By doing so, we can see how the relationships are parallel. My claim is that the subject Levinas describes in *Totality and Infinity*, which he develops in the language of responsibility in *Otherwise than Being*, is indeed one that must be developed. However, as works of phenomenology, these books describe the adult subject. Levinas is then describing at once a subject that already is and a subject that needs to be developed. To be an ethical subject as Levinas describes requires that our ego be decentered. If he contrasts this decentered ego with the ego or self produced by modernity, then the kind of subjectivity he describes most likely does not develop on its own. It is not a self that we are already. It is a self that we need to learn to be.

This chapter addresses these questions in particular by looking closely at Levinas's writings on Judaism that specifically contrast the development of a philosophical subject with his description of the ethical subject: Is there really a command from the Other that is in fact an ethical command? If there is, what is its source and how does it derive any authority? It is worth noting first that these particular difficulties in Levinas's project lie in part with his method and his reliance on religious language. He deploys words like "revelation" that perform some of the heavy lifting for him and he does not offer much in the way of explanation. Scholars are then left trying to make sense of this language— does he mean "revelation" in the same way that God is revealed at Sinai? If so, what implications follow from this meaning? Or, when he uses terms like "revelation" does he simply mean to oppose this kind of experience to one of a reasoned calculation? In any case, while what he means remains unclear and his readers are left to speculate, his use of "revelation" is typically adopted to reference an opposition to philosophy. The debate, then, over the relationship between Levinas's writings on Judaism and his philosophical writings, far from being settled, is reinvigorated.

Although some readers might posit that ethics begins with "God" and others might stipulate that it begins with the Other (and without God), frankly, neither of these responses actually answers the question of what gives the ethical obligation Levinas describes any teeth. Regardless of which side someone takes in discussions concerning the status of Levinas's religious language and his writings on Judaism, it is difficult not to notice the similarity of ideas expressed in both bodies of writing. Moreover, Levinas's religious language permeates his philosophical work just as his philosophical ideas pervade his writings on Judaism, a point that I have demonstrated elsewhere. Admittedly, different styles of writing characterize these two bodies of work, and a number of scholars working on Levinas's philosophical project continue to keep them separated. In spite of this constructed separation, the boundary between these bodies of writing becomes increasingly porous. One might even wonder if maintaining the boundary is at all productive for those who continue to interrogate Levinas's project.

In this chapter, I continue the discussion from the previous chapter by engaging several of Levinas's writings on Judaism. In chapter 3, we saw Levinas explicitly describe a subject who is for the Other, what Levinas calls "humanism," thus defining humanism as of and for the other person. By looking to Levinas's writings on Judaism, specifically his talmudic lectures, we might bring into view answers to some of our questions about *his* understanding of ethical obligation. To that end, I am going to blur the boundary even more.

I am not arguing that God, or a belief in a God—any God—is necessary for ethics. Nor am I arguing that Levinas makes this claim. However, dispensing with the necessity of a belief in God for ethics does not entail, for Levinas, dispensing with religion. As we will see in the next chapter, he is clear about the role of Judaism in the cultivation of a particular humanism within the Jewish community. Moreover, arguing for an ethical subjectivity in a philosophical register, specifically through phenomenological description, does not mean that Levinas does not have an idea in mind regarding the warrant for this ethical subjectivity. Nor does it mean that this warrant is necessarily not reliant on a religious viewpoint. What it does mean is that we need to work harder to find a comparable description of Levinas's ethical project in philosophical, or at least non-religious, language. Simply dismissing its religious dimension or ignoring it will not make it go away no matter how much scholars wish it would.

The Phenomenological Account

In the example of my experience at the 2009 conference I attended summarized in the introduction to this book, I described a common response to Levinas's ethical project: the nihilist, or more softly, the skeptic, who simply says, "I do not feel the claim of the Other." Put more strongly, the person might say, "But why should I care about the Other? Why do I not come first?" In the 1992 interview discussed in the previous chapter, "The Awakening of the I," Levinas addresses this exact point. Following Levinas's response that holiness means ceding the place of the I to the Other, the interviewer asks, "What would you respond to someone who said that he did not admire holiness, did not feel this call of the other, or more simply that the other left him indifferent?" (*IR*, 184). Levinas replies that he does not "believe that is truly possible. It is a matter of our first experience, the very one that constitutes us, and which is as if the ground of our existence. However indifferent one might claim to be, it is not possible to pass a face by without greeting it, or without saying to oneself, 'What will he ask of me?'" (*IR*, 184).

For Levinas, the skeptic is in bad faith when he asks the question, "What is the Other to me?" Simply assuming that the Other might ask something of him is the proof that the skeptic is bound to the Other ethically. And yet it is not clear that Levinas has answered the interviewer's question. Levinas might be right that even having the expectation that the Other will ask something of us is already to admit that we are in relationship with the Other. But there are several potential problems. First, it is a mistake to assume that upon encountering a face, everyone would ask, "What will he ask of me?" And what does that mean? Is there still an ethical claim even if someone does not ask this basic question? Second, the question "What will he ask of me?" does not necessarily yield a response that indicates a normative claim that is made of me. "What will he ask of me?" is very different from the interviewer's question which asked how Levinas would respond to someone who said that he did not admire holiness, which earlier in the interview Levinas described as the self ceding its place to the Other.[2] I might worry about the Other asking something of me because I simply do not want to be bothered, but I might still believe that I owe the Other nothing. Asking something of me is very different from asking everything of me. Asking something of me is also different from acknowledging that I indeed owe something to the Other.

What, then, is the warrant for the face? In response to this question, Diane Perpich argues that Levinas scholars have not taken the time to investigate what Levinas actually means by his notion of the "face" nor have they given an adequate argument that explains how the face commands—by what authority does this happen?[3] She explains that the lack of obvious authority leaves us with two horns of a dilemma. Is the ethical "naturally" embedded in face? If so, from whence does it come? And if not, how does the face garner this moral dimension and this moral authority? Scholars, Perpich observes, have simply accepted at face value not only the veracity of Levinas's claim that the face commands but also the moral authority of the command. In providing an account of the face, Perpich hopes to avoid an authority that does not reveal itself to be grounded in the religious, or more specifically, in God.

Perpich's concern echoes the one Levinas issues in the very first line of *Totality and Infinity*: "Everyone will readily agree that it is of the highest importance to know whether we are not duped by morality."[4] Her investigation into the meaning of this sentence leads us to the conclusion that Levinas is concerned with the struggle between morality and self-interest; maybe there is a bit of the skeptic in all of us.[5] As the British philosopher Howard Caygill points out in his 2002 book, *Levinas and the Political*, the answer to Levinas's opening query is offered at the end of *Totality and Infinity*, in the section "Filiality and Fraternity," where he tells us that in fact we are duped by morality unless there is "the infinite time of triumph, without which goodness would be subjectivity and folly" (*TI*, 280).

Between these two bookends where he raises the possibility that we have been duped by morality, we find an extended discussion about war and peace. As the discussion unfolds, we see that it is not the skeptic who is the enemy of morality, but war. Insofar as we each believe that we have certain rights and those rights come into conflict with each other, we will not only fight to preserve them, but we will also believe we are justified in doing so. If we understand war as the inevitable outcome of an egocentric subjectivity, Perpich's claim proves correct. Nonetheless, even if we think we know who the enemy of ethics is, to be sure, we lack certainty when it comes to the authority of the face. We can locate the problem, as Perpich indicates, in Levinas's claim to use the phenomenological method. If the face of the Other is unmediated, that is, not thought—or, technically, not perceived—then what is the phenomenon that Levinas describes?

Caygill's observations on this point are useful. He notes that Levinas's "practice" of phenomenology is not restrained by the structure of *noesis* and *noema*, even though he still believes himself tied to Husserlian method.[6] According to Caygill, Levinas "departs from this teaching by emphasizing the movement of revelation that takes place in the act of *noesis* and that carries it beyond the *noema* that is revealed."[7] Continuing, Caygill refers back to the preface where Levinas tells us: "If, as this book will show, ethical relations are to lead transcendence to its term, this is because the essential of ethics is in its *transcendent intention,* and because not every transcendent intention has the noesis-noema structure" (*TI,* 29). This is to say that while Levinas would like to think of his strategy as phenomenological, it does not fit into the traditional phenomenological structure.

The phenomenological reading—and by this I mean a reading of Levinas's project that is circumscribed within a philosophical framework that does not reckon with the religious language he frequently deploys—while on the right track is necessarily incomplete. This reading of Levinas cannot be ignored or discarded, even though, as this chapter examines, it is not wholly adequate. The relationship between phenomenology and the ethical subjectivity, or ethical obligation, that Levinas attempts to disclose through phenomenology is not unlike the relationship between child development and the ontological structures of an adult that Merleau-Ponty describes in his essay "The Child's Relations with Others."[8]

In this essay, Merleau-Ponty traces the limits of phenomenology: how does one describe experiences that are pre-linguistic? That is, how does one offer a developmental account of childhood, when that account necessarily depends on a description of structures that lie outside language and thus cannot be verified? Similarly, Levinas frequently refers to the ethical as lying outside ontology, before ontology, pre-philosophical, and so forth. What does it mean for philosophy to enter a realm or offer a description of an event that lies outside its realm? Can it be accessed philosophically? This is but one question for the phenomenological reading of his work, but this question leads us to consider why Levinas so frequently deploys language that refers to the religious texts, since he positions religion, which he equates with ethics, in opposition to philosophy and outside of ontology. More significantly, the phenomenological account falls short precisely where it argues its case—it seems unable to move from establishing that we are intersubjective and live in a world of relationships to the normative component of that relationship that makes an ethical claim on me, a claim from which I cannot recuse myself.

Complicating the question of authority, Levinas's writings vacillate between the most basic rendering of this obligation—"what will the Other ask of me"— as an admission that the Other has some connection or claim on me, and the stronger view that not only does the Other ask something of me, but also *I must do something* in response. And there is ample evidence for this stronger version throughout Levinas's writings. Nevertheless, Levinas's claim that it is simply not possible to pass by a face without greeting it seems plainly untrue. Moreover, even if it were true, is that all he means by ethics?

If it were true, why write *Totality and Infinity*? Why not simply make the statement that he made to the interviewer? Why such an elaborate description of ethical responsibility? If all Levinas means is that we are claimed by the Other, but nothing more than being claimed in the form of being interrupted need occur, then his own account of a radical ethics is actually made trivial. Indeed, this reading would allow Levinas's ethics to come dangerously close to justifying a turn to quietism. My point here is to say that even Levinas in this brief exchange cannot get beyond the basic intersubjective dimension of our very existence. The difficulty is advancing the position such that the normative force of the relationship, the one where the humanism he describes as ceding one's place in the sun to the Other, is established as part of that response. We are still left with the question, "Why should I cede my place to the Other?" Or, put differently, "How is it that I am required to cede my place to the Other?" This question lies at the heart of Levinas's ethical subjectivity.

Steven Galt Crowell's forthcoming paper "Why is Ethics First Philosophy? Levinas in Phenomenological Context"[9] addresses this connection between intersubjectivity and the normative. In his analysis, Crowell patiently works through the phenomenology in Levinas's *Totality and Infinity* in order to arrive at an answer to the question Crowell's title poses. However, Crowell's paper includes a crucial dimension that is missing from the other phenomenological arguments. Beginning with an examination of Husserl's *Cartesian Meditations*, Crowell provides the missing link in all of the phenomenological discussions of Levinas's work. He accomplishes this task by including a discussion of Sartre's view of intersubjectivity. He notes, "Before I can constitute the Other as 'singular,' as performatively responsible, through an analogizing apperception from my own singularity and responsibility, I must *receive* this sense of myself *from* the 'face' of the Other . . . Indeed, Levinas was not the first phenomenologist to recognize that normativity is the key to the constitution of alterity, however. To understand the phenomenological significance of his way of 'reversing the terms,' we must turn to Sartre, who took the problem of the Other as far as one can go without such a reversal."[10] A few pages later, he continues,

This means that the constitution of the Other in my sphere of ownness must bring with it not merely the sense of another consciousness, but, the sense of the *normative*, of standards against which the *validity* of my experiences can be judged. For Levinas too my original relation to the Other "makes the world common, creates commonplaces" (*TI*, 76). This is because "the calling into question of the I, coextensive with the manifestation of the Other in the face, [is] language" (*TI*, 171), and my "recognition" of having been called into question is manifested as "speech." Speech is "generosity," it is the "passage from the individual to the general because it offers things which are mine to the Other." In giving, speech "abolishes the inalienable property" that is mine in separation, and "the generality of the object"—that is, its potential for re-identification, its conceptual, and thus normatively governed, articulation—"is correlative with the generosity of the subject" (*TI*, 76). Thus "language does not only serve reason, but is reason" (*TI*, 207). Reason, in this broad sense, arises from my encounter with the Other, not the reverse (*TI*, 173, 201). I am not first of all rational and responsive to norms; I become so through my encounter with the Other. But how? A phenomenological account of the Other must elucidate how *my own* orientation toward the normative arises.

Just here we find Sartre's advance over Husserl. Sartre criticizes Husserl not for failing to account for the alterity of the other subject, but for failing to account for the Other's subjectivity, where "subjectivity" is not equivalent to "consciousness." (Crowell, 17–18)

This point is not only Sartre's advance over Husserl, but also Crowell's advance over the other phenomenological analyses of Levinas's ethics. Where most of the other discussions that turn to a phenomenological account are able to demonstrate the role of phenomenology to secure the intersubjective relation—the Other is fundamental to my world—they are unable to demonstrate how this relation necessarily carries a normative dimension. Thus, by turning to Sartre, Crowell locates one of the missing pieces—the normative dimension—to Levinas's ethical puzzle.

Using Sartre's famous "keyhole" example, posed in *Being and Nothingness*, where a voyeur is looking through a keyhole and then hears footsteps, Crowell describes the voyeur's experience of looking through the keyhole prior to hearing the footsteps thusly:

[That consciousness is pre-reflective] entails that neither its "project"—what it is doing—nor its motives can be named. Sartre makes this point by distinguishing between existential "possibles" and objective "probabilities." To the peering for-itself, the world is present entirely in terms of a set of possibles in the sense of *affordances*: the shadow is *my cover*; the stairs *escape*; the keyhole *access*; the scene beyond *satisfaction*, and so on. Such possibles do not take the form of *conditionals*: I *could* get away by the stairs; I *might* be able to hide in the shadows; the keyhole *potentially* reveals something, and so on. To formulate possibles (affordances) as conditionals is already to conceive a re-identifiable world of which the for-itself is not the sole locus of meaning, whereas Sartre requires that we conceive our voyeur as solipsistic consciousness (Crowell, 20–21).

But then after the footsteps are heard, Crowell notes, everything changes. My project now has a name: I am a voyeur caught in the act (Crowell, 19). My possibles are now objective probabilities and the meaning of them changes—the shadows might not work; looking through the keyhole is incriminating, and so forth. This is why, Crowell explains, the experience of the Other in the natural attitude is threatening. In Sartre's discussion, the footsteps become the bearer of "the Look," and now "caught" in this act, I find myself ashamed:

> My experience of shame does constitute the Other as Other, but the structure of shame entails that such constitution is always a *response* to experiencing a dimension of myself—being an object—of which I cannot be the origin. I cannot give rise to shame in myself, cannot be "ashamed before myself," since without the Other I am nothing objective. . . . "My shame is a confession" (*BN*, 350). That this analysis sounds paradoxical from an ontological point of view—how can I be ashamed before the Other prior to having an Other objectively "there" for me to be ashamed before?—is a primary motivation for Levinas's claim that ontological analysis presupposes the ethical relation.
>
> This response nevertheless gives rise to a second question. Why should the original experience of the Other as subject be precisely *shame*? This does not ask why we human beings are such that we can be ashamed of ourselves. Nor does it ask why it is shame—rather than, say, pride—that reveals the Other as subject. It is not an ethical question but a phenomenological one: what is it in Sartre's description that allows us to understand why the original experience of being seen takes the form of being ashamed? (Crowell, 23–24)

Crowell's discussion includes a phenomenological analysis of what it is like to be before the Other, to realize that the Other has discovered, or might discover, you in your act—thus securing what you have done and inaugurating or inciting a feeling of shame. The point here is that while the other discussions simply address the Other in my world, they do not describe the actual normative relation that emerges in intersubjectivity. One can certainly disagree with Sartre's analysis, but then we are back to missing the crucial link in the phenomenological discussion that moves from intersubjectivity to a normative underpinning that accompanies that intersubjective relation. Without this extra dimension, we are left with a view of intersubjectivity that is nothing special—one that could just as easily be extracted from Hegel, Husserl, or Merleau-Ponty.

This exploration of the phenomenological account in Levinas's ethical project goes a long way toward filling in the gaps that have remained open for quite some time. Until I heard Crowell's paper, I had remained unconvinced by the arguments offered for the phenomenological approach. It was not that I was unconvinced of Levinas's relationship to phenomenology—this relationship is indisputable if not simply obvious. Rather, it seemed that phenomenology had come up against its own limits and was unable to account for the ethical dimension. Crowell's argument not only completes the link between Husserl and Levinas by using Sartre's examples to illustrate the normative component but also improves upon the structure that Sartre presents. Crowell's contribution to this discussion is to recognize the unfortunate formulation that Sartre develops to describe the relations we have to one another. For Sartre, our relations with others are fundamentally antagonistic; social relationships essentially produce conflict. Crowell's insight into the Sartrean analysis is to demonstrate that what Sartre misses is precisely the Levinasian point: that to enter such a space of conflict at all already assumes an acknowledgment of the normative claim that is made on me. Thus, Crowell concludes, "but the very experience of shame shows that the Other is originally 'there' for me in an asymmetrical way, from a 'height.' This, its *radical alterity,* is thus only *intelligible* in an ethical register" (Crowell, 22).

Yet, in spite of Crowell's argument, the phenomenological description still falls short in one crucial way. Static phenomenology is unable to indicate how that experience came to be normative in the first place: What is the originary ground of normativity? Both Crowell's and Sartre's examples make assumptions that they do not explicitly articulate. In Sartre's case, as in the case of most of Western philosophy, the subject in question is a fully formed adult. If we consider Sartre's example of the voyeur looking through the peephole, why does the voyeur experience shame? My question is not why does the voyeur experience shame in this instance, but how does it come to be that the voyeur can experience such a response? If we acknowledge that shame is experienced because the person in question believes him or herself to be seen doing something that will be perceived by the observer as "bad," "wrong," or "inappropriate," then the voyeur must have developed an understanding that he is doing something he should not be doing *prior* to the event. Even if the voyeur was not taught that this particular act was inappropriate, the voyeur must have been introduced to the general categories of right and wrong, good and evil, forbidden and allowed, and so forth.[11]

Crowell admits that the discussion is not about how we come to be beings who are ashamed, or who feel shame, but rather what is the experience of the Other that initiates this feeling. Nonetheless, unless we are going to say that shame is "innate," or "empathy" is "natural"—and we need to be very careful of the moral language we use in relationship to Levinas's ethics—we need some kind of explanation for the grounding of any discussion of ethical responsibility, whether it is the categorical imperative, a social contract, or an ethics as first philosophy.

The discussion of moral education—how we come to be ethical beings—always seems to be the elephant in the room, and thus we assume either that the ethical response happens somehow, like magic, or it opens the space for many to assert without recourse that they are "simply not compelled by the face of the Other."

My point here, then, is that Crowell's argument supplements the phenomenological account by revealing that it is fundamentally intersubjective *and* that this
intersubjective relation is normative. However, phenomenology cannot explain
the ground of how one comes into relationship with the idea of normativity in
the first place. If we do not address this point, we simply beg the question—the
Other's face calls me to respond because it calls me to respond. Additionally,
this view does not attempt to address the more radical part of Levinas's ethics
that demands we not only notice that the Other suffers but that we actually do
something to address it. It is here that my discussion turns to an argument that
Levinas's philosophical work, his "ethics as first philosophy," assumes some form
of education, cultivation, or formation—the semantics are less important than
the idea that a child is introduced to normativity and reared to understand this
normative conception as relationship to and responsibility for the Other.[12]

Philosophy, Religion, and an Ethical Warrant

As I turn to the next part of this chapter, let me state what I take to be
the philosophical problem at stake in this discussion. I argue that Levinas's own
turn to education—the means to cultivate a certain kind of subjectivity—is itself dependent on his own view of religion. That is, Levinas can argue that Jews
need to return to Jewish education and reclaim a particular view of subjectivity
and in turn an idiosyncratic form of humanism because he holds an idiosyncratic view of Judaism on which he bases his argument. I demonstrate in this
part of the chapter that Levinas's warrant for persuading the Jewish community to embark on this return is located in the notion of an original covenant.
Jews do not necessarily need to believe that this covenant was an actual historical event. Rather, it is taken as a guiding condition of Judaism and thus insofar as individuals identify with Judaism as a religion, they assent to this biblical humanism. What then is the mechanism by which those who are not Jews
will become ethical subjects as Levinas describes? Is it an educational model
similar to the one we find in Jewish education? And does it matter that there is
likely no comparable "event" like the receiving of the Torah at Sinai that binds
all non-Jews together thus providing a warrant for this educational model to
be implemented?

Contrary to the focus of nearly all of phenomenology if not most of Western philosophy, we do not emerge into the world as fully formed adults! As I
mentioned previously, we can see, for example, that many of the structures that
ground Merleau-Ponty's *Phenomenology of Perception* are first introduced in
"The Child's Relations With Others," his long essay on child development. Indeed, much of what is peculiar in Merleau-Ponty's account of our relations with
others can be explained by reading those structures in light of his consideration
of the child. Merleau-Ponty's study documents how one moves from childhood

to adulthood, thus making sense of the static account of these structures, and most specifically, how intersubjective life happens in spite of what appears to be a "natural" propensity toward solipsism.

The tracing of this development is not unlike the one we find of moral development in Rousseau's *Émile* where Rousseau also indicates that we have a "natural" propensity to identify the suffering of another person and be averse to it. However, Rousseau identifies two possible responses to this suffering (there are probably more than two, but Rousseau is concerned with only these two). The first possibility is to see the suffering of the Other, take pity, and then be moved to want to do something to stop the suffering. The second possibility is to see the suffering of the Other and simply close the Other off from us so that we do not have to see her suffering. Rousseau is clear in *Émile* that while our aversion to the suffering of another is natural, how we respond to that suffering must be taught—or cultivated.

What does this mean for Levinas? Most significantly, it means that Levinas, like Rousseau, believed that the subjectivity he describes is one that will be taught. We see this clearly in his essays on Jewish education. It also means that the ethical relation is not one that happens spontaneously as fully formed adults who simply come into contact with an Other—or a compelling philosophical argument for such an obligation. Rather, a certain kind of education positions us for this relation. Finally, it means that for Levinas, philosophy and phenomenology have their limits: they can only describe so much. For the rest, or for some ideas, we might need to turn to religion.

In December 1964, shortly after he published "Signification and Sense," Levinas presented his talmudic reading "The Temptation of Temptation" to the Colloquium of French Speaking Jewish Intellectuals. This reading explores this relationship between religion—read here as an origin of responsibility—and philosophy.[13] This talmudic reading ultimately serves as a critique of philosophy, asking us to consider philosophy's limits and in so doing, it also suggests that a covenant is the origin of ethical responsibility. What makes this talmudic reading so provocative is that it becomes a meditation on, if not an indictment of, philosophy. Indeed, Levinas recalls that the editors of the Talmud sometimes used the terms "philosopher" and "the Sadducee," interchangeably to refer to the one who says to Raba, "You should have listened in order to know whether you were able to accept . . ."; that is, to refer to the one who emphasizes the need for knowledge. Levinas does not correct the rabbis nor does he defend the philosopher. Rather, he queries, "An anti-Jewish Christian?" In the end, Levinas offers in this commentary the most explicit critique of philosophy and the sovereignty of the ego, revealing both the paradox of ethical origins and the limits of philosophy.

The talmudic passage with which Levinas concerns himself addresses the moment of creation and the revelation of the Torah at Sinai. His commentary addresses too many points of interest to consider in this present discussion, not the least of which is its placement in the tractate Shabbat, which concerns the festivals and the observance of the Sabbath. The point on which I do want to focus concerns the implications of Levinas's reading of the "temptation of temptation" as "the temptation of knowledge" (*NTR*, 34), which he sees as a fundamental shift in emphasis from the original covenant when the Israelites accepted the Torah.[14]

He begins his discussion with the provocative claim that the temptation of temptation—which he describes as the temptation of knowledge—"may well describe the condition of Western man. In the first place it describes his moral attitudes. He is for an open life, eager to try everything, to experience everything, 'in a hurry to live, impatient to feel.' In this respect, we Jews all try to be Westerners" (*NTR*, 32). And a few pages later he observes:

> We want a knowledge completely tested through our own evidence. We do not want to undertake anything without knowing everything, and nothing can become known to us unless we have done and seen for ourselves, regardless of the misadventures of the exploration. We want to live dangerously, but in security, in the world of truths. Seen in this manner, the temptation of temptation is philosophy itself . . . the solid basis of our old Europe. (*NTR*, 34)

Levinas's concern about Jewish assimilation reverberates throughout his work and is most apparent in his essays on Jewish education, which I will turn to later. The citation above is especially intriguing insofar as he is insinuating that Jews are essentially not Westerners—that is, at the outset of this commentary, "being Jewish" is set in opposition, or at least in contrast to, "being Western." What then is this Western mode? Levinas describes it as the need to act with certainty, or as much certainty as possible. To act otherwise, that is, to act without knowledge is viewed as simply childish and/or naïve. Additionally, he defines philosophy as the subordination of any act to the knowledge that one may have of that act, where the act comes about after careful deliberation, calculation, the weighing of pros and cons. He indicates that naïveté is the counter to philosophy. Indeed, he comments elsewhere that philosophy is the study of naïveté. And in his 1975 essay, "God and Philosophy," he recapitulates many of the same themes that he covers in this talmudic essay. As a result, we arrive at the "inability to recognize the other person as an other person, as outside all calculation, as neighbor, as first come" (*NTR*, 35).

Returning then to "The Temptation of Temptation," we see his explicit turn to religion as the inauguration of responsibility for the Other, an inauguration that itself cannot be proven. But the point that Levinas makes here with regard to naïveté on one side and philosophy on the other is that this dichotomy, or this relation, grows out of something prior to it. That is, we discover that the temptation of temptation correlates to the dichotomy between philosophy and naïveté, and this dichotomy presupposes something prior.

In response to the Western mode of knowing before doing, Levinas reads the talmudic passage as offering an inversion of this order of knowledge and acting—doing before hearing. And more importantly, he reads this inversion as originary, as founding the very possibility of knowing at all, as founding this dichotomy. Thus, whatever this originary moment is, it must also precede reason. Levinas preempts the possibility of an infinite regress—turtles all the way down—by introducing revelation into the discussion, and he reminds us that if revelation is to have any use it must tell us something that reason itself cannot discover.

We find ourselves, therefore, in a bind: on the one hand, what does it mean to discover these elements of revelation and moreover, what does it mean to accept them and thereby run the risk of having been duped by the Devil (*NTR*, 36)? On the other hand, and this point is crucial, if these elements are accepted *because* they already recommend themselves to the discernment of the one who accepts them, "then they are in the domain of philosophy. They would already be in its domain even if reason were to decide *only upon the authority of the messenger.* The paradox is that Revelation nonetheless claims to overcome the apparently insurmountable waverings and doubts of Reason" (*NTR*, 36, emphasis added). And here we have to ask if his reference to revelation in this talmudic reading carries the same meaning as his reference to revelation in *Totality and Infinity,* a text that also requires us to ask after the warrant for the claim made on us by the Other.

We should note here the striking similarity between the themes in this commentary and the themes that he takes up in his philosophical writings—e.g., responsibility for the Other precedes choice and freedom. In the context of thinking about this choice to receive the Torah, to receive "a freedom of responsibilities," he asks, "Is one already responsible when one chooses responsibility?" (*NTR*, 37). That is, if the acceptance of the Torah is itself the inauguration of responsibility, was responsibility present prior to this acceptance? What then is this acceptance? It is not "choice" as we typically understand it if it lies outside the structure of both knowledge and freedom. But nor can this acceptance have been forced on the Israelites through violence—ethics cannot issue from that kind of violence. "The teaching, which the Torah is, cannot come to the human being as a result of choice. That which must be received in order to make freedom of choice possible cannot have been chosen, unless after the fact" (*NTR*, 37). What then is this acceptance or consent?

Levinas concludes that "[r]eason rests on a mode of consent that cannot be reduced to the alternative of liberty-violence and whose betrayal would be threatened by violence" (*NTR*, 37). He suggests instead that revelation serves as a reminder of a consent that is prior to the freedom/non-freedom dichotomy. As such, revelation does not coexist with other kinds of knowledge, with reason that issues from this originary acceptance. Revelation precedes, indeed it conditions, reason. Thus, in the study of knowledge—epistemology—the Torah plays a fundamental role. It inaugurates reason and all knowledge that issues from it. For Levinas, this cannot be reduced to naïveté, since naïveté is contrasted with reason; naïveté is such because it is characterized as "an unawareness of reason *in a world dominated by reason*" (*NTR,* 38, emphasis added). If we follow the relation between revelation and reason, we see that the acceptance of the Torah not only conditions but also gives meaning to the real, thus claiming that "in this anteriority lies hidden the ultimate meaning of creation" (*NTR,* 40). And then he asks, "What is the meaning of creation: God did not create without concerning himself with the meaning of creation. Being has a meaning. The meaning of being, the meaning of creation, is to accept the Torah" (*NTR,* 41). That is, the acceptance of the Torah is the act that gives meaning to reality. It is not that God would punish the Israelites but rather the act of refusing Torah would simply "bring being back to nothingness."

We find a similar reading in Avivah Zornberg's *The Beginning of Desire: Reflections on Genesis,* where she tells us that the interpretation offered by Rashi, the 11th-century rabbinic commentator, argues that the "main business of [the second day] was the radical transformation of reality from the encompassing oneness of God to the possibility of more than one."[15] The movement of all of creation is a movement of separation and individuation, a movement of identity. The movement of separation, though, often leaves one without a ground. By its very definition, to be individuated is to be separated from something. In this case, the separation may be separation from God and all that separation means. And another commentator, Resh Lekesh taught: "God made a condition with the works of the Beginning—If Israel accepts the Torah, you will continue to exist; if not, I will bring you back to chaos [*tohu va-vohu*]."[16] The acceptance of the Torah at Sinai reveals the Judaic theme "to do and to hear." This expression is understood in English as "To do and *then* to hear," that is, "to do and then to understand." Why is this significant? The acceptance of the Torah without knowing what the Torah is demonstrates faith. More precisely, it is by living an ethical life that one understands what an ethical life is and the necessity of living life as such. But this acceptance is not merely predicated on blind faith.[17]

According to rabbinic interpretation, "standing at Sinai" affirms what God is to create (has created), and therefore saves the world. The face-to-face with God is connected to finding a foundation. The commitment to the ethical puts these early inhabitants back in relationship to God. The giving of the Torah at Sinai necessitates, as recounted in Deuteronomy 5:4, the ability to stand "face to face" with God.[18] Zornberg's discussion powerfully illustrates this relationship between standing and separation, and the terror of returning the world to the chaos and emptiness before creation. Her gloss on the commentary demonstrates the ethical significance of the covenant made at Sinai.[19]

Like the rabbinic commentators who came before him, Levinas also concludes, "The unfortunate universe also had to accept its subordination to the ethical order." That is, the universe *is* such because ethics was accepted. The question of ontology—how being realizes its being—consists in how the Torah was received. It consists in "overcoming the temptation of evil by avoiding the temptation of temptation" (*NTR*, 41). That is, being realizes its being by avoiding a return to the egoism of philosophy, of self-sufficiency, and the sovereignty of the ego asserted via one's desire for knowledge. In this acceptance of the Torah, the acceptance of the ethical, the sovereignty of the ego is subordinated to the Other.

In the last part of this lecture, Levinas returns again to the question of childish naïveté. His interest in this particular question betrays that he is clearly troubled by it. Why would he not be? The unique nature of the event is the giving of the Torah, which means that one accepts the Torah before one knows it. How, then, do we know that we are not duped by evil? What protects us from this danger? For Levinas, this originary moment of accepting the Torah is beyond good and evil in that it precedes this dichotomy. Everything we do is conditioned by an original "agreement" in which a group of people—those who became the Jews—assented to the view that they would put the Other first, that they would live by the ethical. Rather than see this originary moment as childish naïveté, Levinas sees this resistance to the temptation of temptation as a "perfectly adult effort" (*NTR*, 42)—the adult effort that was exhibited at Sinai. And yet unable to "prove" the existence of this originary moment, the talmudic text will nonetheless call the paradox of this inversion—the origin of trust prior to all examination—an "angel's mystery" (*NTR*, 42).

To be clear, revelation for Levinas is not about God *per se*. The acceptance of revelation *is* the turning toward the Other. Indeed, as expressed in this talmudic lecture, Levinas views these as one and the same: revelation = the acceptance of the Torah = the light of the face = the epiphany of the other person, which he declares is "*ipso facto* my responsibility toward him: seeing the other is already an obligation toward him. A direct optics—without mediation of any idea— can only be accomplished as ethics. Integral knowledge or Revelation (the receiving of the Torah) is ethical behavior" (*NTR*, 47). For Levinas, then, to examine without acceptance, that is the real reversal; knowledge without faith is "logically torturous," it is a corruption of morality (*NTR*, 48).

Toward the end of the essay, Levinas raises the skeptical question to philosophy itself when he wonders if it will be ". . . said that this alliance was not freely chosen" (*NTR*, 49). He responds to his own query that to ask this question is already to assume that "one reasons as though the ego had witnessed the creation of the world and as though the world had emerged out of its free will. This is the presumptuousness of the philosopher" (*NTR*, 49). Can philosophy prove otherwise? The answer is not necessarily clear. However, in his 1975 presentation to the Colloquium of French Speaking Jewish Intellectuals, published later as "Damages Due to Fire," Levinas confesses that for him "philosophy is derived from religion. It is called into being by a religion adrift, and probably religion is always adrift."[20] Commenting on this phrase in his biography of Levinas, Salomon Malka adds the following gloss to Levinas's reflection: "Philosophy can lead us only to the threshold of a mystery, into which it cannot enter."[21] Though he appears reluctant to admit to this, philosophy has limits.

Let me state that I am sympathetic to the concerns that scholars raise regarding the use of this religious language and on the reliance of this language of religion itself to become a pat answer to difficult questions regarding Levinas's project. That said, let me also state that as a philosopher I acknowledge, and I think we all do acknowledge, that philosophy cannot answer all questions, inside or outside Levinas's writings. My claim, of course, is not that all of Levinas's ethics comes from God. I am not arguing that Levinas delivers a set of commandments like the Ten Commandments, nor am I arguing that the warrant for ethical obligation comes from God. My argument about the status of the religious writings is the following: Levinas believes that a different subjectivity is needed to address the crisis of humanism he identifies. He believes that this subjectivity originates in Judaism and that it is unique to Judaism, and certainly he could be wrong about this point. He believes that Jewish education is the method for the Jewish community to reclaim and cultivate this subjectivity. And he believes that certain views in Judaism and the community identity of Judaism—accepting, for example, the covenant at Sinai—provide the warrant for his appeal to the Jewish community to rear their children in this way.

The justification comes from the set of community practices that trace their history back to a set of beliefs and a set of other practices that define Levinas's understanding of Judaism. However, he believes in this subjectivity for everyone. He believes that this kind of subjectivity is not limited to Jews and thus the ethical subject can be described in philosophical language. What cannot be addressed adequately in philosophical language is how that ethical relationship comes about, precisely because it is not a rational response to the Other. It is cultivated; it is preparedness. Rosenzweig's gloss on this point in his essay on Jewish education, "The Commandment: Divine or Human," is worth considering. In the same way that if one has an ailment and asks a surgeon what to do, the surgeon would reply, "cut it out." If the same person approached a dietician, she would be more likely to be told to change one's eating habits. How we are trained to solve problems is often similar to how we are trained to approach ideas.

As Rosenzweig humorously recounts, talk of religion or God will be received by different folks in different ways: the student of William James will categorize religious experiences by psychology of religion labels; the student of Freudian psychology will have one explanation that will differ slightly from the student of sociology: individual delusion versus mass delusion! Rosenzweig responds to all of these possibilities by simply stating that the law in Judaism is not experienced as that handed down directly by God. It is experienced as an expression of feelings and reflection of the community: "We know [the Law] differently, not always and in all things, but again and again. For we know it only when—we *do*."[22] A few sentences later he clarifies this point with the following line: "Not that doing necessarily results in hearing and understanding. But one hears differently when one hears in the doing." In the days when the story of Balaam's talking ass is discussed in the synagogue, the story's fairy tale qualities are usually ignored. It means something different when discussed in the congregational community. On every other day, not so much![23] The political theorist Bonnie Honig suggests that Rosenzweig's point can be put this way: "Someone must be listening [to the miracle that speaks out of the Torah]—in fulfillment of the commandment to do so, we must open our ears . . . But, if we can hear what speaks to us, it is because we have put ourselves into a context that opens our ears."[24]

As Levinas depicts it in the 1964 lecture, the angel's knowledge is the prior consent and the immemorial past to which he refers not only in this talmudic essay but also in his philosophical writings, most notably, in his 1974 magnum opus, *Otherwise than Being*. We could also explain it in this manner: This prior consent, the immemorial past, is the "we will do"; my turning toward the Other, relinquishing my place in the sun, being responsible for the Other, giving bread to the Other, this is the commentary, or to put it differently, it is the "we will hear." Is this the warrant for his ethics? If so, what does it mean for those who do not accept revelation? Whose lives are not conditioned by the acceptance of the Torah at Sinai? And in light of where we have gone wrong, or turned away from this ancient message of doing before hearing we can ask if the Jew needs to stand again at Sinai—or better, if everyone else needs to stand there a first time? I would say yes, figuratively. Referring back to Honig's reading of Rosenzweig, to "put ourselves into a context that opens our ears" is precisely what Levinas believes Jewish education accomplishes.

Returning to the question of phenomenology I posed earlier in this chapter, we might find some insight in Michael Fagenblat's elegant book *A Covenant of Creatures*. Fagenblat argues that instead of viewing the phenomenological readings in opposition to the Jewish readings, we should instead see the phenomenology as offering not simply a philosophy of Judaism, but a phenomenology of Judaism. Using Jon D. Levenson as a guide, Michael Fagenblat's reading of creation, which parallels the one offered by Zornberg, supports this position.[25] Quoting Levenson, who reminds his readers that ". . . *the point of creation is not the production of matter out of nothing, but rather the emergence of a stable community in a benevolent and life-sustaining order*," Fagenblat argues that this view of creation is exactly what Levinas meant by the *il y a*.[26] This mysterious and puzzling term first appears in his 1946 essay by the same name.[27] Fagenblat suggests that the *il y a* is a "phenomenological interpretation of the famous elements in Genesis 1:2 that are already there before the act of creation: the *tohu wa'bohu,* variously translated as the 'unformed and void,' 'a formless waste,' or 'welter and waste.'"[28]

Fagenblat utilizes this interpretation to support his argument that for Levinas the *il y a* signifies a time before ethics. That is, the story of chaos preceding creation is not a story about natural creation; it is a story that provides a moral account of the origins of the world.[29] Putting this claim more strongly and supporting my argument above, Fagenblat asserts that Levinas's famous and most widely used phrase, "ethics precedes ontology," is "best understood in terms of the covenantal structure of creation."[30] It is not that creation is simply ethical but rather that creation, in Levinas's understanding of the term and that of Judaism, implies a covenant. Fagenblat concludes this interpretation of creation with the following claim: "What matters for Levinas is not whether this structure of ontological culpability is called secular or religious but that the covenantal structure of creation is acknowledged."[31]

Before continuing my own discussion, I wish to call attention to one more point that Fagenblat makes in this book. In his chapter "Secularizing the Covenant," he recalls that his book is making the following argument: that "what Levinas calls 'ethics' is best understood not as a secularized philosophy of religion in general but as a secularized moral theology of Judaism in particular."[32] That chapter argues that "the term 'religion' itself, in Levinas's philosophical writings, is hermeneutically drawn from a specifically Judaic understanding of the term."[33] The significance of this point is that many scholars point to Levinas's use of the term "religion" as signifying something other than Judaism, that is, something other than religious. They say that if he had meant religious in a conventional sense, he would have used "God," which of course he does, but those references are often set aside as irrelevant. To be clear, Levinas is not stating that morality or ethics derives from God in the way that we often hear the relationship between religion and ethics discussed. My point, and I believe this is Fagenblat's point, is not to say that Levinas is offering a theology. He is not. But to concede that this is not a theology, that is, that God is less important or not important in the origins of the ethical, does not also mean that religion in some traditional or specifically Jewish sense of the term is rendered insignificant. Fagenblat's argument ties together the fundamental and indispensable role of religion in Levinas's own understanding of the ethical and thus we are led back to the question of how one becomes an ethical subject.

Returning to the discussion of the talmudic lectures, we can point out that if we connect the essays on Jewish education to these talmudic readings we can also note that the warrant, or justification, for the return to Jewish education is simply the covenant that Jews made with God. In order to make good on the covenant, in order to ensure that the ethical covenant continues, Jews rely on Jewish education. At some point—mythically or not—a group of people stood at Sinai and accepted the Torah. Yet, it was not only *that* they accepted the Torah, but also *how* they accepted the Torah that made them Jews. The key is the reversal of our modern understanding of moral action—knowing and then doing. For Levinas, the emphasis should be placed on "doing before hearing," which distinguishes him from the philosopher who puts consciousness, or reason, or the ego, first.

Jewish education, in turn, relies on a return to this original covenant, to an original way of being Jewish that has been warped by modernity, by assimilation, and by philosophical reason (or argument) masquerading as wisdom or ethics. Insofar as Jews identify as Jewish, Levinas's warrant to return to Jewish education is in place. The difficulty, it seems to me, is what this means for everyone else. It is not clear that the non-Jewish community has assented to anything comparable. The most similar kind of common origin would be a social contract, but even if that were the case, it is not the case that everyone has agreed to the same contract. Moreover, there are fundamental differences between a covenant and a social contract. At the very least, there are differences between the covenant that guides Levinas's thinking and the kind of social contract that is familiar to liberal political theorists. In a beautiful summary of the difference between covenant and contract, Fagenblat writes the following:

> [T]he second feature of the covenantal ethics of [later Levinas] is its passivity or choicelessness. Later Levinas regards the ethical relation as prior to the freedom of the will, which is exactly how we should understand covenantal faith. One is not free to desist from trusting, to desist from this bond with the other, even if one can and indeed, one ought to work within such trust by shaping it in various ways. Covenantal faith is not contractual. It is not like a contractual arrangement among liberal individuals in which parties freely enter into a mutually obligating relationship and in which the validity and value of that relationship depended on the freedom of the parties to enter it. Rather, in the case of the covenant, as Jon D. Levenson says, "the wrong choice results in nothing short of death." That is exactly the sort of covenantal faith Levinas is talking about. As in "ethics," so it is in the covenant—exit amounts to an abrogation of life. Within covenantal faith there is no such thing as life prior to moral life, for life itself always already implies ethics.[34]

Fagenblat's discussion, which also incorporates Levenson's interpretation, follows directly the rabbinic reading of the midrash on the receiving of the Torah. As we saw with Zornberg's rehearsal of this commentary, the rabbis read the acceptance of the Torah in the same manner, namely, that to refuse the Torah is to be plunged into the abyss; not by God, but by the refusal to live according to an ethical code.

The above passage draws out the point that the phenomenologists have overlooked. The Other as a source of my life, that is the "fact" that my life is a life only because of an Other, does not imply an ethical relation unless one assumes this kind of covenantal faith. That is, the phenomenologists want us to have faith that the relationship with the Other implies a responsibility for the Other, but they cannot establish this point, nor do they admit that they are relying on faith.

My point here is not to say that one now needs to believe in God or that one needs to become Jewish. Rather, my point is that beneath the phenomenology of the intersubjective relationship there lies a view of the human that cannot be penetrated by a raw philosophical phenomenology. It is only by turning to the religious dimension that pervades Levinas's thinking and thus his ethical project that we can locate what it means to say that my relationship to the Other is a responsibility that is not chosen and from which I cannot recuse myself. To refuse the covenant, to refuse my responsibility for the Other is "to refuse the good of life itself."[35] The Jews turn to Jewish education in order to perpetuate the original covenant through which they have assented to live their lives in a certain manner. If that is the case, what does this mean for those who are outside Judaism? Does this mean that Levinas has secularized the covenant by describing the ethical subjectivity philosophically—or universally? If so, what are the implications of that move?

In his essay "Nameless," reprinted in *Proper Names*, Levinas describes three truths that correspond to us living more humanly.[36] The first is that "people need infinitely fewer things than they dispose of in the magnificent civilizations in which they live" (*PN*, 121). He is reminding his Jewish readers of the fragility and failure of their assimilation, when between 1939 and 1945 they lost everything from food and clothing to books and synagogues. The second truth asserts, "in crucial times, when the perishability of so many values is revealed, all human dignity consists in believing in their return. The highest duty, when 'all is permitted,' consists in feeling oneself responsible with regard to these values of peace. In not concluding, in a universe at war, that warlike virtues are the only sure ones . . ." (*PN*, 121). That is, maintaining one's belief that in spite of the presence of war, ethics is still the "truth."

And finally, the third truth, and the one that I want to note in particular: "we must henceforth, in the inevitable resumption of civilization and assimilation, *teach the new generations* the strength necessary to be strong in isolation, and all that a fragile consciousness is called upon to contain at such times," and here Levinas names the maquis, those who resisted French collaboration with the Nazis (*PN*, 121, emphasis added). I simply want to draw attention here to the link between teaching and resisting evil.

Later in this same essay, under the subtitle "The Jewish Condition," Levinas offers the following connection between religion and the ethical and it is worth quoting at length:

> The fact that settled, established humanity can at any moment be exposed to the dangerous situation of its morality residing entirely in its "heart of hearts," its dignity completely at the mercy of a subjective voice, no longer reflected or confirmed by any objective order—that is the risk upon which the honor of humankind depends. *But it may be this risk that is signified by the very fact that the Jewish condition is constituted within humanity.* Judaism is the humanity on the brink of morality without institutions. (*PN*, 122)

It is difficult not to ask if this is what Levinas hopes for—a morality without institutions? An ethics without politics? Without need of politics? An ethics only after there is no more war?

At the very end of this essay Levinas offers a picture of morality that is at once bleak and optimistic. On the one hand, we have anti-Semitism, which he equates with extermination—anti-Semitic language is an exterminating language (*PN*, 123). The Jew sits simultaneously as the object of absolute annihilation, nihilistic destruction, but also as the hope for humanity, for it is the morality that came from "the hither side of civilizations" that brought those forth and blessed those civilizations, that bring forth that morality again. Like his essays on Jewish education, he locates Judaism as the site of this ethical relation, and it is Jewish education that will deliver it (*PN*, 123).

Levinas made this point almost ten years earlier in his 1958 essay, "Israel and Universalism."[37] Responding to a lecture presented by Father Daniélou, Levinas takes issue with Daniélou's assertion that the fate of all religions, when confronted with others, is to choose between charity and truth (*DF*, 176), that is, between a kind of collegiality and conviction. Levinas agrees that acknowledging the commonality that can be found in the three monotheistic traditions is a goal for which we should strive, and that our conscience should be found in that commonality. Nonetheless, he reminds his audience that the Jew does not feel this tension between truth and charity as sharply, and this lack is not because the Jew rises above it, or sees her truth as *the* one truth.

Rather, Levinas emphasizes that Judaism is above all about action, not dogma; truth and charity are not in conflict because it is not truth that is ground of Judaism. Here, he cites Jeremiah 22, which reads, "Thus said the Lord: Do what is just and right; rescue from the defrauder him who is robbed; do not wrong the stranger, the fatherless, and the widow; commit no lawless act, and do not shed the blood of the innocent in this place" (Jeremiah 22:3). Because of this emphasis on action, on care for the poor and vulnerable, rather than dogma or truth, "the Jew can communicate just as intimately with a non-Jew who portrays morality—in other words, with the Noachide—as with another Jew . . . The rabbinic principle by which the just of every nation participate in the future world expresses not only an eschatological view. It affirms the possibility of that ultimate intimacy, beyond the dogma affirmed by the one or the other, an intimacy without reserve" (*DF*, 176). He then declares, "*this is our universalism*" (*DF*, 176, emphasis added). And he continues, "In the cave that represents the resting-place of the patriarchs and our mothers, the Talmud also lays Adam and Eve to rest: *it is for the whole of humanity that Judaism came into the world*" (*DF*, 176, emphasis added).

Anticipating the ideas that in a few years will appear in *Totality and Infinity* and nearly twenty years later in *Otherwise than Being*, he avers, "The idea of a chosen people must not be taken as a sign of pride. It does not involve being aware of exceptional rights, but of exceptional duties" (*DF*, 176–177). Out of this proclamation, Levinas announces his view of moral consciousness and singular responsibility: "It is the prerogative of a moral consciousness itself. It knows itself at the centre of the world and for it the world is not homogeneous: for I am always alone in being able to answer the call, I am irreplaceable in my assumption of responsibility. Being chosen involves a surplus of obligations for which the 'I' of moral consciousness utters" (*DF*, 176–177). These same ideas— election, singularity, substitution, responsibility—will be expressed in his two major philosophical books, most notably the philosophical writings identified with his "later" work, but it is significant to note that at the time this essay is written, neither of those books has appeared in print. It is in this short essay that we see the germ cell of his view of Judaism, even if it is an idiosyncratic rendering of Judaism, in its focus on action, which means care for the poor, the suffering, the stranger, widow, and orphan. For Levinas, Judaism ultimately does have a universal expression and he asserts powerfully that it was brought into being for all humanity. It is a fundamental part of Judaism, but one need not be Jewish to act in this way. It is our actions that will unify us and in which we will find a common ground.

In spite of Levinas's own insistence, and that of some of his readers, that his philosophy is not normative, his criticism of Buber challenges this claim.[38] Levinas is frequently explicit that response is not simply a "pre-cognitive" response, the response that is necessary for all other ethical theories to make any sense; it is also action. Though he rightly and necessarily does not specify what that action is or how it will be determined, he is clear that "before the face of God we must not go with empty hands." At this point, one cannot help but recall the discussion of war and ethics in the Preface to *Totality and Infinity* and wonder what is at stake theologically in that discussion. If we are not to be duped, the possibility of peace must be certain—but is it ethics that brings this about? Recognizing this problem, we can turn to a question that Martin Kavka poses in an essay on Judaism and phenomenology: Is the epiphany of the face the ground of ethics or its goal? I think for Levinas the answer is both/and. If it is the case that Levinas is tracing the priority of the ethical to the acceptance of the Torah, to a covenant whereby an agreement is made to live in a particular way, then there is a sense in which the face of the Other is ground, but it is ground that will issue a way of living such that being able to see the face entails responding to the face.

The crisis of humanism as we saw in chapter 3 turns on an egocentric subjectivity and Levinas offers in response a subjectivity that turns toward the Other, a subjectivity that he roots in the ancient biblical tradition. He is able to propose that the Jewish community turn to Jewish education to reclaim this subjectivity because insofar as one identifies with the Jewish community, one shares this past, this immemorial past where the Torah was accepted at Sinai and a commitment to do before hearing, to follow the Torah, was made. If Levinas is promoting this same subjectivity in his philosophical work, then several questions need to be addressed. How will this subjectivity be achieved? If it is not achieved through Jewish education, what kind of education will accomplish this task? Will this be a communal endeavor the way that Levinas promotes in his essays on Jewish education? Or, is this something that will be done individually, at points here and there, with a hope that it will influence others? What is clearly lacking outside the Jewish community is a means or a mechanism for a similar commitment, like the covenant that was made at Sinai. It is not clear that Levinas intends to persuade everyone at once, unless we consider the community of scholars—or philosophers—who read his work to be like those Jews who identify with their ancient past. In spite of that absence, however, his philosophical writings suggest that he hopes to change our thinking with regard to the conventional view of the subject.

5 The Promise of Jewish Education

Train up a child in the way he should go and even when he is old he
will not depart from it.

—Talmud: Kiddushin 29a

What then does God do in the fourth quarter?—He sits and instructs
the school children, as it is said, Whom shall one teach knowledge,
and whom shall one make to understand the message? Them that are
weaned from the milk.

— Babylonian Talmud, Tractate Avodah Zarah, 3b (see also Isaiah 28:9)

In his biography of Emmanuel Levinas, Salomon Malka opens the chapter on
Levinas's years as the director of École Normale Israélite Orientale (ENIO) with
the following quote:

> After Auschwitz, I had the impression that in taking on the directorship of the
> École Normale Israélite Orientale I was responding to a historical calling. It was
> my little secret . . . Probably the naïveté of a young man. I am still mindful and
> proud of it today.[1]

His confession echoes Theodor Adorno's warning twenty years earlier in his
1966 radio interview published as "Education after Auschwitz." Responding to
the atrocities of the Holocaust, Adorno opens the essay with the declaration that
"the premier demand upon all education is that Auschwitz not happen again."[2]
Barbarism is not something that poses merely a threat of a relapse. Adorno insists Auschwitz was the relapse. He describes the only meaningful education
as "an education directed toward critical self-reflection." And, like Levinas, he
implores us to turn our attention to young children: "Since according to the
findings of depth psychology, all personalities, even those who commit atrocities in later life, are formed in early childhood, education seeking to prevent
the repetition must concentrate upon early childhood."[3]

Yet, while Adorno and Levinas share the same concerns and indeed while
both recognize the necessity of focusing on the way we educate our young children if we are going to prevent another Auschwitz, their respective views of education and what education should do differ. Adorno's interest lies in creating
an environment that cultivates individuals who can resist authoritarian think-

ing. Resistance to authoritarian thinking, however, will not by itself mitigate the danger that he fears. Although the critical thinking that Adorno advocates may help someone resist authoritarian thinking, critical thinking alone will not help someone become a person who resists authoritarian rule. Levinas focuses his attention on cultivating a subjectivity that will not only prevent the conditions that create a murderous self in the first place but who will also respond accordingly if such conditions are created. Adorno's prescription, though it is necessary, is not sufficient.[4]

Reviving Jewish Education

The concern Levinas communicates in the essays collected in *Difficult Freedom* is strikingly similar to the concerns Rosenzweig voiced in his essays on Jewish education.[5] Although there is much scholarship documenting the connections between Levinas and Rosenzweig, this scholarship focuses primarily on the role Rosenzweig's *Star of Redemption* played as an inspiration for the themes that guide Levinas's analyses in *Totality and Infinity*.[6] I have not yet encountered scholarship that explores the connections between Levinas's essays on Jewish education and the concerns that motivate those essays and Rosenzweig's writings in this same area. This is not to say that Rosenzweig's essays influenced Levinas. I do not know that they did nor have I found any indication that they did. It is nonetheless striking that Rosenzweig's concerns, expressed well before World War II and Nazi Germany, parallel those expressed by Levinas. Their conclusions, however, are very different, and thus it is worth taking a brief look at Rosenzweig's essays on Jewish education.

In his 1917 letter to Hermann Cohen, titled "It is Time: Concerning the Study of Judaism," Rosenzweig explains that the problem with Jewish education is religious schooling as it is manifested in the "largest and most influential sections of our intelligentsia" (*On Jewish Learning* [hereafter *OJL*], 28). They have received "their religious instruction from a few years of 'religious classes,' and some High Holiday sermons," thus indicating that Judaism—and its corresponding education—has been reduced to a series of tasks rather than being practiced as an organic part of one's life. We see this concern most clearly when Rosenzweig contrasts the difficulty of developing Jewish religious instruction from that facing Christian religious instruction. He points out that

> [w]e are not concerned with creating an emotional center of this world to which the student is introduced by other school subjects, but with this introduction into the "Jewish sphere" which is independent from, and even opposed to, his non-Jewish surroundings. Those Jews with whom we are dealing have abandoned the Jewish character of the home some time during the past three generations, and therefore for them that "Jewish sphere" exists only in the synagogue. Consequently, the task of Jewish religious instruction is to re-create that

emotional tie between the institutions of public worship and the individual, that is, the very tie, which he has lost. (*OJL*, 28)

In this discussion, Rosenzweig articulates the unique problem facing the Jews. No matter how much the Jews "possess" their own world, this world will always be within another world. It will be a Jewish world within a non-Jewish world.

The problem with assimilation, as Rosenzweig notes, is that in order to become part of the larger world, one must leave the world he or she inhabits. As a result of assimilation, the Jewish world has been reduced to a set of literary documents and rabbinic writings. Yet, while these writings are "a signpost for historical Judaism," Rosenzweig tells us that it is the Jew who still turns to the prayer book who understands what the essence of Judaism is (*OJL*, 29). That is, the prayer book is a sign of living Judaism, not simply studying it. Because Judaism must be lived, the Jewish world is not to be viewed as a step on the way to acquiring, or better acquiring, the surrounding world. Significantly, Rosenzweig anticipates Levinas's assertion that although the German can read the Bible in the German language—like Herder or Luther—"the Jew can understand it only in Hebrew" (*OJL*, 30).[7]

In the ensuing pages, Rosenzweig lays out his curricular plan for Jewish education, recognizing full well the difficulties he will face implementing it. Although he recognizes the problems with introducing the content, arranging for students to go to Shabbat services, and so forth, the real problem for Rosenzweig is finding teachers who are trained with a university education. These teachers must be trained in both theology and the science of Judaism. That is, they will be teacher-scholars, on equal footing with the rabbis because of their theological training, yet will also have additional education.

If Rosenzweig's letter to Cohen lays out the curriculum necessary for Jewish learning, his 1920 letter to Eduard Strauss, titled "Towards a Renaissance of Jewish Learning," reveals the philosophy that underlies this teaching. Rosenzweig begins by stating that it is not more Jewish books or books on Judaism that we need, but more Jewish human beings (*OJL*, 55). In the wake of Jewish assimilation, Rosenzweig asks after what it means to be a Jew. To be a Jew does not preclude one from being German, in the way that being German precludes one from being French. Rather, to be Jewish is not to be Christian, not to be heathen. Judaism, as Rosenzweig describes it, is a way of being human, it is a way that one breathes, it is a "something that courses through the arteries of our life, strongly or weakly, but at any rate to our very finger tips . . . [it is] a greater or lesser force flooding one's whole being" (*OJL*, 56–57). Judaism is not grasped in religious literature, it is not entered as a creed on a civil document (e.g., marriage license), it is not something undergone. For Rosenzweig, Judaism is lived—it is part of one's very being, it is the way that someone comports oneself. One *is* it (*OJL*, 58).

Yet, Rosenzweig insightfully notes that Judaism is more than simply a way of being. It is also something that stands outside of the individual—it existed before the individual and will continue to exist long afterward. It is because of this existence that we have Jewish literature—the body of writings that Judaism comprises. And it is because of this body of writing that Jewish education is at issue. If Judaism were simply a matter of being comported in a certain way, one could be anything; but part of what it means to be Jewish is also to be versed in this literature. He notes that Hebrew does not have a word for reading that does not also include learning (*OJL*, 58). To live in the moment is not to read—it is simply to live. It is because we develop into something, that we are projected toward something, that we have books—that we need to learn. The child wants to learn—and she asks; as does the child that is in us, the child that needs to be awakened and develop into a living thing.

Rosenzweig recognizes that Judaism is both lived experience and the experience of learning, of reading, that allows us to develop that lived experience. The child might "practice" an observance of the Sabbath, but it is not enough simply to light candles and say blessings. The child must eventually live life in a certain way and know something about the life that she is living. Life, Rosenzweig tells us, stands between two points, between the past and future. It is the flame of the day that burns toward the future and illuminates the past. The worry for Rosenzweig is that Jewish study and learning are dying among the Jews and his greater concern is that these things are dying because we have no teaching profession—no scholars and no learning. He laments, "Teaching and study have both deteriorated because we lack that which gives animation to both science and education—life itself" (*OJL*, 60).

The emancipation of the Jews and Jewish assimilation created a void between the past and present. Jews no longer live a Jewish life; they no longer live in the present. The gap between those who keep Jewish law and those who do not grows wider and accentuates the difference between Jew and Jew more than between Jew and Gentile (*OJL*, 61). More significantly, he notes that the three ways that Judaism was lived have changed radically. The law, the home, and the synagogue in the time of emancipation are no longer the sites of an organic Jewish life. The vast majority of Jews do not adhere to Jewish law, the home is no longer the life force of Judaism, and our occupations are no longer natural extensions of Jewish law and home. Though many will visit the synagogue—for a memorial service or marriage—the synagogue does not "wash over and around [them]." Jews have come together in their common struggle for civil rights and in so doing have become apologists for rather than celebrants of Judaism. He thus offers a new model of Jewish education, which he describes as follows:

[d]esires are the messengers of confidence . . . For who knows whether desires such as these—real, spontaneous desires, not artificially nurtured by some

scheme of education—can be satisfied? But those who know how to listen to real wishes may also know perhaps how to point out the desired way . . . For the teacher able to satisfy such spontaneous desires cannot be a teacher according to a plan; he must be much more and much less, a master and at the same time a pupil. It will not be enough that he himself knows or that he himself can teach. He must be capable of something quite different—he must be able to "desire." He who can desire must be the teacher here. The teachers will be discovered in the same discussion room and the same discussion period as the students. And in the same discussion hour the same person may be heard as both master and student. In fact, only when this happens will it become certain that a person is qualified to teach. (*OJL*, 69)[8]

In this description, education transforms those engaged in the experience and "real" education occurs in those fleeting moments in a classroom where listening to others and discussion with others take place. For Rosenzweig, it is less important that the desire be satisfied than that we can meet at the seminar table and that we can desire in common with others (*OJL*, 70).[9] In his essay "What Does it Mean to Receive Tradition?" Martin Kavka explains that "desires," as Rosenzweig deploys the term here, refers to the desire to possess something whole, to become whole, and that confidence, as Rosenzweig states, is the position of readiness, to be prepared for the future without having a map of that future. Kavka concludes that for Rosenzweig, confidence means "this faith that desire can bear fruits, that a link to the past is really possible."[10] Although Rosenzweig's interest focused on adult Jewish education and thus the text at the seminar table is a Jewish text, it is not out of bounds to argue that the goal of both K–12 and higher education is similar to Rosenzweig's—to enflame and free the mind.

Five years after assuming the directorship of the ENIO and only six years after he was released from the German POW camp, Levinas publishes his 1951 essay "Reflections on Jewish Education" in *Les Cahiers de l'Alliance Israélite Universelle*.[11] He opens this essay with the bold statement: "The existence of Jews who wish to remain Jews . . . depends on Jewish education" (*DF*, 265). The statement should not be surprising or provocative. Teaching and education permeate Judaism from the commandment "to teach these things to your children" to rabbinic readings that function pedagogically. In the very next sentence Levinas clarifies this claim. He describes the kind of religious instruction that would be familiar to Catholics and Protestants as insufficient for Jewish education (*DF*, 265). That is, in his discussion of education, Levinas, like Rosenzweig, identifies a kind of education that is unique to Judaism.

To be sure, Levinas tells us, there are many ways to debate what the essence of Judaism is. But this particular debate is not his concern. Rather, his point is that Jewish education is not about teaching the lessons of a catechism (*DF*, 265). What, then, is the link between Judaism and education? Ultimately, Levinas identifies this relationship in very specific terms. Jewish education is about the formation of a subject devoted to humanism. The texture of this education is found in the reading of the ancient and sacred texts, an education that depends on knowing Hebrew since the most ancient of the modern religions cannot be separated from its ancient language (*DF*, 265).

We find, then, in this earliest of Levinas's essays on Jewish education, an emphasis on the importance of learning Hebrew. He justifies the weight given to Hebrew by reminding his readers that Judaism remains a minority in all parts of the world. If the religious teachings are detached from the ancient language, it is as if Jewish education has been reduced to a catechism. The very life that animates the words will have been removed and hidden with no means for the students to recover it: "In a world in which nothing is Jewish, only the text reverberates and echoes a teaching that no cathedral, no plastic form, no specific social structure can free from its abstract nature" (*DF*, 265). Conversely, Christianity, which is alive everywhere and confirmed in a concrete existence, including in the very calendar which governs the cycle of our lives, can content itself with a religious instruction that is simply "summary notions" (*DF*, 265). It was only a matter of sheer luck and family memories that allowed Judaism to stay alive in the 150 years of emancipation—what Levinas notes has also been assimilation. As a result, he observes that "family memories do not make a civilization," and Judaism's so-called luck might have run its course (*DF*, 266).[12]

Looking at Jewish studies objectively, Levinas registers a concern that the waning interest in Jewish studies, in learning Hebrew among other Jewish interests, lies in the view that Jewish studies do not carry a prestige equal to that of comparable studies in the surrounding secular culture (*DF*, 266–267). Jewish studies carry an air of being "old-fashioned" and not exciting.[13] For Levinas the irony of this disengagement is that it overlooks the contemporary nature of Judaism. If Judaism is fundamentally about truths that respond to the demands of life, then these truths must be situated in the immediate context in which one finds oneself. Judaism is not a static religion, but a dynamic one, evident by the very conversations that animate its sacred sources. But part of that dynamism is located in the very way in which Hebrew, not the translation or transliteration, but Hebrew itself, works. To be sure, Levinas is not interested in a traditionalism or piety, both of which stymie religious discourse and yield orthodoxies, not doctrines. Rather, he is interested in revitalizing those parts of Judaism that carry with them the fundamental Jewish values found in Judaism's great texts, e.g., the Bible, the Talmud, and the Midrash. His confides that Jewish souls must be nurtured, but this can only be done if the minds [*cerveaux*] are nurtured also (*DF*, 267).[14]

As we move through Levinas's essays on Jewish education, we cannot lose sight of the connection he continually makes between nurturing minds [*cerveaux*] and nurturing souls. Levinas does not reduce the ethical subject in Judaism to the clichéd bumper sticker that reads "Character counts." Rather, the development of the ethical subject is intimately tied to the development of an intellectually sophisticated mind, which he believes is produced through a sustained engagement with the complexities of Jewish texts. If we understand why he thinks Jewish education is both unique and indispensable, we can appreciate his reason for stating outright that this turn to a science of Judaism does not mean turning to philosophy—and here he means Western philosophy—which he believes Judaism has been doing for far too long already.

In Levinas's view, Judaism capitulated to Western thought, in particular the Enlightenment, rather than assert itself as a legitimate voice in the development of the intellect. It subjected its sources to philosophical scrutiny and justification, thus sanitizing it of all that made it unique. The philosophy of the Enlightenment barreled through modernity and either absorbed everything in its path or pushed it aside (*DF,* 268). In spite of how the Enlightenment presents itself—as the answer to all questions and the question to all answers—Levinas's observations remind us that critical apparatus and critical reflection are not synonymous with the cultivation of a religious civilization nor do they guarantee the cultivation of an ethical one.

What then does a return to Jewish education mean? There are many ways to "study" Judaism; however, to study Judaism as a distracted observer is not to study these texts with a view that they might teach us something: "To raise Judaism into a science, to think Judaism, is *to turn these texts back into teaching texts*" (*DF,* 268, emphasis added). With great insight Levinas observes that the West had not considered the truths that might be found in talmudic texts—or only when these truths correspond to how we already think. That is, the West does not look to the Talmud for wisdom, for insight, or for new knowledge (*DF,* 268). Returning to the Talmud means returning to Judaism its intellectual rigor and its intellectual weight, but to do so without treating it as though it were just another text—like Shakespeare or Goethe. The balance then lies in combining the feelings of Judaism with an intellect of Judaism, thus preventing Judaism from being reduced to either an overzealous exaltation or a mere academic endeavor. Balancing this endeavor between these two poles made it necessary for Levinas to reassure his audience that the Jewish school does not betray the ideals of the secular school and might even amplify those ideals.

Repeating many themes from this 1951 essay, in his 1956 essay, "For a Jewish Humanism," Levinas argues that insofar as the Jewish school supports what he calls "Jewish humanism"—"that which cannot remain indifferent to the modern world in which it seeks a whole humanity"—it lends support to what gives meaning to Judaism in the modern world.[15] The aim of the Jewish school, then, is not simply to bring a Jewish education to Jewish children in order to maintain Judaism as a religion; the aim of the Jewish school is to bring children into the kind of education that will reinforce the Jewish humanism found in and promoted by the Jewish sources. And early in the essay he tells us that while the notion of a Jewish humanism remains secular, Judaism sits at the crossroads between faith and logic.

Citing Mendelssohn, Spinoza, and Maimonides, Levinas corrects the view that monotheism is a revealed religion and instead calls it a revealed Law, indicating that its truth is universal—like reason (*DF*, 274).[16] This monotheism, however, is not concerned with preparing humanity for individual salvation. Indeed, Levinas rejects the idea that we are preparing for a private meeting with a consoling God. Rather, Levinas situates the drawing of the presence of God into humanity as a just act, a moral act. He equates the vision of God with a moral act: "This optics is an ethics" (*DF*, 274–275).[17] Rather than lead us to God, this religion leads us to humanity: "Monotheism is a humanism" (*DF*, 275). He reminds his readers that quietly motivating the Jewish resistance to convert to Christianity is the belief that the human truths of Judaism were being subsumed into Christianity and thus losing their distinctly Jewish character. That is, as tempting as it might have been to convert, and as dangerous as it was at times not to convert, Levinas believes that underlying this resistance was the sense that the only way to keep Judaism alive was to instantiate it physically— to remain Jews. To convert would have signaled the complete disappearance of Judaism. The Jewish ideas subsumed into Christianity would no longer be remembered as originally Jewish (*DF*, 275). He concludes this essay by identifying the problem with assimilation and the homogeneity that Jews desired and for the most part achieved as the loss of that which made them unique—"the secret of their science" (*DF*, 275).

Throughout these writings on education, and this essay is no different, Levinas maintains that studying Jewish texts in their original, Hebrew language provides the vehicle for a "difficult wisdom" concerned with truths that correlate to virtues. Further, he identifies as a distinguishing feature of Judaism that it holds as one of the highest virtues the knowledge of its own sources (*DF*, 275). That is, Judaism's uniqueness consists not only in that it commands the teaching of itself, but also that this teaching has built into it the discovery, preservation, and enactment of a Jewish humanism. As a result, he sees Judaism not as parochial, nor as a mechanism for separation, but as precisely the opposite—as that which is "indispensable to human harmony" (*DF*, 276). It should not surprise us then that his identification of Jewish humanism becomes the foundation for promoting the Jewish day school. He locates in the Jewish school the primary space in which Jewish humanism will be kept safe.

In the same year that Levinas published "Reflections on Jewish Education" (1951), he also published the essay "The State of Israel and the Religion of Israel," in which he identifies that feature which makes the State of Israel unique from all other modern political states.[18] Here Levinas tries to differentiate not only the State of Israel from other states but also the religion of Israel from other religions. Incorporating his analysis of a collection of essays brought together by Chaim Grinberg, Levinas comments that he is struck by the ease with which the essays move from religion to ethics (*DF*, 217–218).[19] He adds that he does not see these essays as simply promoting dogma with moral veneer; instead the dogma is morality itself (*DF*, 218).

He summarizes the collection with the affirmation that belief in God does not *incite* us to social justice; instead he equates the two, referring to belief in God as the "institution of that justice" (*DF*, 218). This justice is not an abstract principle. Anticipating themes that will appear in full force in 1961, he asks if the whole aim of religion is not ultimately to see the face of the Other (*DF*, 218). To his own question, he boldly replies that what makes the State of Israel special is that it finally offers an opportunity to carry out or fulfill the social law—the moral law—of Judaism (*DF*, 218). Again, emphasizing the ethical dimension of Judaism, the Jewish people, and the State of Israel, Levinas argues that the need for their own land was not an end in itself for the Jewish people. Rather, it was a means to an end—to have one's own land, to live by the laws of Israel, by the laws of Judaism, means "they could finally begin the work of their lives" (*DF*, 218), where here what Levinas means by the "work of their lives" is the work of ethics.

Notably, this early essay stands out in that Levinas offers a strong statement against religion as mere ritual practice and he warns against making such distinctions that separate those who are religious—those who practice their faith—from those who are not. Such distinctions, while they might have had purpose at the dawn of the diaspora, serve no purpose now except to blind us to what is at stake in the religion of Israel—the practice of social justice. Levinas is skeptical of those who have only the most vague feelings of religiosity; yet, he is equally worried by those whose religious fervor does not move them to social action (*DF*, 218–219):

> Justice as the *raison d'être* of the State: that is religion. It presupposes the high science of justice. The State of Israel will be religious because of the intelligence of its great books, which it is not free to forget. It will be religious through the very action that establishes it as a State. It will be religious or it will not be at all (*DF*, 219).

Returning to Grinberg's collection, Levinas finds an answer to his question— "But how are we to read these [great] books?" (*DF*, 219). It is the Torah, after all, in which we find the values of democracy and socialism, and the inspiration for an "avant-garde state" (*DF*, 219). But why remain tethered to the Torah? Is the Torah not out of date? What can it teach us today? For his answers, he refers to Yeshayahu Leibovitz's essay "Religion and State."

As Levinas reads Leibovitz, the Talmud provides the human example to the law of which the Bible speaks. These books together can help us deduce the justice required for all situations. Here Levinas distinguishes Judaism from its religious counterparts and he mirrors the themes found in his companion essay on education. The great books of Judaism do not cleanse human life of the complexities that comprise human relations. The stories and the commentaries demand rigor in our attentiveness to them. They will not dispense answers easily or simply. But they will offer us guidance if we pay close attention, and indeed our job is to figure out how these stories of the past can teach us something about our present-day situation. The act of study binds the Jewish state to Jewish religion (*DF,* 219–220).

We see then how Levinas connects three themes: the relationship between Judaism and the ethical—or the impulse to social justice; the universality of this dimension of the religion; and the relationship this particular aspect of the religion has to education. He insists that what has been lost in Jewish education and thus in the religion is the way in which we let the texts speak to us—the way in which the text has something to teach us. We must, therefore, return to rabbinic exegesis, which made the text speak (*DF,* 220). In this return, the text becomes a teacher, or at the very least, a source of teaching rather than a mere object of study. To see the text in this way is to practice Judaism in its original spirit (*DF,* 220).

Only six years after the war had ended and Levinas returned to Paris, his writings reflect a firm commitment not only to Judaism itself, but also to Jewish education as the means by which this particular form of Judaism will be perpetuated. We should bear in mind that the essays I just discussed were published ten years *before* he published *Totality and Infinity.* If understood in this manner, with this chronology in mind, it becomes increasingly difficult to dismiss the religious language in the latter text as simply a placeholder for a concept that cannot otherwise be named (lest it might carry the ontological connotation Levinas wishes to avoid). The religious language Levinas utilizes cannot simply be interchanged with any other word. He chooses these words for a reason. It is increasingly difficult to claim that the meaning of these words in his philosophical writings is radically different from how he uses this language in the essays published under the category currently called "writings on Judaism." He is clear in these essays that religious inspiration—specifically Judaism—is equivalent to the possibility of seeing the face of the Other (*DF,* 218).

These themes reformulate ideas that he introduced early in the essays collected in *Difficult Freedom,* but they are poignantly expressed in his 1954 essay, "Assimilation Today," where he connects the Dreyfus Affair to the years of National Socialism, both of which are not only horrifying parts of Jewish history but which also put into question the relationship Judaism had to the principles of 1789.[20] Expressing great pain, he reminds his readers not only *that* assimilation failed but also *why* it failed—"It failed because it did not put an end to the anguish felt by the Jewish soul. Assimilation failed because it did not placate the non-Jews, or put an end to anti-Semitism; on certain points, it stirred up heated reactions and arguments once more. Anguish and anxiety still surreptitiously alter apparently free behavior and every Jew remains, in the largest sense of the word, a Marrano" (*DF,* 255).

Referring again to Chaim Grinberg, Levinas cynically observes: if Jews were not converting to Christianity it was not because they believed in Judaism but rather because they did not believe in anything religious (*DF*, 255–256). He then astutely, and pessimistically, notes that the most serious crisis with regard to assimilation is that it is slowed down only by the irreligiousness of those who might convert or assimilate (*DF*, 256). We could frame Levinas's point in this glib fashion, which might even remind us of a Borscht Belt joke: the good news is that since Jews do not believe in anything, they are not converting to Christianity in much larger numbers than they might otherwise; the bad news is that Jews do not believe in anything, including Judaism.

The discussion of the separation between church and state, between the private life of conscience and the realm of public life, which Levinas takes up in this essay could not be more pressing than it is today, here in the United States. He reminds us that the vice of a philosophy of assimilation is its forgetting, or its ignorance, of the ways that secularized forms of religious life lie at the heart of the so-called secular state (*DF*, 257). For many in the secular state, the state's religious framework need not be made explicit, indeed, it need not even be thought—"one breathes it naturally" (*DF*, 256–257). As we see only too well in the battle lines being drawn over public education, health care, and so forth, the separation is not firmly implanted simply as a result of the juridical separation between church and state (*DF*, 257).[21]

Israel then presents an opportunity not available to the Jew previously—an opportunity for life in the State to converge with the life of conscience. But also, as a result of Israel's reality, "the error of assimilation becomes visible. The Jews' entry into the national life of European states has led them to breathe an atmosphere impregnated with Christian essence and that prepares them for the religious life of these states and heralds their conversion" (*DF*, 257). The secular states, which are founded on a Christian structure, create a Christian atmosphere that is perceived as secular.[22] It is to the Jew who resists being drawn into this pool, who tries to swim against this current, that the secular is revealed as religious. Thus, the Jew must make a decision, a decision that includes reviving a Jewish science, which must include returning to Hebrew. And again, as Levinas does in every other essay on Jewish education, he reminds his readers that this return, this reclaiming of Judaism, does not refute the principles of 1789. Rather, in Levinas's view, the Jewish sacred texts teach a universalism that is not reliant on particularity. Their message is indeed a message of human solidarity, a nation united by ideas (*DF*, 257). Avoiding the question of believing in God, which is a different question, Levinas asks the most pressing question for Judaism: "Do we still want to be Jews?" Essentially he is asking whether Judaism still offers what it originally promised (*DF*, 258).

Affirming the same themes from Levinas's essays that dominated in the 1950s, Catherine Chalier, Levinas's former student, contrasts Levinas's discussion of the relation between the interiority and exteriority of the ethical to that in Kant's discussion.[23] Although she observes that for both Kant and Levinas ethics depends on the fact of God's absence, Chalier also notes the difference in their relationship to their respective religions: Kant to Christianity and Levinas to Judaism. For example, Chalier reminds us that Kant's philosophy makes frequent references to Christianity and even "gives a privileged status to that religion to speak of Christ as a model for pure moral intention."[24] She further recalls that for Kant interiority is the determination of the moral action—what motivates the moral subject—while for Levinas the determination is exteriority, the actions that are in fact done. In a state of need, the suffering person cannot wait until the final hour when the agent's motivation is ascertained to be pure; the person needs to be fed.

Chalier's analysis effectively shows how the interiority of Kant's system can be mapped onto key themes in Christianity—namely, the anxiety over one's own salvation—while Levinas's emphasis on exteriority reflects the underpinnings of Jewish ethics—namely, the responsibility toward and care for the Other.[25] In so doing, she discloses how Western philosophy is often either a veiled religiosity (in the extreme view) or uncritical with regard to how religion has influenced the structure of what we identify as the philosophical canon. Her observation with regard to one of the central philosophers of the Enlightenment parallels Levinas's observation with regard to the world at large—the secular world is not such to the Jew. Rather, it is structured in a similar fashion to Christianity. But those who are not of an identity that explicitly runs counter to this structuring do not necessarily experience this secular world as religious in the way that the Jew does.

Chalier's reading, which also emphasizes the role of practice in Judaism, supplements Levinas's view. Rather than having its focus on the salvation of the self, resulting from one's belief in God, Judaism requires that we act for the Other. He is concerned with the complete destruction of ethics which revealed that the ethical obligation to the Other had been covered over, that the way we teach our children morality is to teach them mere rules of behavior. Levinas's concern is to address what he sees as a plain fact—that Western ethics failed and the most horrific site of that failure was Auschwitz. In spite of itself, the humanism produced by modernity lost precisely that which made it human, namely the religious—read here as ethical—dimension, bearing in mind that religious for Levinas specifically refers to the tie that binds one person to another. That is, religion is not an "individual" experience of the transcendent. Rather, the transcendent defines the possibility of being pulled out of one's own ego toward another, to put the Other before oneself, to be compelled by the command of the responsibility for the Other.

Humanism and Anti-humanism

The questions Levinas raises in the early education essays from the 1950s motivate his 1973 essay, "Antihumanism and Education," published almost twenty years after "For a Jewish Humanism," and only one year prior to the publication of *Otherwise than Being*.[26] Levinas opens this essay by connecting the Western view of humanism with a conception of freedom that is protected by the liberal State. We see him struggling with the same questions about humanism and humanities education that continue to haunt most contemporary discussions of education. Additionally, this essay most explicitly invokes Jewish education as the best response to the evil that the world saw unleashed in the twentieth century.

He begins by describing the movement of humanism as beginning with a respect for the person, the blossoming of human nature, "the cultivation of creativity in Art, intelligence in Science, and pleasure in daily life" (*DF*, 277). The introduction of just law follows from our freedom to pursue our own pleasures, even as this introduction also reveals the limit of law. On the one hand, law is necessary to safeguard our freedoms and to maintain peace among the nations and with other states. It provides the possibility for individuals to have a private life (*DF*, 277). On the other hand, humanism can see only the law of the state or the laws of nature. Humanism not only moves through and is transmitted by certain kinds of work and the study of certain books, but it also worships the principles for which humanism stands (*DF*, 277).

Levinas reveals his distaste for this kind of humanism when he notes that the focus on the beautiful transmission of these ideals led to a focus on the beautiful language in which these ideals are expressed. The noble ideals and principles themselves were "lost in rhetoric and ideology" (*DF*, 277). Simply reading literature with complex moral narratives was confused with the view that this made one a better person—to read was in fact "to do good." The other confusion, which persists with regard to humanities education, connects being an educated person in the classical sense of the term with having a developed moral character.

Levinas admits that there is nonetheless a connection between the humanism of the belles lettres and the biblical ideal of humanism. The attachment to books that is the hallmark of the humanism that he criticizes is certainly fundamental to Judaism, which is tethered to the Torah, the Talmud, and other sacred writings. Judaism, too, is vulnerable to degenerating into ideology (*DF*, 278). This connection though is only apparent. He asks, "Can the whole of Western humanism pass for a secularization of Judeo-Christianity? Have the rights of man and of the citizen and the new spirit that conquered in the eighteenth century not fulfilled in our minds the promises of the prophets?" (*DF*, 278).[27]

These questions reveal precisely what is at stake in his discussion. In the move to secularize Judaism's ethical impulse and assimilate it into this Western humanism, Judaism let go of what made it unique—or rather, it let go of what remained unique to Judaism. It severed the particular link it had to the prophets, specifically, the rabbinic tradition through which Levinas claimed the voices of these prophets reverberate. This forgetting however enabled the possibility of a

Judeo-Christian friendship, a noble friendship secured by the noble and courageous actions of men and women during World War II. But this friendship masks the fundamental differences that remain, above all at the level of doctrine and belief. The Jew lives in a world that has been fashioned by Christianity and in Levinas's view the Jew has not overcome what it means to be in this position. Nonetheless, liberal humanism offers a level playing field on which Jew and Christian can be equal, or at least on which the Jew can feel that she is the Christian's equal. This is why, Levinas confesses, this crisis of humanism is of grave concern to him (*DF,* 279).

We arrive at Levinas's central concern: the crisis is a crisis in and solved by Jewish education, which has lost its meaning. This crisis, however, is not that Jews became detached from Judaism but rather that Judaism surrendered to Western humanism—to its ideals, hermeneutic methods, and abstract universalism. As a result, rabbinic exegesis, which is the hallmark of a Jewish reading of scriptural writings, was not simply lost or forgotten but rendered inappropriate, irrelevant, and outdated. Judaism's signature method of reading, of engaging a written text, was disqualified and it was done so by relinquishing itself to Western humanism thus allowing this new humanism to forget its roots in the ancient traditions in which its principles were first forged.

This difference that identifies Judaism as distinct is precisely the reason why the Jew made this move. The modern Jew, in Levinas's view, did not want any differences. With the move to this liberal humanism, which claims to be universal, idiosyncratic religion no longer served any purpose. Repeating the same concern from his 1950s essays, Levinas admits that Judaism had lost its social effectiveness and its intellectual meaning—the two traits that he believes make Judaism and the study of Jewish texts unique. As a result, simply to be of "Mosaic confession" was to consign oneself to the past, to the outdated, to the old and irrelevant—and worse, to the subjective (*DF,* 280). To put it more disparagingly, but also probably more accurately, it is to be viewed as provincial, unsophisticated, and unreflective, opting for a religious—read here as irrational—sensibility over scientific reason.

As Richard Kearney writes in the preface to his recent book *Anatheism,* the God-question keeps returning. The question brings with it a new set of criticisms as we see in the recent spate of attacks from public intellectuals like Christopher Hitchens to scientists like Richard Dawkins to comedians like Bill Maher, all of whom want to paint religion in its entirety with the same tarred brush.[28] In the views of these critics, to be a religious person necessarily renders one thoughtless, simple, and dumb—if not worse: unethical, bigoted, and violent. They present this view of religion in contrast to atheism, which they want to claim is not guilty of the same crimes.

All of these thinkers, as astute as they are, seem to have overlooked the more obvious point that ideology, in whatever form it takes—religious or not—can be dangerous, intractable, and violent. One need only look to Stalinism, Tiananmen Square, indeed, even Hitlerism to see that there has been much violence committed in the name of a political ideology that has been detached from a religious adherence to God. Moreover, it could easily be argued that much of the extreme violence done in the name of religion was really a mask for the political ideology that supported it. That is, was it the religion—religious doctrine—that demanded the violence or was it the thirst for power that is independent of religion that demanded the violence? I suspect it was the latter, and the simple erasure of religion (well, maybe not so simple) will not erase an ideology that most likely will take its place.

For Levinas, the move away from Judaism led Jews down a dangerous path where they abandoned the idea of living lives as ethical models and rejected the role of Judaism as a light unto the nations. In contrast to the intellectual acuity that used to define Jewish education, Levinas admits that Jewish education had become mere religious instruction—like a catechism—in which the ideas were detached from their source, separated from the civilization that birthed and nurtured them. They were now lifeless ideas (*DF,* 280). This break from the past means that the teaching is also divorced from the cultivation of the student into someone concerned for all humanity. That is Levinas's greatest sorrow.

Like Rosenzweig before him, Levinas also laments that Judaism became only a "mental reserve" rather than a religion that would be an organic part of daily life. Religious instruction was reduced to a few hours a week and to a *bar* or *bat mitzvah.*[29] What is most pressing for Levinas, unlike Rosenzweig, is the connection that Levinas perceives between this loss and Judaism's separation from the unique humanism that originally informed it (*DF,* 280). Because Jewish civilization is stored in written texts, the loss of Hebrew education within the Jewish schools means that this civilization remains hidden, inaccessible, and forgotten. It is then viewed as having no use, though its value remains a lost secret. Levinas tracks this loss to "the Emancipation" (what he will often refer to in shorthand as "the principles of 1789") that gave Jews their citizenship even as it asked them to give up publicly their particularity as Jews. It is not that Levinas wants to relinquish the privileges—or rights—that accompanied this emancipation. Rather, he recognizes that insofar as Emancipation was grounded on a Christian structure, which the secularists ignored, Jews were increasingly encouraged to become more like Christians. The difficulty in straddling the universal promise of rights and the particular ways in which one lives as a Jew also allowed the Jew to move farther away from Jewish education and the ethical life it would help cultivate, which Levinas views as a part of Judaism that is less contingent on specific Jewish practices. To give up keeping kosher does not necessarily entail giving up reading Hebrew and being for the Other.

Responding to what Judaism had become, Levinas argues that the crisis of humanism such as we have seen in the inhumanities of the twentieth century highlights the view that Jewish education should mean something other than religious instruction. His recitation of a laundry list of those inhumanities raises questions not only about what Western liberalism promised but also about what modern humanism delivered: World War I, the Russian Revolution refuting itself in Stalinism, fascism, Hitlerism, the 1939–1945 War, atomic bombings, genocide, and most certainly the philosophical discourse of Heidegger, which subordinates the human to the anonymous gains of Being—and despite Heidegger's "Letter on Humanism," lending credence to Hitlerism itself (*DF,* 281). The fragility of Western liberalism was revealed by the inhumanities of its time, and Levinas pointedly asks, "Is it a basic inability to guarantee the privileges of humanity of which humanism had considered itself the repository?" (*DF,* 281).

This crisis of humanism revealed the Jew as such. That is, while the Jew had attempted to move into the background, to become like everyone else, to live in the universal world set out by Western humanism, the crises of the twentieth century revealed to the Jew precisely the fragility of a humanism that is divorced from religion and thus claims to be for everyone. In turn, he asks if there is a fragility to humanity in humanism (*DF,* 281). And he answers simply, "Yes." In the truest sense of the term, the Jew became a martyr and as such revealed that the "meaning of humanity is not exhausted by the humanists, nor immune to the slippage that is at first imperceptible but can ultimately prove fatal" (*DF,* 281). Western humanism has failed because it is fundamentally flawed—it simply cannot capture all of what makes us human, nor can it protect humanity from those who would persecute others.

The aftermath of World War II was not the first time that the Jews responded to their surrounding world with a recognition that something profound was missing from their life. Levinas offers several examples of the ways that Jews tried to incorporate a dimension of "being Jewish" into their Western lives— the French Jewish Scouts movement, the Maimonides school, and so forth. His point is not that the Jews wanted to announce themselves as persecuted but rather it revealed a recognition among the Jews that the surrounding humanism did not capture or deliver all that was human. These acts, Levinas surmises, were attempts by Jews to keep alive what it means to be persecuted so that the Jew does not become a persecutor (*DF,* 282). It was an attempt to move toward a doctrine that was better able than Western humanism to deliver meaning to being and life (*DF,* 282).

Levinas's concerns about both humanism and liberalism extend to the recent critiques launched against them. His exposition brings him to a point where he finds himself set between these two poles—the fragility of a failed humanism that promotes universal values on one side and the response to the inhumanity of the twentieth century, which he calls anti-humanism. Yet he wants his audience not to misunderstand his mistrust. His is not a mistrust that abandons all human ideals. Rather, he wants to put into doubt the humanism as has just been described. He wishes to protest the belles lettres and the allegiance to them, which give the appearance of having a conviction of principles—his worry is that revolutionary literature becomes confused with the revolution itself. It is a protest against "the decency that covers hypocrisy, the anti-violence that perpetuates abuse . . ." It is an anti-humanism that in response to the failed Western humanism "protests against all-powerful literature and finds its way even into the graffiti that call for such literature's destruction. It is an anti-humanism as old as the prophecy of Ezekiel, in which the real prophetic spirit is offered as the only thing capable of putting an end to such writing" (DF, 283).[30] Yet Levinas warns of this temptation also. The appeal of Ezekiel is an appeal to unhappiness (DF, 283), and just as he worries about the power of rhetoric in the belles lettres to confuse those who read them into believing that reading is the same thing as doing, so too, Levinas worries about the purely rhetorical power "that builds its nest in pathos," a very dangerous nest in which to nurture education. This kind of pathos just as easily leads to complacency, which is the resolute enemy of education.

In the penultimate section of this essay Levinas assures his readers that "the crisis of humanism cannot be reduced to being opposed to the belles-lettres. Antihumanism does not confine itself to this denunciation of literature and an eloquence that disguises misery" (DF, 283–284). Real intellectuals are able to remind us of the cracks in our civilization, not cover them over. They are able to identify these shifts in meaning, especially when these shifts point to the potentially crumbling foundation. But if intellectuals identify these shifts, our mistake lies in asking them to act as moralists and repair the structural defects they identify.

For Levinas, if we go beyond the Said—within which the intellectual communicates—we will find the responsibility for the Other, a commandment before it is pronounced. That is, we will find an originary message on which the collection of belles lettres is formed. Thus Levinas questions not only what Western liberalism promised and what modern humanism delivered, he also worries about the recent critiques launched against them. That is, even thinkers like Foucault would offer a compelling critique of modern liberalism and reveal liberalism's hypocrisy—this critique could also be considered a form of anti-humanism. However, for Levinas, the kind of critique that someone like Foucault would offer would not in the end deliver the anti-humanism that he desires, a humanism of the Other. We see this point made most clearly in that same section of the essay when he takes on the sex, drugs, and rock-and-roll culture of the 1960s. It is difficult not to hear him sounding like an old-fashioned "fuddy-duddy," who is just not hip with the times. His concern, however, is not with the behaviors that follow from sexual liberation per se; that is, he cannot be dismissed as an ascetic. Instead, Levinas's concern focuses on the libertine approach to these behaviors, which in the end is about the satisfaction of *only* one's own sexual pleasure.[31] He astutely observes that while this might be a kind of anti-humanism, that is, a critique of the hypocritical liberalism that prevails in the twentieth century, it is not the anti-humanism that he seeks.

He finds himself, then, positioned between these two poles mentioned earlier—the fragility of a failed humanism on one side and the anti-humanism that responded to it on the other. He is not unaware that by situating himself in this position, he locates himself at the more conservative end of a political spectrum in the battleground of the culture wars. He recognizes that the young people in the Jewish community are more inclined to choose or desire, like their non-Jewish peers, a life of "if it feels good do it" and "it's all about me" than to choose a life that is "for the other person." In spite of what appears to him an impossible dream, Levinas turns to Jewish education, which upholds Judaism's view that children should not be educated in moral confusion—with no distinction between good and evil. Indeed, it is part of our responsibility to ensure the existence of this dimension in their lives. They must be raised to be open to the misfortune of others and to be willing to respond to those who suffer. Thus, it is significant that while Levinas is clear about the moral upbringing of children, he confines what he means by "moral" to that which has to do with the suffering of others and the false happiness that typically accompanies immediate gratification (*DF,* 285).

The most significant point in this essay is his belief that through Jewish education, the young people of his day would be more able to swim against the current that might otherwise simply carry them along. For Levinas, Jewish education fundamentally teaches that justice is the response to the other person and that an education based on the Talmud would not ignore the sexual dimension of our lives but would help portray it in all its complexity, ambiguity, and indeed occasionally its tragedy. And here Levinas makes his final dig at the belles lettres for the simple and sentimental manner in which love and sex are often described. But his point here is that while he wishes to situate himself in contrast to the libertine approach to life, he also wants to distance himself from the brutality of a totalitarian State that would also impose constraints on our personal behavior. His goal is not to control sexual behavior—that misses the point. For Levinas, Judaism at its core is fundamentally humanist/anti-humanist in that it focuses our actions on justice toward the Other. To live one's life in this humanistic way will necessarily lead to a change in other behaviors.

This crisis revealed the loss incurred by Jews as they embraced a so-called secular life and adopted the modern liberal tradition of France. Instead of being the echo of the surrounding civilization, Levinas implores French Jews to take the lead. Thus, in the face of these atrocities, Levinas notes, "the opportunity for Jewish education is valuable precisely because it swims against this current of homogeneity that appears to be carrying us along" (*DF,* 285). His mistrust of Western humanism is a protest against "the declamation that takes the place of necessary activities, against the human decency that covers hypocrisy, the anti-violence that perpetuates abuse; but equally against the violence of the verbal indignation of revolutionaries themselves who immediately become inverted into a cultural pastime as they turn themselves into revolutionary literature" (*DF,* 282–283). Levinas's view of Jewish education is precisely that it is not a homogenizing process. He believes this approach to Jewish education will cultivate independent thinkers who are able to think creatively and with sensitivity toward the other person. At the end of this essay, Levinas states simply that Jewish education is

> the conviction that a limit must be imposed on the interiorization of principles of conduct, that certain inspirations must become gestures and rituals. There is no frontier in the depths of human interiority that can arrest mental reserves when one sets out to "spiritualize" . . . Jewish education does not rely on the ineffective brutality of constraints imposed by the totalitarian State in order to maintain a law within freedom and guarantee freedom through law . . . These are practices carried out to please God only to the extent that they allow one to safeguard the human in man. Is this a particularism? Of course. But it is not some limitation or other that is brought to bear on national allegiances, civic duty and fraternity. It is a particularism with regard to doctrines, anthropologies, axiologies and theologies. It involves no separation from men. (*DF,* 288)

He distinguishes Jewish education from other forms of education, for example, belles lettres, by claiming that it contains within it not simply a few geniuses whose work we try to repeat, but also the breadth of experience amassed over thousands of years; it calls us to return to its wisdom—the Word, when elevated, is the Word of God (*DF,* 286). It calls for a new (or old) relationship to the law and moral obligation. Hence, by tracing the roots of the problem back to 1789, Levinas links the problems of Jewish assimilation, Jewish humanism, and Jewish education to the development of the French republic and the consequences of the liberalism that it produced.[32] Although he recognizes the tremendous benefits of the French Republic to the Jews, he also recognizes the dangers. It is in this ambivalence that Levinas locates the *difficult freedom* of being Jewish—the temptation of the secular world in which the Jew lives, the temptation to forego what seems old and obsolete only to adhere to these same values in a flashier package, the tension created by living a particular life within a public space that demands homogeneity. It is in these essays on Jewish education that we find Levinas struggling with all of these themes and trying to reach an audience that is also struggling. These essays both identify the problem and the solution—the Jews have lost their way, they have become too Western, and by that he means they no longer put the Other before themselves and thus they no longer serve as a light unto the nations, to become a model for others to do the same.

Levinas's writings on Judaism, including those essays on Jewish education and his writings on Jewish universalism, demonstrate that it is the universalism of the Enlightenment and the Universal Rights of Man (*Les Principes de*

1789 and *La Déclaration des droits de l'Homme et du Citoyen*) that both tempt and repulse him, attract and scare him. Levinas's response to this education, however, is not the response of a younger Stanley Fish, who proudly claims that the humanities have no value save the pleasure they produce in the reader; nor is it the response of the moral perfectionist who sees the task—and ability—of humanities education to perfect the human virtues. Levinas's response is of a different order. He is not concerned with moral perfectionism, that is, he is not concerned with a self that is virtuous or morally upright insofar as that self follows a fundamental moral principle like Kant's categorical imperative. Nor is Levinas interested in a moral perfection that is solely about the cultivation of a self as such—a self with a well-trained body, a self that does not waste its talents, a self that is patient, perseveres, or is prudent. This is to say, he is not concerned with a self that is concerned with itself.

For Levinas, modernity's description of the subject in terms of freedom and rationality is opposed to a positive understanding of the human as vulnerable and dependent. (There is a view of the subject as vulnerable and dependent, but it is applied to women.) The moral theory that developed out of Western philosophical thought focused on the self—the cultivation of a virtuous person or the development of self-perfection. This move is, for Levinas, necessarily a move *away from* ethics as he defines that term. The moral theory that emerged from modernity's view of the free and rational subject is a smoke screen for the underlying ethical obligation that informs those theories. That obligation remained hidden or dormant until Levinas's ethical project asked us to rethink how we understood both ethics and subjectivity.

What then does it mean to say Levinas equates ethics with being Jewish and thus is nudging everyone toward being Jewish? Throughout his writings, Levinas describes a radically different view of subjectivity, one for which he believes there is an originary warrant and that I would then argue is secured through a complementary education—formal or otherwise. This different subjectivity in turn yields a different relation that the "I" has to the Other. His description reveals that he does not believe reason and introspection to be sufficient to turn us toward the Other nor do they compel us to be responsible for the Other. Levinas traces this humanism to Jewish sources. He believes that this kind of humanism is what makes Judaism unique. He also believes, as we saw above, that Judaism was created to offer this kind of humanism to the world. This Jewish humanism may refer to or recall a dimension of "Jewishness" or Judaism that is essentially universal.

At the celebration of Levinas's 80th birthday, Chalier observed: "the exigency of study is not sufficient in a world scarred by suffering, personal or collective."[33] If she is correct, then she is also right to remind us that the commandment "thou shalt not kill" is a requirement for everyone. We must then "question ourselves . . . about everything our own being kills, through thought, through words, and through deeds, before we think about God, or, more precisely for the idea of Him to gain meaning within ourselves." And the universalism of Levinas's teaching is found in Chalier's statement, that "[herein] lies the highest exigency of [Levinas's] teaching, an exigency from which no one is ever released, an uneasiness which lasts as long as the span of life which is imparted to us . . ."[34] Chalier further recalls that Levinas taught the students who attended those Saturday-morning meetings that one should not enter a house of prayer or study with a cold heart. Neither should one be so self-certain about one's relationship to God. Although one should get back in touch with one's inner life, this move entails reading the Book, and that requires "a master who guides the attention, who makes the letter a teaching experience." The link, then, becomes clear—the highest exigency is not only not to kill, but also to question all the ways in which our own being kills, to get back in touch with our inner life, to return to the Hebraic words, such as *hineni*, here I am. These words, according to Chalier, were brought to life by Levinas's presence and it is "our responsibility to keep them alive."[35]

Levinas recasts "the humanity of man" at stake in those writings from the 1930s—"Reflections on the Philosophy of Hitlerism" and *On Escape*—as a crisis in humanism in his essays from the 1950s. Importantly, he situates this discussion of the crisis within the context of Jewish education and the failure of Jewish assimilation. If the problem was that the Jews had lost their way by giving up their ties to a robust Jewish education and the cultivation of a unique subjectivity this education delivers, then the solution to the problem must be a return to that particular approach to education; it is through this approach to education that the responsibility to keep alive "those words"—the Hebraic words, such as *hineni*—is fulfilled. Levinas then has offered this return to Jewish education as a solution to the crisis of humanism facing not only the Jews but all of humanity. If the Jews are to return to Jewish education to achieve this new subjectivity, then the question that we must ask is, "How will non-Jews accomplish this task if the particular Jewish expression of this responsibility does not resonate with them?" One possibility is to describe the ethical subjectivity in a register that resonates with the non-Jewish world.

6 Teaching, Fecundity, Responsibility

I have always looked upon the relationship between teacher and pupil
as a most sacred one.[1]

—Morris Raphael Cohen

Against the Heideggerian history of myth, the plastic image and
its imitation, history is the sacred history of teachers and fathers—
teaching and fecundity—and not of heroes. It is not that of political
history.[2]

—Emmanuel Levinas

Emmanuel Levinas returned to Paris immediately following the murderous years
of World War II, during which he served as an interpreter before his unit was
captured. He then spent the duration of the war, 1940–1945, first in Frontstalags
in Rennes and Laval, then at Vesoul, and from June 1942 until May 1945 at
Stalag 11B at Fallingbostel near Magdeburg in Germany.[3] Upon his return and
without delay, he went to work for the Alliance Israélite Universelle (AIU) and
in 1947 became the director of the École Normale Israélite Orientale (ENIO).
At the event celebrating the occasion of Levinas's eightieth birthday, Ady Steg,
who was the president of the AIU—the organization under which the ENIO
operated—at the time of the celebration, offered this fable speculating about the
time when Levinas would stand before the heavenly throne.[4]

A Fable

In about forty years, when you appear before the Heavenly Throne, if he
were to ask you:

"Emmanuel Levinas, what have you done with your life?"
You reply, "I committed myself to philosophy and I believed in the good
and the just as I have written in my books."
ADY STEG: "Very well," He would reply to you, "And?"
EL: "I studied with Husserl and Heidegger."
HT: "Heidegger? Hmm . . . And?"
EL: "I studied also with Chouchani."
HT: "Marvelous! Chouchani, it is true, entered the soul of the Talmud!
And?"

EL: "Based on his teachings, I have given numerous Talmudic Lessons to the Colloquia of Jewish Intellectuals."

HT: "Bravo! How indeed is one able to understand the Torah without the light of the oral law! And?"

EL: "Precisely. I have thus been able to comment on the Torah at the École Normale Israélite Orientale of the Alliance on Shabbat mornings."

HT: "At the school?"

EL: "Yes, I have indeed run this school during the last many years."

HT: "Director of the school, you, a prestigious philosopher?"

EL: "Yes, director of the school."

To these words, Cherubs and Seraphs, Ofanim and Archangels begin singing a glorious hymn and you will be led to the right of the Eternal One.

Steg's fable emphasizes something unique in the life of an esteemed academic: that for all of Levinas's academic achievements—and there are many—it will be his directorship of a Jewish day school that impresses the heavenly throne. The fable indicates the weight placed on education—general studies and Jewish education—by those who worked for the AIU, some of whom were Levinas's students while he was the director. When Levinas stands before the heavenly throne and must recount his accomplishments, the Eternal One is impressed by his intellectual accomplishments. But it was his role as director of the ENIO, which trained the schoolteachers who eventually taught in schools in Iran, Morocco, Tunisia, and Lebanon, of which the Eternal One takes note.[5]

Nonetheless, the Eternal One's added question—"you, a famous philosopher?"—was spoken with more than a hint of doubt or suspicion, betraying the more common negative sentiment toward education and those who educate. The view that "those who can't, teach" is still prevalent today, and the attitudes toward education range from resentment—teachers are paid too much (?!) for such cushy jobs—to outright cynicism and contempt regarding the educational system and what it promises. This range of negative attitudes creates a powerful force pushing against education, hindering any possibility of real reform: no one believes that education produces anything positive; only those who are not good at anything else would go into teaching; and teaching is so easy that teachers should not be compensated adequately for doing such a job. In contrast to this view of education and teaching, Levinas saw both as salvific, not only for the Jewish people after their near destruction during World War II, but also for humankind in the larger sweep of history.[6] The future of the world rests on how we educate our young people. Ady Steg's fable is certainly written for effect. Yet it is not lost on any of Levinas's students from the ENIO or anyone who reads his essays on Jewish education that education is not a side hobby in which he engaged. As we saw in the previous chapter, he viewed education as fundamental to his radical vision of ethics.[7]

Ami Bouganim, another of Levinas's former students, echoes these themes in his postface to *Levinas: Philosophe et Pédagoge* when he confesses that "in

France, philosophy does not hold education in much esteem; it is willing to consider it as one of its applications, but in no case as one of its determinations. However, Levinas spent the greatest part of his days on administrative tasks as a school director, melding a real interest in pedagogy with his research in philosophy."[8] Bouganim's essay is rich with insights about Jewish education internationally. He confesses that even in Israel there was little success in facing the de-judaization of its young people. He proudly states that the ENIO was one of the rare places where one could reflect on Jewish education.[9] Although the United States saw the origination of the first Sunday schools and the first Ramah camps,[10] "[n]owhere in the Diaspora did anyone yet consider the perpetuation of the Jewish people in terms of Jewish education . . . Levinas was one of the rare individuals to think the Jewish destiny otherwise than in political terms, wagering on 'an education which does not separate human beings,' *recognizing in ethics the first and last word of Judaism*."[11] Bouganim is also quick to distance the aim of Levinas's teaching from those aims found in traditional religious education:

> [He] did not want to cultivate piety, thus, distancing himself from any "pedagogy of exaltation" where enthusiasm would try to make up for the deficiencies in studying and the failures in intelligence . . . Levinas thought that if Judaism did not speak to the young generations who cried out for Marx or declaimed Heidegger, falling prey to the false messianic promises or to puerile charms, it was because nobody any longer went to the trouble of addressing them on their condition with a somewhat coherent discourse. Only to harness it to education did Levinas wrench the Science of Judaism from the pure and hard philology which, since the beginning of the [twentieth] century, gave off—to repeat Scholem—whiffs of death: "To raise Judaism into a science, to think Judaism is to turn these texts back into teaching texts." (Levinas 1951)[12]

On the one hand, these themes express not only Levinas's dedication to Jewish education but also Bouganim's belief that the relationship between this commitment and his philosophical project pervades the essays he wrote on Jewish education while he was director of the ENIO. On the other hand, I am not sure Bouganim is quite correct in his claim that Levinas was speaking Greek only to those who had forgotten their Hebrew—that is only to Jews who had "lost" their way. He had a secular, non-Jewish audience to which his philosophical writings are also directed.

Bouganim's comments also go directly to the heart of Levinas's essays in *Difficult Freedom,* which when read as a whole powerfully reveal a secularity that is in fact not secular. The structure that appears secular masks the Christianity that pervades it. As a result, one cannot help but see that Levinas's suspicion of Western subjectivity is at its root a suspicion of Christianity, and once again, another of Levinas's ambivalences is revealed. Although he sees a fraternal relationship between Judaism and Christianity, and although he credits individual

Christians whose courage during the Nazi occupation is to be noted and commended, Levinas nonetheless occasionally cites Christianity as not only inheriting but also perpetuating a Western subjectivity that is based on an egocentric ethics and that values individual freedom and salvation above all else. As we saw in the previous chapter, Levinas warns us in these essays that the Jew who pushes against this secular mask cannot help but see behind it; the Jew who does not resist the status quo continues to believe that he is part of a secular, universal state. Yet, the latter believes this only because he or she is not versed enough in either Judaism or Christianity to know otherwise. Bouganim's reading of Levinas is telling and many often forget that the articulation of the Hebrew into Greek is not only for the benefit of those who are not Jewish but also for the benefit of those who are but who no longer know, or never knew in the first place, the language of Judaism.

Totality and Infinity was published in 1961, fifteen years after the lecture course that was published as *Time and the Other*.[13] While it does seem to be the case that many of the themes from the earlier work are given new life in his 1961 book, *Totality and Infinity* cannot be reduced simply to an expansion of the themes in *Time and the Other*. For example, although Levinas gestures toward the ethical relationship in *Time and the Other*, he does not name it as such in that book. Additionally, the references to teaching that are so frequent in *Totality and Infinity* do not appear at all in *Time and the Other*. Although I am unaware of the exact years that Levinas was writing *Totality and Infinity*, it should be safe to say that one reason for this particular difference—the references to teaching that are absent from those earlier writings—is that he was working through these themes in the 1950s, the years when he was also the director of the ENIO, the branch of the AIU that coordinated the actual teaching in the schools and trained future teachers. We should not be surprised then that references to teaching punctuated the philosophical project Levinas was developing at the same time that he was in the trenches teaching the Jewish youth and concerned with "crises" for which he saw education as the solution.

More interesting to note is the similarity in themes that concerned him in both the Jewish writings and the philosophical project of that time period. In both sets of writing he identifies a crisis in humanism for which a new subjectivity is needed. But, he describes this new subjectivity in different registers in his Jewish writings and in *Totality and Infinity*. This chapter considers what it means that *Totality and Infinity* was published after he had been the director of the ENIO for fifteen years and that it was written during the same period he was concerned with themes found in his writings from the 1950s, which were published in *Difficult Freedom*. This exploration demonstrates that teaching is not a simple trope but rather the key to Levinas's philosophical project in *Totality and Infinity*. His interest in education was not only related to the development of his ethical project, but also was fundamental to the project's coherence.

Turning toward the Other

In his essay on Jewish philosophy and phenomenology, Martin Kavka asks if the face is the ground or the aim of ethics.[14] The question Kavka raises points to one of the most difficult problems in Levinas's project: "How does ethical response come about?" Regardless of how we answer Kavka's question, the problem remains. Whether the face is the ground or the aim, the question of how one becomes a Levinasian subject—a subject that can see the face of the Other and respond—persists. Indeed, it is a question that haunts Levinas's project and always seems to lurk in the background of the commentaries on and criticisms of his ethics. This section looks briefly at Levinas's references to teaching in *Totality and Infinity*. These references are few and scattered throughout the text, and they are at every point undeveloped. Yet, I would maintain that their presence is nonetheless significant. Just as Levinas called for the Jewish community to return to Jewish education as a means of reclaiming the ethical tradition that is unique to Judaism, so too, Levinas employs a model of education—of teaching—for the self to become an ethical subject.

We should bear in mind that several of the essays discussed in the previous chapter were published ten years before *Totality and Infinity*. Levinas had directed the ENIO for about fifteen years before *Totality and Infinity* was published in 1961. Clearly, he was writing this book while also writing about themes that included the failure of assimilation, the question about the relationship between the universal and the particular, and the promise of education. For this reason, it would be more surprising if references to education and teaching were not found in this text. Nonetheless, it has not been the case that the place of *Totality and Infinity* within the context of his writings on Jewish education has been studied adequately, if at all.[15] With this chronology in mind, it becomes increasingly difficult to think of his references to teaching in *Totality and Infinity* as a mere trope or metaphor. These references are fleeting, but not insignificant.

Levinas's references to teaching in *Totality and Infinity* can be placed into three distinct categories. The first is the set of references early in the text where Levinas describes the Other in terms of a teacher or master. That is, this first set of references to teaching establishes the relationship to the Other as a teaching relationship. One of the earliest references appears in "Transcendence as the Idea of Infinity," a subsection of "Metaphysics and Transcendence" in the first part of the book. He writes, "The relation with the Other, or Conversation, is a non-allergic relation, an ethical relation; but inasmuch as it is welcomed this conversation is a teaching [*enseignement*]. Teaching is not reducible to maieutics; it comes from the exterior and brings me more than I contain."[16] Here the relation with the Other is referred to as a conversation, thus it is characterized in terms of speech—the Other speaks to me. By occupying a position of an interlocutor, the Other also teaches me. Levinas clearly intends to distance the ethical relation—where that which comes from outside is emphasized—from the pedagogy of Socrates, where truth is pulled out from one person by a series of questions being posed. The relationship to the Other will always exceed any knowledge that can be brought forth from within.

This description mirrors the one Levinas offered twelve years earlier in his 1949 essay "Transcendence of Words: On Michel Leiris's *Biffures*," where he writes, "The presence of the Other is a presence that teaches; that is why the word as teaching is more than the experience of the real, and the master more than a midwife of minds. He wrenches experience away from its esthetic self-sufficiency, from its *here,* where it rests in peace. And by invoking it he transforms it into a creature" (*OS,* 148). This comment follows his discussion of Robinson Crusoe, in which he shatters the mythology of Crusoe as an insular individual who lived a solitary life. To the contrary, Levinas recalls not only the character "Friday," but the language—speech—between them.

The second set of references is found in the section called "Ethics and the Face," where the face of the Other is described in terms of the ethical relation. Because Levinas has already cast the relationship to the Other as a teaching relationship, the ethical relation can now be seen as a relationship of teaching.[17] This move is specifically the move from a description of the Other phenomenologically to a description of that relationship as fundamentally normative. The move is neither obvious nor inherent—it must be established. But insofar as Levinas carries the teaching relationship forward, we can see the parallel he draws between the ethical relation and the teaching relation. The ethical relation is always already a teaching relation.

In these early references to teaching, Levinas binds the relationship the "I" has to the Other to that of teacher and student. Recalling the discussion of education in the first part of the paper, we can see the significance of teaching to the Jewish tradition. The teacher is not only valued, but also valued more highly than the parent. Teaching is fundamentally part of the tradition, which presents itself as being commanded to be taught to the next generations. Repeatedly, these references to teaching are found throughout the biblical tradition, and the role of teaching is taken up again in the rabbinic commentary, which makes the Hebrew Bible Jewish.

These two sets of references feed the third category, which we find in the final section of the book, "Beyond the Face." In this final section, we also see how Levinas reverses the way we might typically understand the teaching relation. As Levinas characterizes the relation, the Other is the teacher. We see this point most clearly in the description of filiality and the relationship between the father and son. Typically, we think of the parent as the teacher, and of course, in many ways this is the case. In his discussion of fecundity, Levinas characterizes the child as a Stranger (Isaiah 49)—and throughout *Totality and Infinity,* he repeatedly proclaims his responsibility to the Stranger (*TI*, 267). In this description, then, it is the son, cast as Other, who teaches the father.

Here, the lesson that the child teaches the parent is of a different order—it is a lesson that calls the parent to ethical responsibility, to place the child before the parent; it calls for the parent to set aside his or her own ego and turn toward the child, just as the "I" must turn toward the Other. The birth of the son turns the father not only toward the son in responsibility for him but also outward, toward the community, toward the other Others. The father is responsible for his son but also for his son's responsibility—the child cannot exist on his own and thus "he can be brought up, be commanded, and can obey . . ." (*TI*, 279). Levinas's discussion of fecundity—the birth of the child—described in *Totality and Infinity* is also the birth of teaching: the child teaches me. Birth is the fecundity of teaching and responsibility; the two are intertwined. Part of the responsibility that the father has to the child is in turn to teach the child, to bring the child up to be responsible for Others—and this point was made clearly in my discussion of Levinas's essays on Jewish education in previous chapters of this book.

We can begin to see how these references to teaching and the discussion of the parent-child relationship in *Totality and Infinity* are connected to his earlier discussions of Jewish education in his essays of the 1950s. It is clear from those essays that the school—the teacher—and the parent have a fundamental role to play in the cultivation of an ethical subject. Certainly we could argue that his view only applies to the Jewish community, but that would not only make no sense, it is not supported by his own references to teaching and parenting. Indeed the epigraph for this chapter emphasizes this point: history is the history of teachers and fathers, teaching and fecundity.[18] By importing the trope of teaching into his philosophical project—into the language of the Greek universal—what I contend Levinas has done is import the significant role that teaching plays in the development of the ethical subject in Jewish education into the philosophical project that describes his view of radical ethical subjectivity and directed it toward a wider non-Jewish audience. It is not only that he has attempted to translate the notion of Jewish ethics from the Hebrew to the Greek, but he is also attempting to translate the method by which one accomplishes the task. It simply cannot be the case that only Jewish children need to be reared to turn toward the Other and that this responsibility does not apply to anyone else. Among other problems, this view would run completely counter to the very way in which Levinas describes ethical subjectivity.

Although Levinas's discussion of eros, fecundity, and filiality has been criticized from all angles, and while many of the criticisms are certainly with merit, they also tend to miss the point.[19] In her critique of Levinas, the feminist theorist Luce Irigaray seems unwilling to acknowledge that for Levinas fecundity is not simply the physical birth of a child. Rather, the birth of the child inaugurates the ethical relation—in Levinas's words, the father is responsible for the son. Fecundity avoids being reduced simply to natural reproduction, but neither is it erotic creativity—even if that is the creativity of sexual love; rather it is the creation and re-creation of *responsibility*. Fecundity implies responsibility for the Other, and progressively for others. In order for the phenomenology to work, the child needs to have been introduced to some kind of moral upbringing. The Levinasian subject did not enter the world sui generis. Just as Merleau-Ponty's ontological structures regarding the Other can be traced back to his essay describing the child's relations with others, so too, Levinas's ethical subject assumes some kind of introduction to ethical responsibility.

As we see in *Émile*, Rousseau acknowledges that an innate capacity to see the suffering of the Other is not enough, for the child could develop in one of two ways. To put Rousseau's concern in modern terms—the child could develop such that his aversion to suffering compels him to want to bring that suffering to an end and thus help the other person, or the child could develop into a person whose aversion to the suffering compels him to do everything he can to avoid it. Only through a proper education (though certainly we can raise questions if the one Rousseau proposes is proper) can the path of wanting to help the suffering Other be secured. Thus, Levinas's turn to the family structure, though problematic, does get at a fundamental question that emerges out of his work: How does the individual become the subject who can be interrupted by the Other? While it might not be the case that we all raise children, it is indeed the case that we were all raised by someone—for better or for worse—and we were introduced to the moral world at the same time that parent or caregiver was called to ethical subjectivity by the child.

In the collection of interviews published under the title *Ethics and Infinity*, Philippe Nemo asks Levinas, "You see in [filiality] a properly ontological feature and not merely a psychological accident or perhaps a ruse of biology?"[20] Levinas replies, "I believe that psychological 'accidents' are the ways in which ontological relations show themselves. The fact of seeing the possibilities of the other as your own possibilities, of being able to escape the closure of your identity and what is bestowed on you . . . this is paternity" (*EI*, 70). Levinas then states, "It is not necessary that those who have no children see in this fact any depreciation whatever; biological filiality is only the first shape filiality takes; but one can very well conceive filiality as a relationship between human beings without the tie of biological kinship. One can have a paternal attitude with regard to the Other. To consider the Other as a son is precisely to establish with him those relations I call 'beyond the possible'" (*EI*, 70–71). For Levinas, then, the *first* moment of the ethical relation is found within this erotic and then parental relationship. And we see here the movement from ethics to politics, from the original micro-society of a family to larger formations. Levinas refers to the Other in the ethical relation in *Totality and Infinity* as his teacher and he refers to the ethical relationship par excellence—that of father and son—a relationship of teaching. Returning to his interview with Philippe Nemo, Levinas responds precisely to this point. "Filiation and fraternity—parental relations without biological bases—are current metaphors of our everyday life. The relationship of master to disciple does not reduce to filiation and fraternity but it certainly includes them" (*EI*, 71).[21]

In his writings following *Totality and Infinity*, Levinas appears to drop the familial references, with the exception of his use of "maternity" in his later writings, most notably in *Otherwise than Being* (1974). My argument is that Levinas turns to a stronger view of the ethical subject than what he initially describes in his 1961 work and that this subject is dependent on an educational process that shapes her. The claim that Levinas's 1961 project fails is partially correct. Rather than argue that it fails completely, however, I would instead claim that Levinas exchanges the father-teacher for simply the teacher, even if not stated as such. What seems clearer in the writings after 1961 is Levinas's emphasis on an ethical subject that is not simply "interrupted" by the Other, but who is also shaped in such a way that the subject is willing to cede her position to the Other. Additionally, we should not overlook the turn to Levinas's use of the prophetic, particularly in *Otherwise than Being*, where the prophet functions most effectively as an interruption—as an Other who teaches.

Nonetheless, Levinas's description of the ethical relation in *Totality and Infinity* as a relation of teaching appears most significantly in his discussion of the relationship between the father and the son, which he refers to in *Totality and Infinity* as the paradigmatic ethical relation. Teaching, as indicated by the above citation, is the presence of the Other as revealed in the face of the Other. That is, the face of the Other is a face that calls to us and teaches.[22] Education and transcendence meet in the ethical relation to the Other. For Levinas, then, the biblical commands that enjoin the "I" to respond to the Other exemplify the ethical relationship: "Thou shalt not kill"; "Thou shalt love the stranger"; and "Thou shalt love thy neighbor as thyself." These biblical commands require that the ego project out of itself toward the other. Transcendence is connected both to God and to ethics.[23] Thus, even if we find the phenomenological account of the face compelling, this account nonetheless rests on a previous experience of the ethical. And even if we agree about this previous experience as informing the subject, Levinas seems to be arguing that this subjectivity is a new subjectivity, a new humanism (or old, rooted in biblical Judaism)—one that we need to learn, one that we need to develop. Teaching then becomes not simply a trope, but the very ground of his ethical project.

Recalling the essays on Judaism and in particular Jewish education, we can see two significant points. The first is that Levinas is naming the inhumanities of the twentieth century a crisis in humanism, which he then reformulates as a loss of ethical subjectivity. He is calling on the Jewish community to return to Jewish education in order to reinvigorate Judaism with this Jewish humanism—this ethical subjectivity. And notably, he makes the point that this ethical subjectivity is not only for the Jews; it is the universal part of Judaism and it is the obligation of the Jews to share this part of Judaism with others.

I maintain that *Totality and Infinity* is Levinas's first attempt to do precisely this—to articulate this Jewish humanism, this ethical subjectivity, into Greek, into a philosophical language that can be understood and appreciated universally. Levinas appeals to the Jewish community that they return to Jewish education, that it is the youth who need to be raised differently than they are currently. Similarly, his description of this new ethical subjectivity that he promotes in his philosophical project relies on cultivation, on child rearing, and on education. It is not the case that one reads Levinas and makes a decision to become Levinasian—this, in fact, would be too Kantian, a choosing of duty over inclination or an exertion of the will. Rather, the philosophical intention is to reorient its readers to a new subjectivity, one that counters the anti-humanism that held sway over twentieth-century intellectuals for far too long. Can this be done simply by reading his philosophical work? I cannot say for sure, but my guess is that the answer is that it cannot. This is not to say that Levinas is more like Aristotle and less like Kant—Aristotle, though he recognized the need to cultivate good practices, was interested in the cultivation of a virtuous person. Levinas is not concerned with moral perfection but the development of an ego that is for the Other—and this, for him, cannot be accomplished by a rational choice.

Scripture, Teaching, and Ethical Response

Levinas's employment of the midrashic tradition and biblical narratives serves a pedagogical function.[24] For Levinas, it does not matter if his readers see or accept his invitation as such. To the extent that one engages the philosophical text as he wishes, one is engaged in this ethical project. One can forego this responsibility or obligation in reading, just as one can forego this responsibility in one's life when confronted by the face of the Other. To forego responsibility does not mean that one is recused from it. In any event, Levinas sees the ethical relation in terms of the response to the Other, and this response to the Other is the response to God. To be engaged in his ethical project, then, is by his own definition to be brought into religion and therefore in relation to God. One could say this is simply an issue of semantics—Levinas calls religion a relation that could certainly be viewed in secular terms. However, for Levinas, the ethical relationship cannot be separated from the profundity of the approach to the Other. The move to the Other is precisely the interruption of our *conatus essendi,* our drive to preserve ourselves over all others. To approach the Other with the idea that the Other comes before me is, for Levinas, the quintessential moment of transcendence and of being in contact with the divine. Ethics, as Levinas defines it, *is* religion—and here he distinguishes religion from spirituality, which can allow a shift from the human to the non-human. Finally, for

Levinas, the humanism that permeates Judaism is universal, and this humanism can be found and accomplished in textual exegesis.

I concede Levinas's claim that he does not turn to the biblical verse for proof; rather, he uses these examples to illustrate. Regardless, his illustrations are far more powerful with the use of these tropes than they would be if attempted secularly. Although he cites from other literary sources, and certainly he sees other literary sources as conveying a similar message to the one we find in the Bible, the Bible's sole task is to teach us to be responsible for the Other. The Bible's power to convey this message is not simply a difference of degree from other literary vehicles; it is a difference of kind. And we could suggest several reasons for this difference. One might be that the Bible is universally known, even if not read by everyone in the same manner. And so we could say, if not the Bible, then what? If the Bible does not provide a universal message, what literary text does?[25]

However, the issue for Levinas is not that the Bible is universally accessible or that it is universally accepted. Levinas views the Bible in terms of its one universal mission—to direct us toward the Other by modeling this responsibility within its narrative and by requiring us to engage with the text as if it were an Other. Although other books also examine the human condition and attempt to direct us to our responsibility to the Other, the Bible is unique in that this role is its only role. Additionally, most importantly, in Levinas's view, this role is itself religious. As Richard Cohen points out, "This is also why the Yiddish term for synagogue, '*shul*,' literally means 'school.' Not because praying is learning, though it is, but because learning is a kind of prayer, a holy service, a link to transcendence. A text is sacred not because it is inviolable, but precisely because it transfigures, engages, and in this way is 'alive.'"[26] To engage with the Bible, then, is to engage in a transcendent act.

Levinas honors the talmudic tradition that keeps the text alive. Exegetical reading prevents the text from becoming a mere document, or even a mere book, "that is to say just a thing, and in once more allowing it to resonate with the great and living voice of teaching."[27] This teaching aids in attuning us to the face of the Other. So we see how he invites us into his philosophical work. Without a doubt, he would not want us to confuse philosophy with a sacred text, and he is often explicit that philosophy falls into the category of the "said." Nonetheless, his rhetorical use of biblical tropes and references calls on us to read his philosophical work with the same attention, care, nuance, and sensitivity that we might read the Scriptures.[28] We are called to pay attention to the gaps, the interpretations, and the references rather than pass over them quickly as simple literary devices. And we are called to incorporate these references into our interpretations of his work.

We might say then that Levinas infuses his philosophical discourse with these biblical references not simply because they come to mind more readily than, say, a quote from Proust, but because he has engaged the Scripture exegetically and inserted this interpretation into this philosophy such that we are now all exposed to it. When Levinas inserts a phrase from Isaiah or a reference to Cain, he has exposed us to his reading, a midrashic or rabbinic reading, of the Bible. He does not simply insert a phrase; he inserts it strategically. He places the reference where it fits with his description of the ethical relation and the call to human fraternity. Since the meaning of his references is not obvious, the reader needs to massage the text and its reference to understand why Levinas placed this particular reference within the context of a philosophical discussion. For example, Levinas's reading of the Cain and Abel story is not a straightforward interpretation. Levinas's reading of Cain in terms of Cain's failure to acknowledge his own responsibility for Abel is a unique interpretation. Levinas's strategic placement of these references obliges us to pay attention to his distinctive reading of Cain and to see Cain's actions in a new light.[29]

The "pedagogy" at work in Levinas's writings reflects Levinas's own interest in Jewish education and it provides an implicit directive of how the ethical subject he describes is cultivated.[30] Levinas's view of the ethical relation, then, points to a pedagogy that would include reading the biblical narratives Jewishly. Through Levinas's incorporation of these texts into his philosophical argument, each reader is introduced to the readers who came before him or her. The confrontation with the text is therefore a confrontation with the whole of the past (*BTV*, xiii). We can now see how he repeats in 1981 a theme found in his 1973 essay on Jewish education. As I cited previously, Levinas says,

> hence the way that readings continually refer to origins across history going from pupil to master; hence the discussion in gatherings between colleagues questioning one another from century to century, the whole thing integrating itself as tradition into commented Scripture, and always calling anew for a reading that is both erudite and modern. Hence the commentaries of commentaries. (*BTV*, xiii)

And as I mentioned previously, Levinas sees the conversation that takes place within midrash *as modeling the very conversation that he hopes his philosophy can promote,* a conversation he outlines as the distinguishing feature of Jewish education. If he can incorporate this model of commentary into his philosophical work, then he not only connects his readers to the larger interpretative conversation of Judaism, but also to his understanding of Jewish humanism. We, his readers, thereby become part of the history and the history lessons that have been taught, and we do so prior to our choosing to do so. We, his readers, participate in Levinas's understanding of Jewish education, without ever setting foot in a Jewish day school.[31]

In his interview "On Jewish Philosophy," Levinas illuminates the connection between philosophical discourse and the role of midrash in interpreting the Hebrew scriptures. His interviewer first expresses surprise at Levinas's comments that indicated that he saw the tradition of biblical theology and that of philosophy as immediately in harmony (*IR*, 239). Levinas addresses this surprise by explaining how he sees this connection. For Levinas, the lived experience of Judaism—not its piety, but its underlying mode of being—is above all a sense of belonging to humanity, a sense of belonging to a supreme order of responsibility (*IR*, 240). It is a life in which he also sees non-Jewish books as expressing a similar concern or a similar responsibility—a concern for the meaning of life. The list of these books includes *Hamlet, Macbeth, King Lear, The Miser*, and *The Misanthrope*, in addition to the novels of Tolstoy and Dostoyevsky.[32]

In Levinas's view, these novels are not philosophy per se; rather, they express the same concerns that occupy philosophy, but in a different language, a different idiom, or a different register. By drawing this distinction, Levinas appears to have divided the written word into two categories: philosophy, on the one hand, and literary texts, on the other. Yet, all who read his philosophical work notice the frequent references to literary sources, including the numerous citations from the Jewish holy texts. This powerful characteristic of midrash coupled with the universal emphasis that philosophy can add to it may help us understand why Levinas connects his philosophy to this religious conversation. His use of these citations encourages us to ask what we are to make of the Scriptures and of the holy texts in Judaism. Should we classify them as simply another form of literature, on par with secular literary texts? Or, do they constitute a third category that falls somewhere in between philosophy and rhetoric? If the latter, then what is their status relative to these larger categories? Additionally, his distinction allows us to see why Levinas believes philosophy to be limited in very particular ways. If we recall the discussion about the humanities from chapter 1, we can begin to see why Levinas emphasizes Jewish education, which includes midrash and Talmud, even as he displays a deep admiration for non-Jewish sources.

Singularity and the Talmud

In their essay "The Babylonian Talmud in Cognitive Perspective," Jeffrey Kress and Marjorie Lehman outline the pedagogical implications of the Babylonian Talmud (the *Bavli*)[33] and thus come close to addressing the secularist's question. The authors claim that the *Bavli*'s character—"a unique document unlike any literary work produced during its time or thereafter—is the result of the distinct style of dialogue utilized by its redactors to weave together an array of disparate sources from different time periods."[34] The authors characterize the organization[35] of the document as one in which *sugyot*[35] of "different generations are presented as communicating with one another."[36] In contrast to the Mishnah where the different positions are presented discretely, as independent of each other, the positions in the *Bavli* are presented as connected; the style is dialogical and argumentative. That is, the different positions are presented in direct contact or communication with each other. Additionally, the authors continue, the "components of the argumentative framework are ambiguous, tangential, and elliptical. Many arguments are non-linear in nature. This has led scholars to question why the redactors of the *Bavli* chose to edit their available source material in accordance with an argumentative style of discourse that requires so much effort on the part of the reader to understand."[37]

The goal of this article is to demonstrate how certain components known to be significant in cognitive development are actually "performed" or incorporated into the style of reading demanded by the *Bavli*. The authors' intention is to show the significance of modeling the kind of interaction encouraged by or reflected in the *Bavli* for educational practice. The authors, faculty members at the Jewish Theological Seminary, are interested in these questions as they apply to Jewish pedagogy and Jewish education. My interest in their essay and the conclusions they draw lies in how similar the descriptions of this pedagogical style are to what Levinas describes in his references to teaching. Additionally, this model is significant in that it counters the traditional model of teaching that we find described throughout much of Western philosophy, a model that garners force through Rousseau and then culminates in the individuality championed by Nietzsche in *Zarathustra*.

Citing other scholars who have commented on the argumentative structure of the *Bavli*, Kress and Lehman refer to one of the most significant components of this structure: its opposition to self-evidence and "'the confident assertion of a single truth.'"[38] Taking up this point, the authors add that "had the *Bavli* intended to function solely as a dogmatic and canonical religious text, one 'truth' would have emerged. The fact that sequences of deliberation produce polyphony of opinion on any given subject, instead of a retrievable truth, testifies to an acknowledgement, on the part of the editors of the *Bavli*, that there is no definable truth. In other words, if the truth is clearly known, there is no reason to argue against it."[39] The authors cite David Kraemer's view that "the *Bavli* strives to convince the reader of the viability of all the perspectives presented therein, even if such opinions contradict one another."[40]

Kress and Lehman then turn to Menachem Fisch's conclusions. The incorporation of his conclusions ties their work to philosophical models of truth. Fisch's scholarship specifically uses philosophy of science as a lens through which to view talmudic argumentation. What do these different models tell us about the limits of human knowledge and therefore of truth? Since human knowledge and ideas are necessarily limited and therefore imperfect, there are no objectively true facts.[41] All ideas must be "tested in relation to their [respective] intended objectives and constantly pit against alternative systems."[42] The strength of an argument depends on the strength of the argument that can be made against it. The authors note the significance of Fisch's observation. He identifies a traditionalist strand of opinion that is continuously challenged by a self-doubting, undogmatic, and reflective voice. The counter-discourse, which Fisch labels as the anti-traditionalist voice of the Talmud, is the voice of the rabbinic elite "aspiring to teach future rabbinic elites to reason rationally about the content of their legacies in the same way open-minded and self-doubting agents (scientists) were shown . . . to act rationally when striving knowingly to improve upon systems on which they work(ed)."[43]

In the move to make the connection between the structure of the Talmud and cognitive development, Kress and Lehman initially rely on the conceptual frameworks of Vygotsky and Siegel, which focus on the communal dimension of knowledge. For both Vygotsky and Siegel, the cognitive development of the individual "must be understood within the patterns of relationships and interactions in which such development takes place. Vygotsky's framework intends to "show how 'individual responses emerge from the forms of collective life."[44] The authors then turn to the work of Lotman and Bakhtin, "who stress the importance of interaction between readers and the written work," in order to demonstrate how the work of Vygotsky and Siegel apply to the study of the text. This bridge between these two sets of scholarship demonstrates that the communal or social aspect of education and the production of knowledge is primary.

By turning to Bakhtin, the authors are able to incorporate the text as a "member" of the community. That is, the text becomes part of the social relation, not as something to replace another human member of the educational community, but as a supplement. In the case of the Talmud, we have a more interesting example. As the authors have already indicated, the *Bavli* demonstrates or models this very communal aspect of knowledge within its own structure. Thus, if one uses the *Bavli* and then models a pedagogical style on it, multiple layers of instruction are enacted within the learning environment. All of these layers in turn reinforce the significance of the social dimension of education *and* the importance of the text in drawing out that dimension. Here we find the link to Levinas's philosophical project.[45]

Judaism's commitment to include the minority position as part of its theological canon not only allows Judaism to resist being characterized as monolithic; it also provides the very substance and model for the educational process. Levinas's description of the pedagogical dimension regarding the self's relationship to the Other is similar to his understanding of Jewish education.[46] How then can we rethink education so that it is neither anti-intellectual nor ignorant of the responsibility we have toward the Other?

Writing on similar themes, Lee S. Shulman opens his essay "Professing Understanding and Professing Faith: The Midrashic Imperative" with the following question, "Is there a distinctly Jewish way of knowing?"[47] Although Shulman does not definitively answer this particular question, he does explore pedagogical possibilities of a Jewish way of knowing, required by the very structure of the Talmud. He begins with one of his favorite stories from the Talmud to illustrate his point. In the story, a man wishing to express his newfound religious commitment wants to observe the very next Jewish holiday, which happens to be Sukkot, the feast of the Tabernacles. He tells his rabbi that he would like to build his own *sukkah*. The rabbi tells him that he cannot simply build a *sukkah*: "That is not how we do things in our tradition. In our tradition you have to first study the laws before you are prepared to fulfill them. You are not ready to build the *sukkah* until you have immersed yourself in the entire volume of the Talmud that deals with the topic of *sukkah*. You must spend the next year studying this tractate. One year from now it will be time for you to build your *sukkah* and you will be able to build it following all the instructions of the Talmud."[48]

Shulman's point in sharing this story is not about the argument between theory and practice, studying versus doing. Rather, his point is completely the opposite. What appears to be a straightforward lesson in building a *sukkah* turns out not to be so straightforward. In a sentence that could just have easily been written by Levinas about the function and modeling effect of midrash, Shulman comments about the Talmud: "Wrapped around the text are commentaries in Hebrew comprising some 1,000 years of debate and argument concerning the meaning and application of the core texts."[49] The proper observance of Sukkot as directed by the Talmud, which includes the building of the *sukkah* in addition to eating and sleeping in it, brings up many more questions. The commentary then begins to address these questions, though with each response, many more questions are raised. Thus, the impulse of the Talmud—of studying Talmud—begins to appear less like an exercise in the quest for truth and more like an exercise in engagement—with the text, with the commentators, and with the dialogue that is produced by those commentators. The ancient commentary is made relevant to the present day when a rabbi includes a Talmud passage homiletically in her *d'var Torah* and connects it to a problem that is currently pressing on the community or the larger world. In this way the rabbi helps her congregants see how ancient wisdom might teach us something today.

Like Kress and Lehman, Shulman does not explicitly offer midrash and talmudic learning to those outside of Judaism, though he does present at least one example of a learning experience of a student he encountered, as a correlate to the weave-like style of learning that he believes Judaism provides. Yet many points that Shulman makes can be compared to the discipline of philosophy. The idea that the commentaries are spread out over time and that often these commentators never met or even lived at the same time is similar to how many scholars view the history of philosophy.

Much of the history of philosophy can be viewed as a conversation, sometimes taking place within the same time period when one philosopher is actually able to reply to the criticisms of his position.[50] Similarly, we as teachers do the same thing nearly every day in our classes. Every time I teach a philosophical text, whether it is a pre-Socratic fragment, a Platonic dialogue, an eighteenth-century essay by Kant, or a twentieth-century essay by a French philosopher,

I ask my students if they can think of an example to which they can apply this theory. How does Plato's political system compare to ours? How can we learn from Kant's vision of "perpetual peace" or the categorical imperative? Can you think of ways in which you discipline yourselves, as Foucault describes in his book? That is, my aim in class is always threefold: what do we think the philosopher is trying to say, what are the multiple ways in which we might understand this philosopher's text, and how might we relate the philosopher's view(s) to our present conditions in the world? My point here is not to say that philosophy is identical to the Talmud—I do not think it is. But I do think certain kinds of philosophy and certain ways in which we can study philosophy come close to resembling the conversation found in the Talmud and the impulse to have that conversation taken up by its readers. What I think is missing from most of philosophy, and this is crucial, is the ethical impulse that runs through the Talmud. I do not think that the ethical impulse is naturally present in philosophy but I do think it can be engaged pedagogically.

As Shulman notes after observing several classes on his visit to Messiah College, "This [the pedagogy of homiletic] was a pedagogy I understood emphatically. It was the *d'var* Torah, a homiletic move that disposes students to think actively about the connections between textual interpretation and making a difference in the world that we call *tikkun olam* in the Jewish tradition, the repair of the world."[51] My concern is that Judaism carries with it an underlying imperative to act in particular ways—ethical ways—that are concerned with repairing the world. I cannot say that this is the case for all religions nor can I say that it is the case for fields of study that are not religious, e.g., philosophy and other humanistic studies. Nonetheless, I remain interested in how these ideas can be brought into conversation—what it might mean to engage the secularist with a pedagogical method fundamental to and maybe even uniquely found in a Jewish text.

In the same interview mentioned above, Levinas tells his interlocutor that the Scriptures do not, for the Jews, exist apart from the interpretations that are attached to them. These interpretations are found in the collections of *midrashim* and the Talmud. One needs to know only a little bit about Hebrew and the construction of the Hebrew texts in order to see why these interpretations are significant. First, there is the "technical" reason. Biblical Hebrew does not contain vowels, although it does have vowel aspirations. Biblical Hebrew is a language based on roots; different combinations of letters have a general meaning and their specific meaning alters slightly, depending on the vowel aspiration that is inserted. Biblical Hebrew also lacks punctuation. So, one can see, just by the simple absence of vowels and punctuation, that difficulties and conflicts in interpretation immediately emerge. The rabbinic model of midrash tries to address these problems by offering possible explanations and interpretations. This part of midrash addresses the "technical" problems with the holy text.

Levinas is not concerned with this aspect of the written language. Rather, he emphasizes another characteristic of midrash—its excess. Even if one could deduce what is referred to as the "plain" meaning of the text, that meaning would still be enigmatic. The written word always signifies more than it says. Even literary texts, such as those of Shakespeare, Molière, Dante, and so forth, signify beyond their plain meaning and "invite the exegesis that is spiritual life" (*BTV,* xi). Levinas does not attribute the enigma of the verse to the simple imprecision of the text that therefore gives rise to misunderstandings (*BTV,* xi). Nor is it the insufficiency of language to communicate its ideas. It is not simply an instrument that is either effective or not. Rather, the text will always have more to say, and its saying will always engage me with the Other. Language becomes the coordinator between myself and the Other. It questions the assumed naturalness of self-care and calls to my attention the care of the Other.

The Jewish tradition recognizes that the text simply asks to be interpreted. In Levinas's hometown of Lithuania, where he lived a life that he recalls as steeped in the Jewish tradition,

> [t]here was a demythologizing of the text, but also a search for a pretext for thought, down to the very letter of the text. That was the essential aspect of that way of reading. There was also a demythologizing of what was already demythologized, a quest for meaning to be renewed. It is as if the verse were saying over and over: "Interpret me." (*IR,* 240–241)

To approach the Torah "Jewishly," then, is precisely to approach it through the rabbinic commentary on it. The holy texts engage us; they implicate us in their narrative and they ask us to respond to them. The rabbinic conversations found in the collection of *midrashim* are not simply about the holy text. They are engaged directly with the text. By engaging with the text in the manner that they do, they draw out the voices in the text that might otherwise remain hidden. The Bible is considered a holy text, and Levinas, following the rabbinic tradition, believes that through midrash the holy voice of God, as alterity, opens itself up to us. Midrash opens up the voices in the Torah that are muted in the text, either because they are explicitly absent from the narrative structure or because the narrative structure lacks clarity. Midrash lifts these voices out of the text and then brings them to bear on the narrative. By enabling our access to these Others, midrash brings us closer to the ethical and, thus, closer to God.

The Scriptures, and the reading of them, constitute a third category that, for Levinas, cannot be neatly contained by either of the two categories mentioned above: literature or philosophy. Levinas explains that philosophy is directed at a different audience; he even refers to it being directed at a different kind of mind:

> [philosophy is directed at] minds which are *not* forewarned and which require totally explicit ideas, a discourse in which all that is normally taken for granted is said. A discourse addressed to Greeks! A way of speaking that is added to and animates that more confidential, closed and firm way of speaking which is

more closely linked to the bearers of meaning, signifiers which will never be released from their duties of the signified. (*IR*, 240–241)

He offers this description of philosophy as its distinguishing feature and as that which distinguishes it, primarily, from a holy text. However, within this same response about midrash, Levinas offers a gloss on the manner in which philosophy is similar to a Jewish text. We see his change in perspective when he says that one day philosophy was discovered to be multiple and have hidden truths. It was discovered that it has "levels, and goes progressively deeper, that its texts contradict one another, and that the systems are fraught with internal contradictions. Thus, it seems to me essential to consider the fact that the Jewish reading of the Scripture is carried out in the anxiety, but also the hopeful expectation, of midrash" (*IR*, 240–241). The last point is the most interesting, for it suggests that insofar as one approaches the philosophical text with an awareness of its levels, its depth, and its internal contradictions, one might be approaching it in the style of midrash, that is, in a style similar to that of the Jewish reading of Scripture.

Levinas's interviewer concedes that he was also thinking that philosophy and religion are not two different theses or worlds. Rather, they are two different languages; there is the language of philosophy and the language of religion— or in this case, the Hebrew Bible. To allow this similarity between the two supports Levinas's belief that philosophy can be approached with the method of reading similar to one that is used when approaching a Jewish holy text, just as midrash keeps the Torah alive by preventing its easy thematization. It prevents this thematization by posing questions and offering alternative readings of the text; recognizing that philosophy is multiple and approaching it as such will also keep it alive.

In *Otherwise than Being*, however, Levinas offers a different view of philosophy, one that places it directly in conflict with the description we see above, and also in direct opposition to his concept of the ethical. In this text, Levinas introduces us to his concept of the "saying." He contrasts the saying to the said, the latter indicating that which is thematized and static. The saying is fluid, exemplary of the approach in the ethical relation. Levinas indicates in several places that the interpretative model of midrash is similar to his concept of the saying insofar as the saying is an excess, that which lies beyond the said. In Levinas's words, the saying opens me to the Other.[52] The saying expresses the infinite aspect of the other person. Justice or law—"the said"—arises out of the saying. Philosophy, understood as parallel to law, and therefore in the category of the said, is derivative of religion—understood here by Levinas as the saying. By expressly equating philosophy with the said, and in other places describing midrash in terms of the saying, Levinas, in this book, has set philosophy in opposition to midrash. How, then, are these contradictory descriptions to be reconciled? What role does philosophy play for him?

We might say that for Levinas Scripture and philosophy are ultimately joined in their "*essential* connection in human civilization *tout court*, which is measured or hoped for as peace among men" (*IR*, 241). Both Levinas and his interviewer emphasize that philosophy and Scripture articulate this concern differently, in different languages, as it were. And they both admit that, in the end, the concern is nonetheless the same. However, the difference cannot simply be understood in linguistic terms. The real difference is ethical. In Levinas's view, midrash is interdependent, interconnected, and intersubjective. It implicates the reader in a dialogue and exposes the reader to the other voices in the text, not simply for a literary purpose, but for an ethical one. Thus, if philosophy could also implicate the reader in its narrative, that is, if it could invite the reader to engage with the text in the way that midrash does, philosophy would then contain an element of the saying; it would itself become ethical. And, more importantly, it would be able to translate the ethical into a universal language.

Religion, then, is not the opposite of philosophy; that is, it is not irrational belief or faith as opposed to rational thought. Rather, Levinas sees religion *as* transcendence. In this sense, we can see why Levinas would articulate the relation to God as implicitly ethical, or that devotion to God is devotion to the other person (*IR*, 243). This view is fundamental to the Jewish faith, in which the relation to God is held to be inseparable from the relationship to the Torah (*IR*, 243). Moreover, for Levinas, this view of religion is not reducible to an ethnic particularism. On the contrary, Levinas sees this view of religion as universal. The key to Judaism's universalism lies in its emphasis on ethics. Since a truth is universal when it applies to every reasonable being, and a religion is universal when it is open to all, for Levinas, the Judaism that links the divine to the moral has always aspired to be universal (*DF*, 21). The concept of "chosenness" in Judaism does not refer to nobility or class. It does not refer to privileges. Rather, "election," a better word choice here, refers to responsibility, and one's "place" is determined by whether one decides to accept or reject that responsibility. Does one see oneself as obligated with respect to the Other or not? To recognize this fact about oneself elevates one to an exceptional status, one of increasing responsibility (*DF*, 22).

Interestingly, Levinas does not directly answer his interviewer's question, "is philosophy simply a secular product of religion?" In some sense, it cannot be simply that. On the one hand, Levinas defends religion's need to resort occasionally to philosophy. Religion cannot accomplish the ethical task on its own. On the other hand, it is the religious texts that provide the universal ethical dimension to philosophy. Religion, then, needs the universality—the universal language—that philosophy provides, but philosophy needs the religious dimension provided by the Jewish holy books. In the end, Levinas concludes that philosophy and religion are two methods linked by their approach to transcendence—an approach to God, an approach to the other person. Philosophy becomes ethical when it meets religion rather than turns away from it, and Levinas speculates that in all meaningful thought, transcendence is manifested (*IR,* 246). This might explain why he sees his philosophical project as an articulation of the Bible, rather than an alternative to it. The biblical references that permeate his philosophy serve this end. These references connect the reader of his philosophy to a very specific conversation. As a result, it is fair to ask why Levinas does not make an even firmer distinction between the two categories of philosophy and religion.

Here we can acknowledge those who have noted that Levinas's philosophical writings perform what he writes about in his Jewish writings—namely, the translation of the Hebrew into Greek.[53] As mentioned above, Levinas refers to philosophy as derivative of religion, and additionally subordinates philosophy to religion (Judaism), even though he admits that biblical verse often displays a philosophical accent. Levinas links philosophy to ontology. It remains at the level of being. So the subordination of philosophy to religion coheres with his view that ontology be subordinated to ethics. As a result, he turns to the biblical narratives as illustrations of his philosophical arguments.

As we saw earlier, the biblical commands that enjoin the "I" to respond to the Other exemplify the ethical relationship: "Thou shalt not kill"; "Thou shalt love the stranger"; and "Thou shalt love thy neighbor as thyself." Levinas's employment of the biblical verse is more than simply illustrating that the Other is mortal and that there is an injunction not to kill the Other. His employment of the biblical phrasing provides a force to the statement that might otherwise be absent. Levinas's own comments indicate that for him this statement expresses more than simply a prohibition not to kill. It

> becomes a fundamental definition or description of the human event of being, a permanent prudence with respect to the violent and murderous acts against the other which are perhaps the very assertion of a being, as if the very imposition of a being's existence were already to jeopardize someone's life. (*IR,* 62)

We see a similar force in the infrequent but strategically placed references to Cain. The references, found in *Otherwise than Being* and several essays, always draw attention to "Cain's sober coldness." Levinas's interpretation of Cain's behavior and his subsequent response to God is unorthodox. He does not wish to highlight Cain as simply the first "killer." Rather, he sees something more profound and potentially more dangerous in Cain's behavior. The issue at hand is not that Cain killed Abel—although, certainly Levinas would not deny that killing Abel was horrific. Rather, Cain's reply to God indicates that he felt no connection to human fraternity.

Levinas's interpretation of Cain as someone disconnected from human fraternity is not only more interesting, but also more penetrating than traditional interpretations of Cain. To say that God punished Cain because Cain killed Abel does not offer us much with regard to moral lessons. We learn that murder is wrong with the delivery of the Ten Commandments. Levinas's interpretation is more arresting, for it alerts us to the fundamental flaws in our relationships to others, namely, the alienation and disconnection that indicate a lack of ethical subjectivity, an undeveloped humanity. Levinas astutely identifies that the real problem with Cain is not simply that he killed his brother, but that in his reply to God's question "where is your brother?" Cain reveals that he did not understand that he had any responsibility toward his brother at all. He reveals that he is completely disconnected from human fraternity. In Levinas's terms, he *could not* see the face of Abel. However, the biblical passage alone does not demand this reading. This point could only be gleaned by the commentary on the narrative—either through Levinas or the rabbis. It is not a point that stands obviously on its own. In a sense, Levinas employs the midrashic model and inserts his interpretation into his philosophical work without acknowledging he has done so. And by doing so, he exposes his readers to this model.

We can use the above discussion to explain why Levinas turns to biblical figures and phrases to help illustrate a point. Levinas's discussion of midrash discloses the most significant aspect of this kind of reading, namely, its pedagogical capacity. As the earlier citation indicates, each reader is confronted with the readers who came before him or her. The confrontation with the text is a confrontation with a history of lessons, from the whole of the past (*BTV,* xiii). Levinas's view of midrash might go far to explaining why, for him, a phrase or reference from any other literary work would not suffice. The Bible is simply not another literary text, as we see in the story of Cain and the lesson that Levinas gleans from it. The stories in the Bible move forward with the characters, flawed as they are, developing responsibility, that is, ethical subjectivity. Neither Cain, nor for that matter Adam, could acknowledge their responsibility for their own actions. Biblical narratives and the stories of the sages and others are taken, by Jews, neither as authoritative myths nor as simpleminded children's tales. Rather, they are taken as exemplary *paradigms*.[54] As the biblical narratives move forward we see Noah and then Abraham repeatedly uttering, "Here I am," indicating they are ready to serve. They are responsible and will take responsibility.

In Levinas's project, it is this ethical responsibility that defines human subjectivity. The Bible, then, illustrates the origins of human subjectivity: "The Bible teaches us that man is he who loves his neighbor, and that the fact of loving his neighbor is a modality of meaningful life, of a thinking as fundamental—I would say more fundamental—than the knowledge of an object, than truth as knowledge of objects" (*IR,* 63–64). Levinas's use of the biblical phrasing imparts more than simply the mortality of the Other; in order to convey this meaning he turns to the midrashic model, the interpretative model that sees in excess of the "plain" meaning provided by the written word of the text. Certainly, this point could be made through other literary vehicles. However, for Levinas, the biblical narrative displays a unique stance, and therefore engages us more profoundly.

We see this unique stance reflected in the comments by talmudic scholar David Stern who recounts that one reading of midrash claims that the study of Torah—in other words, midrash—is as much a path to holiness as is following *halakhah*.[55] Levinas echoes this point in "Revelation in the Jewish Tradition," where he notes: "the study of the commandments—the study of the Torah, that is, resumption of the rabbinical dialectic—is equal in religious value to actually carrying them out. It is as if, in this study, man were in mystical contact with the divine will itself" (*BTV*, 141). We find further support in Stern's observation that the "study of Torah, the activity of midrash, does not . . . constitute an act of directly interpreting God as though the text itself were literally divine. Instead, one could almost call midrash the interpretation of Torah as a figure or trope standing in for God."[56]

So by placing these tropes within the context of his philosophical work, Levinas invites his readers to enact the very event he attempts to communicate. Through his philosophical work, we can come closer to God, and we are, therefore, closer to the ethical. When we encounter the biblical tropes, we are invited to engage them. We are called to understand the use of the trope and why it was placed in the text.

The wisdom of the Bible as understood Jewishly becomes part of the philosophy; God, or ethics, and philosophy are intertwined. The Bible teaches, and the Bible read Jewishly, that is, through exegesis, teaches even more effectively. As mentioned above, this teaching is a form of transcendence and turns us to the ethical—to the face of the Other. And more importantly, in Levinas's view, it teaches in a way that other literary vehicles cannot. It is not the case that all literature, or high art, intends to attune, or succeeds in attuning, us to the ethical. Levinas's philosophy, layered with pieces from Scripture, invites us into the Jewish reading of the Bible in order to demonstrate the very practice of engaging with the Other. In this way, the performative dimension of the Hebrew Scriptures takes priority over the philosophy *within* his philosophical text. His project cannot achieve what it aims—i.e., to implicate us in the very language of the ethical—without exposing us to that language, i.e., the language of the Jewish religion. His philosophy teaches, and its infusion with a specific religious language enables it to do so in a unique voice.

For Levinas, then, this Jewish way of reading the text might be the most effective way, though certainly not the only way, to expose our students to the *idea* of alterity, that is, to other voices and the voices of the Other. At the very least, this method would expose them to the idea that there are voices, in the text and in the world, that are often muted if not outright silenced. Moreover, the process of questioning that we find particularly in the talmudic tradition is intended not only to teach students to question in order to be attuned to the material at hand. The Jewish tradition of learning also recognizes something unique about the journey one takes in the educational process. The questioning between the two study partners requires each participant to admit that there is always something more to be known. This process intends to develop humility and a certain integrity regarding truth on the part of the students. And the interaction between the study partners aids in developing the respect one has for the Other, in addition to building a close bond of friendship. And the interaction between the study partners aids in developing the respect one has for the Other, in addition to building a close bond of friendship. But most importantly, even if they learn nothing else, the study partners learn that dependence is healthy and productive. All of this is grounded in the initial obligation to the Other that informs the relationship. The subject who enters into this tradition does so as a "we," in partnership with an Other. Finally, this practice explicitly recognizes that education is filled with transcendent moments and that to study is to be in touch with the divine—sentiments expressed by educators, though not usually in these words.[57]

References to education pervade Levinas's writings from beginning to end, and he locates the solution to the crisis of humanism specifically in Jewish education. For Levinas this means Torah, Talmud, and Hebrew. If considered between the writings in *Difficult Freedom* and the writings collected in *Humanism of the Other*, we can see that the ethical subject for Levinas is one that is developed—taught, if you will. And while I am sympathetic to this view of the subject, I am not without my concerns. Like a Kantian system that seems to rely on a thoroughgoing ethical community—lest one need to lie to the Nazis when they come asking for the Jew hiding in the attic—the Levinasian subject is one that seems nearly self-sacrificing. To turn to the Other, to cede one's place in the sun, will prevent wars if all are successfully educated—and I think this is what Levinas has in mind. Yet, I can imagine the hesitation—"I'll do this, if you do that"—which begins to sound more like a social contract, an exchange of favors, or worse a game of "ethical chicken," in which one side decides to hold out with the view that the other will eventually succumb, rather than the pre-rational turning to the Other he describes.[58]

My point here is less to say that I think Levinas is wrong in his promotion of a new subjectivity; in fact, I think he is right. Rather, my point is that Levinasian ethics is indeed difficult, maybe even impossible. My concern is that many commentators have made Levinas's ethics seem easy or natural: Levinas is merely describing who we already are; we have just simply ignored it or covered it over. Ethics in the Levinasian sense then almost becomes a bit of magic that I cannot control—although the responsibility that I do not acknowledge will always impinge on me: maybe I will or maybe I won't give you some of my bread. In light of what happened in the camps, it seems that an ethical subjectivity that is as capricious as the one I just described would be farthest from his mind.

Instead, I consider the possibility that his philosophical project and his writings on Judaism describe an ethical subjectivity that is far more complex and difficult to achieve. Additionally, I contend that it involves a commitment many of us might not be ready to make and might never be able to make. We cannot simply read his books and then "become Levinasian," whatever that might mean; nor can one be a subject as Levinas describes without consequence. To become a subject in the way that Levinas describes requires a commitment by those who parent and teach; it is not a commitment made lightly. While it is true that Levinas does not prescribe moral rules such as the Ten Commandments or even a categorical imperative, it is not the case that there are no prescriptions. First and foremost, he tells us that the face of the Other commands me not to murder. But even if I bracket this point, he is not simply describing but also prescribing a different subjectivity, one that amplifies the ethical responsibility for another.

It is no accident that Levinas repeatedly refers to Isaiah, the suffering servant (and eventually the model for Christ) and the one who advocates that Jews become a light unto the nations. Additionally, like the prophets, Levinas repeatedly references the widow and the orphan, that is, tending to the misery or suffering of the Other. Thus, at the same time that Levinas makes the argument for this subjectivity in his philosophical project, he makes a similar argument to the Jewish community. But in addition to the argument for this subjectivity to the Jewish community, he adds three more points: he demonstrates that this subjectivity originates in Judaism, it is what makes Judaism unique, and that Jewish education is a mechanism for achieving this end. Israel, defined as the community of Jews, must become, once again, the light unto the nations. By setting the example, others will follow—maybe only one at a time, maybe in larger groups. Nonetheless, one cannot help but wonder if ultimately Levinas hopes that the non-Jewish community will be persuaded to educate their children in a similar fashion. In the end, he describes the ethical relation with terms like "interruption," and yet his essays on education seem to state rather clearly that in order to be interrupted and respond to that interruption, the subject needs to be cultivated—and that means an education that turns the subject toward the Other.

7   Humanism Found

Let justice well up like water,
  Righteousness like an unfailing stream. (Amos 5:24)

And they shall beat their swords into plowshares
  And their spears into pruning hooks
  Nation shall not take up
  Sword against nation;
  They shall never again know war. (Isaiah 2:4)

God is not in heaven. He is in men's sacrifice, in the mercy men show
for one another.
  Heaven is empty but men's mercy is filled with God.

—Levinas in conversation with Michael de Saint Cheron

This book has argued that Levinas's writings on Jewish education help us understand his fundamental concerns motivating his ethical project. He witnessed a crisis of humanism for which a new subjectivity was required. His philosophical writings argue for this new subjectivity, but the question of how this subjectivity can develop begs for an answer. His writings on Jewish education provide some direction. Yet as they guide us in answering this question, other questions emerge. The most obvious is to ask what his argument means for the non-Jewish community. How does the solution that Levinas offers to the Jewish community translate to the non-Jewish (or even non-practicing Jewish) community? Even if my argument regarding the importance of Jewish education to Levinas's project is sound, we are left wondering what we do now. Can we identify or construct an educational model that is both necessary and comparable to the Jewish educational model which Levinas presents?

In his 1962 book *The Prophets,* Abraham Joshua Heschel explains that he turned to the prophets because philosophy had become too detached from the concerns most pressing to him.[1] Why the Jewish prophets? At the time of the book's publication Heschel had been teaching at the Jewish Theological Seminary in New York, the seminary for the Conservative branch of Judaism. He explains that his work within the academic environment began to feel isolating and self-indulgent. It had lost contact with the "real" world, the world that demands from us our attention. More importantly, he believed that the work of the academy led to a life of "suspended sensitivity in the face of stupendous challenge, indifferent to a situation in which good and evil became irrelevant, in which man became increasingly callous to catastrophe and ready to suspend the principle of truth."[2] The prophets, according to Heschel, are "some of the most disturbing people who have ever lived," for their intense anguish about even the most banal of life's unjust events is relentless.[3]

Heschel's reading of the prophets asks us not to think as much about the truth or the validity of the prophets' claims. Instead, he asks us to think about who the prophets were. What distinguishes them as prophets? What did they feel? He tells us that before we can even begin to address the question of what the prophets mean to us, we must understand what they mean to God: "Prophecy is a sham unless it is experienced as a word of God swooping down on man and converting him into a prophet."[4] He further explains that although he does not wish to discount the method of "impartial phenomenology," this kind of impartiality has no place in his investigation. He confesses that he has long become wary, even suspicious of such impartiality, which indicates either that the situation has no relevance to us or it does, in which case the impartiality is simply a pretense. Reflection is not separate from the prophet's conviction:

> While the structure and the bare content of prophetic consciousness may be made accessible by an attitude of pure reflection, in which the concern for their truth and validity is suspended, the sheer force of what is disclosed in such reflection quietly corrodes the hardness of self-detachment. The magic of the process seems to be stronger than an asceticism of the intellect . . . In the course of listening to their words one cannot long retain the security of a prudent, impartial observer.[5]

Heschel is not discounting the power or necessity of pure reflection. He is simply indicating its limits. If we wish to clarify what the prophet asserts, then we call in pure reflection; if we wish to know what it is like to be a prophet, i.e., his existential character, then pure reflection will not be sufficient. As Susannah Heschel observes, "Rather than debate theological interpretations, the prophets denounce hypocrisy and insist on justice as the tool of God and the manifestation of God. Neither religious ritual nor belief holds meaning for the prophets as ends in themselves; what God wants, Amos insists, is not worship but an end to war crimes and exploitation in the marketplace. For the prophets, justice is the means of redemption, including our redemption of God from the constraints of religion, human mendacity and complacency in the face of evil. They also are adamant that evil is never the climax of history."[6] According to Abraham Joshua Heschel, "the prophet was an individual who said 'No' to his society, condemning its habits and assumptions, its complacency, waywardness, and syncretism."[7]

In this chapter, I turn to the role of the prophetic in Levinas's writings, especially in his later work, in order to suggest that his view of the ethical that permeates his work from the 1930s until his death in 1995 resonates with the role of the prophet in the community (even if not named as such)—the one who calls the community to responsibility. By examining Heschel's treatment of the prophets, we can see how the prophetic consciousness might have guided the development of Levinas's philosophical project. Heschel's reading of the prophets may help us understand how for Levinas the references to the Hebrew prophets carry a different status than a reference to Shakespeare. I argue that Levinas's frequent references to the Hebrew prophets, in particular Isaiah, one of the most significant of the Hebrew prophets, in *Otherwise than Being* is not an accident nor is it simply a rhetorical flourish. His references to Isaiah complete his clarion call—prompted by his all too prescient insight in his earliest essay—to bear witness to the ethical, to speak out against injustice, and to act for the Other. It is the distinction and description that Heschel offers above—the prophet is the one who said "No" to his society—that, I argue, Levinas exploits. Levinas's use of the prophetic in his later work, particularly in *Otherwise than Being,* is not for the purposes of mere explication. He is not interested in a discussion about what the prophets meant. Nor does Levinas employ the prophetic texts as a means to invoke the simply religious dimension of Judaism—the laws of *kashrut,* ritual, or the adherence to the Sabbath. Rather, Levinas is interested in how he can import the power of the prophetic and its command not to be indifferent into his philosophy.

Levinas's Prophets

In his essay "The Spirit of Jewish Prayer," Abraham Joshua Heschel alerts us to a problem in modern Jewish life. Heschel begins this essay with the declaration that although services run smoothly, full of "pomp and precision . . . decorum, voice, and ceremony," they are devoid of life. Ironically, the place of worship is lacking soul.[8] Judaism has developed a new habit of "praying by proxy," where the congregants "let" the rabbis or cantors do the praying for the congregation.[9] In order to correct this problem Heschel explains that we must first know what prayer is, and in order to answer this question, we must first know who we are when we pray and what it is we are praying for. He asks, "What is it that a person is conscious of in a moment of prayer?"[10] This question is better understood in terms of the rabbinical expression, "Know before Whom you stand."[11] He maintains that to live without prayer is to live without God. It is to live without a soul.[12] Yet, he argues against the position that prayer is simply emotion or emotive, even though he admits that certainly emotion is a component of prayer. In his analysis, "before Whom" makes reference to God and "you stand" refers to the act of prayer as an act that "happens between man and God in the presence of God."[13] To pray is to expose oneself to God, to enter into that relationship with God.[14]

In Heschel's characterization, this relationship with God does not remove us from this world; rather, prayer is how we "bring God back into the world."[15] And although prayer in Judaism can be either praise or petition, the former ranks foremost.[16] In his discussion about the ways that prayer is regulated—who can pray, when one can pray, and so forth—Heschel acknowledges the "perpetual danger of prayer becoming a mere habit, a mechanical performance, an exercise in repetitiousness."[17] He argues that we need to find a way to balance the regularity of prayer with spontaneity—though he admits that this is a difficult problem to solve. He uses the comparison of halakhah and aggadah—Judaism needs both, and they map onto the body and the spirit—neither of which should be disparaged. Yet maintaining these polarities also keeps the tension between them present. How then does one approach the text with the proper *kavanah* (disposition or mindset)?[18] Citing Maimonides, he states, "Prayer without *kavanah* is no prayer at all."[19]

To impress upon us the significance of approaching prayer properly, Heschel refers to Berakhot, the first tractate of the Mishnah, the same talmudic passage that Levinas references in his discussion of the importance of talmudic study.[20] The regularity of prayer and the laws that govern us move us into a position to pray, even when "we do not feel like doing so." For Heschel, it is not that education or study adds to prayer; rather, the very notion of prayer includes a particular mental disposition. Most importantly, Heschel tells us that we pray in order to pray—that is, we do not pray for the sake of something else. Thus, there is a command to pray, a command to put ourselves into a proper frame of mind and body such that we can pray, such that we can be in the presence of God and such that we can continue to make commitments to God in good faith—but we have lost the ability to know what words mean, to know that words have a soul. We do not know how to gain insight into that life.[21]

Like Heschel, Levinas explores a similar problem with Jewish prayer in a contemporary world in his essay "Education and Prayer."[22] Revealing his continued struggle with the tension and the relationship between reason and revelation, philosophy and religion, Levinas originally titled this essay "*Philosophie et Prière.*" He introduces this essay with the following assertion: "Prayer is one of the most difficult subjects for a philosopher, as it is for a believer" (*DF*, 269). Certainly not an understatement, even today! He begins by telling us that on the one hand he maintains prayer's centrality to Judaism; but on the other he wishes to accord prayer a secondary position.

In this discussion of Jewish prayer, he affirms that the centrality of community, while still indispensable for prayer's meaning, has nonetheless been lost from prayer itself. And he tells us that while prayer has first place in Judaism, he wants to grant it second place. The function of prayer is for the individual to renew his or her links with the community of Israel, which is now dispersed through space and time (*DF*, 270). Levinas repeats the fable from Berakhot where God is putting on his own *tefillin* each morning (*DF*, 270). If the Shema is our affirmation of God's uniqueness, this fable is the "celestial counterpart" to the Shema: When God prays, God says, "Who is like you O Israel, a nation unique on the earth?" Israel is unique to God just as God is unique to Israel. For Levinas, this exchange implies not mutuality, but an affirmation of Israel's own uniqueness and thus an affirmation of humanity. In Levinas's view, essential to the Shema is not only the connection between God and Israel but also the one among the people of Israel themselves. That is, Levinas "hears" in the Shema a call to humanity that is both united and unique, universal and singular.

Although prayer is often thought in terms of the individual, for Levinas prayer transcends the individual. It is what makes Judaism religious. That is, it tethers Jews to their history and ties them to the community. According to Levinas, it is prayer that paved the way for Jewish nationalists, for it is in prayer that Jews are bound to Israel as a people and then as a nation. But in the paragraphs that follow this discussion, he takes a more circumspect look at the priority of prayer and asks what implications this has for the contemporary world and contemporary Jews. In this section of the essay, he frankly asks after the role of prayer in the modern world.

Modernity is often positioned in opposition to the sacred. Levinas asks us to consider what the call of the modern world is and if there is a way for Judaism to respond to this call. He recognizes that many who have left the fold of Judaism are among the brightest and most active of humanity. Yet, they also believe that religion cannot provide salvation as long as "reason and justice are left unsatisfied" (*DF*, 271).[23] Old-fashioned Judaism, as Levinas refers to it, is dying off and he calls for his readers to return to Jewish wisdom. However, this return must be to the Jew of the Talmud rather than the Jew of the psalms. Reason, he asserts, must take precedence over prayer.[24]

In the final paragraph of this essay, Levinas asks his readers to consider what really moves them with regard to Jewish truth. Where, he asks, do we find "the most dazzling confirmation of our truth?" And he replies that it is not found so much in the offices of the synagogue, but rather in those flashes of talmudic genius, and it is in this that Jews find their mark of being chosen (*DF*, 272). For Levinas, if we ignore this opportunity to bring talmudic reason into the educational arena and to offer it a privileged status over prayer, thus drawing many Jews back to Judaism, "we risk ending up with a Judaism without Jews" (*DF*, 271). His emphasis on Talmud follows a line that points all the way back to Hillel and the story of Shammai the convert. Hillel's parting words, after telling Shammai that all of Judaism rests on one basic ethical tenet, are "now go and study," indicating that while Judaism and the practice of this ethical tenet might appear easy, indeed it is more complicated. Judaism without study is a Judaism without content. Indeed, Levinas reminds an interviewer many years after publishing this essay that "it is in the *yeshivot* [the talmudic schools] that God takes delight."[25]

Judaism must respond to the modern world by recognizing the role of reason that is already a fundamental part of the religion. But it is in the last few sentences of this essay that what is at stake for Levinas is brought into relief: "The builders of a better world—who, in the name of Reason, ignore the Judgment— are enclosing and walling up our sons like the living bricks of biblical Egypt

tion, and responsibility. Its focus, as many have noted, indicates the shift from the Other so thoroughly discussed in *Totality and Infinity* to the Subject. He now asks us to think of ourselves in the role of the prophet. Thus, his frequent references to the banal (the gratuitous hello) and the extreme (dying for the Other) are not out of sync with each other. His work does not ask us to think in terms of the grand moral gesture, the "big one" that will require us to act. His work reveals that if we do not speak out against the small injustices, if we do not feed our neighbor, if we do not think of the Other as someone to whom we owe everything, we will be incapable of acting when we are confronted with the so-called "big ones."

Levinas's use of the biblical narratives, interpretations of which are dependent on midrashic style, and his frequent references to the Hebrew Scriptures do instructive work for him. This is not to say that other religions should be excluded from this conversation. My point is rather that Levinas's relationship to Judaism situates his work and his project within a larger Jewish context.[29] In Levinas's view, the Hebrew Bible illustrates the origins of human subjectivity: "The Bible teaches us that man is he who loves his neighbor, and that the fact of loving his neighbor is a modality of meaningful life, of a thinking as fundamental—I would say more fundamental—than the knowledge of an object, than truth as knowledge of objects."[30] The Bible, read Jewishly, not only reflects the responsibility of a time before memory and before choice itself, it also teaches this responsibility. And here we see how Levinas's own concerns about how to make the past relevant to the present and to the future intersect with John Dewey's. Taking his cue from rabbinic Judaism, Levinas affirms that the past is not only kept alive in the textual tradition, but it is made present. The wisdom of the old is brought to bear on the new.[31] His intention is not to turn Judaism into a piety. Instead, Jewish learning, which includes prayer, is disruption.

Education and the Midrashic Imperative[32]

In his essay "On Religious Language and the Fear of God" (originally published in 1980 in French in *Man in World*), dedicated to Paul Ricoeur on the occasion of Ricoeur's sixty-fifth birthday, Levinas offers a reading of a passage from the Babylonian Talmud, Tractate Berakhot 33—the same text cited by Heschel. In this commentary, Levinas emphasizes the role of study in our relationship to God. This essay, written fairly late in Levinas's philosophical career, reflects many of the themes we find in his philosophical writing, though here these themes are applied to sacred texts rather than to the ethical Other, per se.[33] Early in this essay, Levinas sets out his task. He hopes to offer a "description of religious language which admittedly, in the last analysis, relates it fundamentally to a thought which is already a discourse (reading and studying the Torah) but which, between the Torah and the discourse allowing transcendence to signify, brings in attitudes of will as carriers of meaning, . . . a discipline which is heteronomous to the point of depending on an educational community . . ." (*BTV*, 87). Torah and Talmud study are communal endeavors. More importantly, they have a pedagogical function. Levinas describes talmudic texts in the following way:

> Compact, elliptical, allusive and, as it were, challenging all rhetoric and all magic of the word (for it to be intelligible, a simple translation requires the addition of syntactic particles and even implied sentence numbers), it is made up of arguments, questions and answers, objections and replies to the objections, all chronologically separated from one another, sometimes by centuries, yet brought together by the logic of the purpose whose mediate inferences are not all explicit. It has an incessant concern for attributing every saying to its historical author. Hence the constant evocation of personal names of the rabbinical scholars who have spoken or who, in such and such a circumstance, behaved in such and such a way. This is not to offer the reader a purely anecdotal interest; it is there for the purposes of teaching. Finally, in the presentation of the discussions there is very often a way of leaving them open, which would not fail to surprise those who believe in the false reputation of the dogmatism attached to the Talmudic Tractates. (*BTV*, 87)

His aim in the above description is to call our attention to the need for commentary. Talmudic passages do not speak for themselves and are often so dense and opaque that they barely speak at all. The sacred texts of Judaism call us from outside of ourselves—so outside that we are required to engage these texts with others. His reference to the rabbinic scholars reaffirms their eternal role as teachers, long after they have died.

Levinas's reading of Tractate Berakhot 33b moves through discussions of compassion and justice, obedience and human disinterestedness, the fear of God, the fear for Man, and then finally, in the concluding section, the fear of God and education. In this final section, Levinas claims that "man learns the humanity of the fear of God through the Torah. The study of the Word of God thus establishes or constitutes the most direct relation to God, perhaps more direct than the liturgy. *Hence the central place in Judaism of teaching in order to ensure the religiosity of religious discourse*" (*BTV*, 97, emphasis added). Judaism calls us from outside ourselves and it teaches us to engage with the Other. One cannot help but ask if the implication of Levinas's comment is to say that study is not only embedded in prayer; it is also in fact more religious than prayer. In contrast with Heschel's reading of the same passage, Levinas deploys this text for the particular purpose of promoting study, or education.

We see indications of this point at the end of this essay when he recaps the problem with the three prohibitions or improper formulations of prayer as found in Tractate Berakhot 33b. His gloss, which focuses on the third prohibition—the issue of repetition: "We give thanks, we give thanks"—is worth reproducing at length:

The return to the "interdict of repeating" is also an opportunity to insist, in concluding, on the idea of discipline, and consequently on the authoritative educational intervention of the community: to excuse the repetition of the formulations of prayer on the pretext of a possible first recitation being purely mechanical, and thus requiring a second recitation with a more concentrated thought, is to give a bad excuse. A purely mechanical recitation is carelessness. The fear and the love of God exclude such "familiar" behavior. An education is needed, and that education can become a constraint. The constraint of the community or of tradition, which has been—or, more exactly, can be—the first word on which everything depends. (*BTV*, 97–98)

For Levinas, then, mindless recitation would not be an excuse for the second recitation, since the familiarity with God that would allow such a mindless act of prayer would be considered carelessness. That is, according to this commentary, prayer cannot by definition be simply rote or mindless, since it assumes a familiarity (not intimacy) with God, the Absolute Other, that we simply cannot assume. Levinas's analysis in these two essays presents a dimension of prayer that is not normally discussed. Prayer is often presented as that which is outside of education, and even outside of reason. But in this essay, Levinas draws on themes from the earlier essay where prayer—the prayer of the psalms—was put in opposition to the reason of the Talmud. Here, Levinas argues that prayer must assume a certain comportment of the self in order for it to be authentic. Prayer calls for education within a community.

Levinas clearly has the Jewish tradition in mind when he speaks of ethics and education in religious language, the language of transcendence. More specifically, Levinas believes that the Jewish scriptural tradition embodies a response and an attention to the particular Other without losing sight of the necessity of the universal. The tension kept in balance is significant to ethical and political acuity. He also holds that transcendence is connected both to God and to ethics. And here we also see why Levinas distinguishes the stories and the characters in the Hebrew Bible from the stories and characters in other works of literature. We see it first when he claims in his essay "The Meaning of Meaning" that the face of the Other is "the meaning of the beyond."[34] He continues,

The meaning of the face is not a species whose indication or symbolism would be the genus. The face is alone in translating transcendence. Not to provide the proof of the existence of God, but the indispensable circumstance of the meaning of the word, of its first statement. Of the first prayer, of the first liturgy. A Transcendence that is inseparable from the ethical *circumstances* of the responsibility for the other . . .

One can detach from it, or isolate from it, and think the idea of God on its own. One can think it or know it while forgetting the ethical circumstances of its meaning and even find within it—but after the fact and through reflection—a religious experience. Religions and theologies live from that abstraction, as do the mystics from that isolation. But so do religious wars. (*OS*, 94–95)

Levinas insists on the concrete, of not thinking God alone, but God as revealed in the face of the Other, a face that demands us to respond to it, a face that says, "thou shalt not kill." To think God alone, rather than in relationship to another human being, is what permits people to hear the voice of God as one that asks him/her to kill another.[35]

Additionally, Levinas worries that thinking God alone distracts us from the ultimate relationship that the presence of God entails, that with the Other. To think God alone reverses the order of priority and potentially distracts us with discussions and arguments concerning the presence of that God. To think of God as the limit of alterity requires that to be in the presence of God is precisely to respond ethically to the Other. Further, there is the view that one brings to the text the very text itself; the text is always already human (and divine). We, its readers, open it up and release that divinity. This reversal mentioned above does not mean that Levinas ignores God. In fact, we see Levinas's reliance on the divine again in his discussion of the biblical command, "Thou shalt not kill."[36]

The incorporation of a religious dimension into secular education, regardless of the religion, is controversial, to say the least.[37] We must remember then what this concept of religion means to Levinas. In several places, Levinas refers to the universalism of Judaism. This is ironic, since Judaism is often thought of as parochial, too particular, in contrast to Christianity, which is viewed as universal.[38] In Levinas's view, "the Judaism that links the Divine to the moral has always aspired to be universal" (DF, 21). The notion of election, which is so fundamental to Judaism, is not about special privileges, granted by birthright, as is portrayed by the persistent misinterpretation; rather, election refers to the special responsibilities, not only open to all who wish to accept this responsibility, but conferred upon Jews by virtue of being an "I" separate from all the others: "I" am obligated (DF, 21). Being chosen, then, is nothing other than recognizing one's "exceptional" position (DF, 22). It is this view of Judaism and responsibility that allows Levinas to promote the "religious" dimension as universal.

We might say that Levinas's philosophical project encourages this meeting. As we saw previously, Levinas makes this view explicit in "Antihumanism and Education," where he argues that the so-called secular humanism is actually Jewish at its very core (DF, 279). The very concepts Levinas sees in Jewish education that are not in conflict with the ideals of the secular school are precisely those same concepts that should transfer to the secular, or public school. Secular humanists have lost sight of the Jewish values from which humanism emerged. And so we can already see how a "secular" Judaism can be encouraged in the public arena.

I do not make this claim naïvely. I am acutely aware of possible dangers of and the obstacles to translating this particular pedagogical style, which focuses on a particular content, into a secular educational environment. However, by considering Levinas's own writings on Jewish education, we might be inspired to think more creatively and with more sophistication about education, teaching, ethics, religion, and the political.

What then is the connection between Levinas's writings on Judaism, and specifically those writings on Jewish education, and his larger philosophical project? My claim is that if his Jewish writings argue that Jews need to become more Jewish, his philosophical writings engage his readers—Jewish and non-Jewish alike—in a similar endeavor. Where his Jewish writings are explicit about what the Jewish community needs to do to address the crisis of humanism, his philosophical writings draw out a philosophical argument for, and a phenomenological description of, this new subjectivity, which Levinas sees as fundamentally Jewish. His writing style engages his readers in a method that is similar to what one might find in Jewish education—an intellectual endeavor that contains within it a persistent directive to turn toward the Other.

As I mentioned previously, I wish to warn against the assumption that one becomes "Levinasian," whatever that means, or ethical in the sense Levinas describes, by reading or even understanding Levinas's books. I do not think this would even be the aim of Levinas's philosophical project. Indeed, to have such a goal would undermine the very way that he understands the nature of education, as addressed in his own essays on the subject. Rather, his philosophical project reinforces the view that education is fundamental to the formation of this new subjectivity. Insofar as his readers become convinced that he is right, they will in turn teach others. They might choose to raise their children differently or they might work to change the educational system.

Education, and indeed a particular kind of education, is fundamental to the creation of the subjectivity that Levinas describes. This kind of subjectivity does not happen overnight; it does not happen because we "get" what Levinas is saying. While reason and introspection might lead us to understanding, they do not guarantee wisdom—an unfortunate conflation made long ago in the history of philosophy, where the love of wisdom (search for truth?) was conflated with possessing that wisdom. It happens because a radically different view of what it means to be human guides the educational process of our children. What then might a non-Jewish education with this same goal look like? Let me suggest one possible example, which asks us to consider how the prevailing pedagogy functions and what we might do to change it.

The state of Texas offers as their English as a Second Language (ESL) curriculum a pedagogical method called "50–50 immersion." This same program is sometimes called two-way language instruction. Essentially, the program works in the following way: Children enter the program in kindergarten or first grade. The classroom is equally populated by native English and native Spanish speakers. Certain days during the week are assigned to be "English only" or "Spanish only." Depending on the day, the teachers wear an apron keyed to the day so that the children know which language the teacher will be speaking when they arrive at school. In the early grades, the children may ask or answer questions in either language, regardless of the day, but they will be spoken to only in the language for that day. The children are paired—native English speaker with native Spanish speaker. On the days when only English is spoken, the children who speak Spanish must rely on those who speak English. The children who speak English are responsible for those who are dependent on them—and vice versa.

The majority of schooling is set up so that children hoard—everything from pencils to knowledge. School is set up as a competition that encourages children to think of the acquisition of knowledge and success in school as a zero-sum game. It does little more than pay lip service to ethical development. The most dangerous irony of public schooling is that it relies on community support precisely to teach certain values that aim to undermine the very community support it needs: for example, inculcating strong capitalist values that oppose taxes, on which public schooling relies. It certainly does not encourage or support anything as radical as Levinasian subjectivity. Most of the "character building" is based on a view of capitalism that is worrisome at best. The values that are extolled are virtues that define the "good worker."

In contrast, the pedagogy in the dual-language immersion program is not added on as a suggested teaching methodology. Rather, the pedagogy is central to the entire educational process. The children must learn to rely on each other and in turn they must also learn that they are responsible for each other. They must learn that knowledge is not a zero-sum game, that learning material and developing their minds are intimately connected with the relationships that they develop to and with the other children—possibly more so than with the teachers.

This particular pedagogical model is unique for several reasons. The program is itself academic—all the children are learning a second language at the same time that they are learning course content: math, reading, language arts, and science. That is, they are learning their regular academic subjects in both English and Spanish. For the native Spanish speakers this means that they are also learning English and the native English speakers are also learning Spanish while learning course content in both languages. The teaching method is intimately tied to the very possibility of learning. The development of responsibility is not something that is taught like a catechism; it is something that grows organically through the process of education. There are days when some children do not understand the language spoken and the other children are called to help them. Vulnerability and responsibility are built into the pedagogical structure. For the time that my own child participated in this program, I recognized that my responsibility extended beyond my daughter. I am responsible not only for her but also for her classmates. I must teach her that she is also responsible for her classmates regardless of whether they are able to return the gesture. It is not occasionally that these other children need help; it is on a daily, even hourly, basis. And in contrast to the now famous lines in John F. Kennedy's 1960 inaugural speech—"Ask not what your country can do for you but what you can do for your country"— this is not a call to service, nor a call to citizenship; it is *election* to ethical responsibility.[39]

This dual-language program is not midrashic—let me be clear about that. Nor does it approach texts as difficult and opaque as the Talmud. However, it intimately ties an instructional method that relies on responsibility for the Other to the success of learning the material. The same can be said for talmudic learning, which tethers the content of the material to the *way* it is learned. The pedagogical style that I identified above is not perfect, and to mimic talmudic learning it would need to include a talmudic style of reading: the texts need to be complex and open-ended; the subject matter must deal with difficult topics that are also part of daily life; the interpretative process must support readings that allow different voices to emerge, to be able to see what is and is not said, to draw out what has been hidden. Children need to be encouraged to speak, interpret, and argue. Nonetheless, this program does ask us to consider how different school would be if the very nature of learning were such that children had to rely on each other, and every day the one who was dependent and the one who was called to responsibility changed. And how different it would be if reading books was about seeing not only what and who are included in the narrative, but also being encouraged to talk about what and who are not.

Recalling the earlier citation from Franz Rosenzweig, we note that transformation takes place in the classroom, specifically in the discussion at the seminar table with others. It is less important that the desire be satisfied than that we can meet at the seminar table and that we can desire in common with others (*OJL*, 70).[40] When approached through the midrashic tradition, the biblical narratives teach us how to read carefully, critically, and sensitively. Is this not the kind of literacy that we want from students who we hope will participate in the democratic process and, quite frankly, who will participate in the social structure? Is this not the kind of attention that we hope will translate into a responsibility for other people? Would it not be even more advantageous to teach our students that religious texts ask us to read them not only with sensitivity and respect but also with a critical eye? The community of inquiry that Dewey promotes points us in the right direction. His idea was to encourage a community of learners who would practice democracy by participating in the very act of learning and who would each be responsible for the Other. But if, as Levinas suggests, politics is derived from ethics, then it is the Jewish tradition from which Levinas's own ethical/philosophical project emerges that provides us with a more effective pedagogical model that encourages us first to engage with each other face to face.

Levinas situates Jewish education as that which *simultaneously* inflames the mind and cultivates an ethical subject who is responsible for the Other. That is, Jewish education is not anti-intellectual, nor does it simply rely on the intellect to cultivate an ethical subject. The aim, then, of Levinas's philosophical project is to employ an educational method that is informed by his understanding of Jewish education as that which cultivates intellectual acuity and also develops responsibility for the Other. His view of the ethical relation not only points to an educational model that includes reading biblical narratives Jewishly; it also relies on this model of education to cultivate an ethical subject. Levinas's insight reveals the role that alterity plays in midrash, since the role of midrash is to open up the text and allow voices that are otherwise muted to be heard. Thus, for Levinas, reading Jewishly is precisely to read such that one is open to the Other. Although the process of questioning that we find in the talmudic tradition is intended to teach students to question the material at hand, the Jewish tradition of learning recognizes something unique about the journey one takes in the educational process—it reveals an approach to education that is less concerned with the notion of absolute truth. Instead, its role is to engage the mind and to join the learners in a community of education. It might be that this role is what philosophy always intended—that philosophy was concerned less with a single truth than it was about identifying wisdom by inflaming the creative mind, and that this kind of learning was to be done communally. Unfortunately, this view is not the standard view of philosophy or of education.[41]

The talmudic model of learning outlined above radically challenges the model we find throughout the history of philosophy. It not only resists an absolute truth, it also explicitly teaches this resistance. This point draws the rabbinic model closer to one that Nietzsche might have envisioned. In both cases, the context for teaching would be an opposition to many of the values we find in modernity. These values emerge out of an extreme liberalism that cannot offer a positive vision for the cultivation of humanity but only a view of individuals as free to make choices on their own, and a society that is engineered to guarantee the widest range of these freedoms. Both Nietzsche and the talmudic rabbis would agree that, left to their own devices, people, though free, frequently do not make good choices, or even choices that would best serve themselves. Freedom, while an important value, cannot be the overriding value that determines how individuals are cultivated. Both Nietzsche and the talmudic rabbis have a vision of how to refashion human beings. However, this is the point at which Nietzsche and the talmudic rabbis would part company.

For Nietzsche, "community" is negotiable. Although Zarathustra rejects the life of the hermit, it seems clear that most of his teachings reflect a view of humanity that is at least suspicious of dependence if it is anything other than propadeutic, or temporary. He cannot envision dependence on others as healthy or positive. By contrast, for the talmudic rabbis, the context of the Jewish community, and the larger community in which they live, is non-negotiable. The community is what drives the entire talmudic project in its positive vision of cultivating humanity. What the talmudic rabbis discovered and exploited is the way that individuals not only contribute destructively to relationships, but also positively. Healthy competition, vulnerability and dependence, erotic desire in learning fundamentally drive healthy human relationships. For the rabbis, these are not simply "facts of life," though they are that. They are also what it means to be human. Like Nietzsche, the Jews do not deny their animal nature, nor do they deny the unhealthy tendencies that can accompany that nature. Instead, the talmudic tradition is geared precisely toward constructing a community that takes all of these elements of human life into account.[42]

Levinas demonstrates in *On Escape* that the seductive call of freedom presented to us by modern philosophy is a mythology.[43] First and foremost, our bodies require food, nurturance, and warmth. Our bodies betray us. Levinas's ethics, the response to the Other, which recognizes the possibility of sacrificing one's life for the Other, is prior to any sense of freedom or choice. And here he sees the mythology of freedom in the same way that he sees the mythology of autonomy. Even before the call of the Other, before any ethical response, we are not free. We can see, then, how a pedagogical model of education based on a view of learning that emerges from the Jewish tradition would be founded. And we can see that unless one is willing to step out of the tradition set forth by modern philosophy, and step out of it radically, this kind of pedagogy might not reveal itself. Levinas's implicit identification of the talmudic approach to learning not only radicalizes his philosophical project. It also transforms how we think about education, our understanding of both teaching and learning.[44] Education, and indeed a particular kind of education, is fundamental to the creation of the subjectivity that Levinas describes.

I do not write this naïvely. Although Levinas's essays on Jewish education speak to the Jewish community, there is no correlative in the philosophical community at whom his philosophy books are aimed. Indeed, it would run contrary to Levinas's own philosophical argument and in particular his ethical project to command such a reception. The justification he has for arguing this point to the Jewish community traces its roots back to the covenant at Sinai. It does not matter if that covenant "really" happened. What matters is that a community identifies itself in a particular way, with a particular history, and by a certain set of community practices. Levinas can appeal to the Jewish community based on the very identity they claim to have that binds them together. This justification does not transfer easily to other communities.[45] There is no comparable covenant outside of the Jewish community that binds a community in agreement with regard to how to be as people. Certainly we can talk about the differences among Jews and Jewish communities. But the covenant at Sinai is central to Judaism and this is why Levinas uses it to make his appeal. Yet, one cannot help but wonder what the point of his philosophical project is if not to persuade his readers of the need for this new subjectivity.

Levinas's goal in the essays on Jewish education is once again to call the Jewish community to be the light unto the nations, to hold itself to a higher ethical model than the community in which it exists, and hope that others will follow.

His goal in his philosophical work is to persuade his readers that there is a risk in attempting to achieve this subjectivity that is worth taking. Nonetheless, the beauty of Levinas's project lies in its approach: it is for each person who is persuaded to rear his or her child differently, to educate him or her through a different pedagogical method, and to effect change by becoming an example of the subjectivity Levinas promotes. It is for each person who reads these books and essays to decide if he or she will become part of what Levinas advocates for the Jewish community: to be a light unto the nations, to live by example, and not to be indifferent.

The turn here must be toward education, but education understood differently from the models the West has inherited from its intellectual past—it is a call to election, to be responsible for the Other. Thus, the education that will most likely fit a democratic society might not itself be democratic in practice—nor will it resemble most of the public schools we currently know. There would be more problems than I could enumerate here with regard to implementing such a system in the public schools, not the least of which would be incorporating the religious foundation, like studying Talmud, for example, to secular education. But I think it would benefit all of us to take seriously what talmudic study encourages—partnership, knowledge produced in conversation with another, a plurality of thinking, drawing out muted voices, developing a mind that can entertain complicated moral and legal problems—that can produce a multiplicity of possible ways to respond to those problems while also recognizing the issues of legal and moral justice that necessarily accompany those decisions.

Much has been made of Levinas's insistence on separating his philosophical writings and his Jewish writings. Yet even as he made this claim, he continually blurred this line by importing citations from the Hebrew texts into his philosophy and by inflecting his Jewish writings with a philosophical approach. We can see the unique and significant role of the scriptural references within Levinas's philosophical work. My claim is that the scriptural references are rhetorical, but they are not "simply" rhetorical; they are necessarily so, and they do work for Levinas that other literary vehicles cannot. Most importantly, they engage his readers such that they are invited to "read," or grapple with, the Scriptures in a manner potentially unfamiliar to them. This invitation, in turn, has the effect of turning his readers toward his texts, toward his ethical project, and toward the Other.

The question that emerges from the discussion in this book is the following: What would education look like if we rethought it in light of Levinas's concerns? How might the political be expressed? I described one possible example but it is not within the scope of this book to answer these questions completely. Indeed, that would require a book in itself. My aim here however is simply to make the point that contrary to the accusation that Levinas did not engage the political, he in fact did explore an account of political action, but it was directed at the Jewish community in terms of education. I believe his reasons for this are less a chauvinism than staying true to the points he made in his philosophical work, that it was not for him to tell others what to do, only to make the philosophical case that something needed to be done.

I argued in this book that Levinas's ethics call for, even assume, an account of education that will deliver the ethical subject he describes in his philosophical work. Recalling the previous educational models that were able to diagnose the disease but were not successful at finding a cure, I argue that insofar as Levinas describes an ethical subjectivity that runs counter to one produced by Western philosophy, so too the educational model that will cultivate such a subjectivity must also be radically different. It also must run counter to the standard models that trace their roots back to ideas that are fundamental to Western philosophy. It would seem that a comparable account of the political might also need to be found with a different set of tools.[46] Thus, in opposition to Arendt, I argue that we can find in the educational experience the roots of the political; education does not simply make the new possible, but is itself the emergence of the new. My claim, however, is that if we are not first mindful of Levinas's warnings, if the political, even as education, is not rooted in the radical ethics that he describes, we will simply leave ourselves vulnerable to becoming the perpetrators he warns against.[47]

Notes

Introduction

This introduction and parts of the book benefited from my participation in the Amherst College Copeland Colloquium on "The Future of the Humanities," where I was a Copeland Fellow during the 2011–2012 academic year. In particular, I would like to thank Jay Caplan, Jennifer Cayer, Tom Dumm, Catherine Epstein, Anne-Lise François, Maria Heim, Leah Hewitt, Premesh Lalu, Ruth Miller, Andrew Poe, Austin Sarat, Adam Sitze, Lucia Suarez, and Boris Wolfson. Additional participants included Christopher van den Berg, Daniel Conway, and Teresa Shawcross. The epigraph is from Montaigne's essay "On schoolmasters' learning," *The Complete Essays* (New York: Penguin, 2003), 159.

1. Adorno, "Education after Auschwitz," in *Critical Models: Interventions and Catchwords,* trans. Henry W. Pickford (New York: Columbia University Press), 191.

2. By indirect I mean that an obligation to one's own family could be the result of or fulfilled by our response to a risk posed to others. For example, the father's responsibility to others is fulfilled when he responds to his young son whose mind is now poisoned with hate.

3. There is the additional, but non-Levinasian point, that even if I save my own child, I could still endanger my child by not helping others in need. I say that this point is not Levinasian because it hitches saving the lives of others to the actual end of protecting my own children rather than because I have an obligation to the Other independently of what other harm or good might be an end result.

4. In his 1966 essay, "Education after Auschwitz," Theodor Adorno writes, "By [attempts to work against the repetition of Auschwitz] I also mean essentially the psychology of people who do such things. I do not believe it would help much to appeal to eternal values, at which the very people who are prone to commit such atrocities would merely shrug their shoulders. I also do not believe that enlightenment about the positive qualities possessed by persecuted minorities would be of much use. The roots must be sought in the persecutors, not in the victims who are murdered under the paltriest of pretenses. What is necessary is what I once in this respect called the turn to the subject. One must come to know the mechanisms that render people capable of such deeds, must reveal these mechanisms to them, and strive, by awakening a general awareness of those mechanisms, to prevent people from becoming so again. It is not the victims who are guilty, not even in the sophistic and caricatured sense in which still today many like to construe it. Only those who unreflectingly vented their hate and aggression upon them are guilty. One must labor against this lack of reflection, must dissuade people from striking outward without reflecting upon themselves." See Adorno, "Education after Auschwitz," 192–193.

5. Rousseau, Second Discourse, 2:36. See Rousseau, "Discourse on the Origin and Basis of Inequality Among Men," in *The Discourses and Other Early Political Writings,* ed. and trans. Victor Gourevitch (Cambridge: Cambridge Univeristy Press, 1997).

6. I call this second response the "Gated Community" option. Hermann Cohen's discussion of pity provides an interesting contrast to Rousseau's. Arguing against Spinoza's view that pity arises from the same subjective source that gives rise to envy, Cohen chastises Spinoza for not recognizing the vast chasm that exists between the two. He believes that Spinoza, and others, can only make this mistake if they do not recognize social suffering and only think of suffering as unique to the individual.

7. See, for example, John Stuart Mill's *The Subjection of Women*, which argues that education is the primary cause for women's subordination to men. It is not enough that women are kept in an inferior position to men—socially, personally, and politically; through the educational process, they are taught that being a woman is to like the position in which they find themselves. It is not that Mill provides an educational model; rather, he argues that education is responsible for shaping who we are and how we see ourselves as political subjects. Writing almost one hundred years earlier and influenced by Locke's view that young children can reason at an early age, and responding to figures like Rousseau who would deny women any serious education, the eighteenth-century philosopher Mary Wollstonecraft argues in her *Vindication of the Rights of Women* that we need to reshape the way we educate young girls and women to position them in society in a manner commensurate with their abilities, which are substantially greater than what has been granted them.

8. In a recent essay, Philip Kitcher comments on the history and consequences of this approach to the discipline of philosophy, charging professional philosophers with succumbing to a kind of scholasticism, and thus asks if they wonder why the academy and the general public see philosophy as not even in the ivory tower but rather engaging in the worst kind of obscure self-indulgence. Kitcher asks philosophers to reexamine the boundaries and definition of their discipline. He calls for a pragmatic turn in philosophy, which would take place at the "core" of those subfields that have typically been viewed on the "periphery," e.g., feminist philosophy, philosophy of race, environmental philosophy. I would add to his point that the philosophical tradition known as "continental philosophy," while also guilty of maintaining a pecking order and trading in obscurity, is also subject to the pecking order of what has become the dominant philosophical tradition. Additionally, continental philosophy, though it also does not take feminist philosophy or environmental philosophy as seriously as it could, does a better job of integrating these themes into its central discussions. Moreover, continental philosophy continues to stay true to its roots, interrogating and describing our lived experience, calling into question and reexamining those fields, including philosophy, that try to tell us what it means to be human. See Kitcher, "Philosophy Inside Out," *Metaphilosophy* 42, no. 3 (April 2011): 248–260.

9. Although schools had been mandated since the seventeenth century, the nineteenth century actually saw state funding for public schools for the first time. We see this in Massachusetts with the influence of Horace Mann and the Common Schools.

10. There are of course exceptions to this claim: the classical American philosophers, as I mentioned previously, and some European thinkers, e.g., Adorno, Bergson, Levinas, and Merleau-Ponty, to list only a few.

11. My point here is not to homogenize the humanities and claim they are all the same. Nor do I wish to claim that various disciplines in the humanities, e.g., religious studies, or even philosophy have not called into question this narrative advanced by European philosophy or this subjectivity that Levinas also questions. My point rather

is that this story widely influences Western education, particularly in the United States, and thus informs the way we understand and approach moral development. My thanks to Maria Heim for her question to me that indicated I needed to clarify this point.

12. Levinas indicates in several places that money is neither good nor bad, but rather we can view it as something that allows for or enables us to provide for others.

13. Steven Pinker's recent book, *The Better Angels of our Nature: Why Violence has Declined,* argues that from a statistical point of view, overall violence has decreased, and we currently live in a time which has the least violence the world has ever seen. There is much to discuss just in this claim, but what worries me about Pinker's argument is that he links a decreased rate of violence to modernity and the formation of nation-states. With this move, power and violence gradually shifted from individuals to states. Using this hypothesis, Pinker is able to explain why people in the American South are as a whole more violent than their compatriots in the North: they are less willing "to accept the state's monopoly on force" (Singer's review of Pinker). Thus, Pinker's argument begins to look like a version of Hobbes's social contract—the more power we give to the state the better off we will be. Among the concerns that I have with such an argument is that Pinker seems to ignore raw numbers and the malice associated with something like genocide, even if statistically those numbers are smaller comparatively with the population as a whole. Second, the social contract is often based on self-interest; thus it is not clear that we have decreased violence in a Levinasian sense, but simply have shifted our view about who we judge better able to deploy it from individuals to the state. And third, it is not clear that trusting the state with certain kinds of violence is a good idea—or even that it makes us less violent. Much of the cruelest violence, even if not the largest quantitatively, has been committed by the hands of the State: Stalinism, the bombs dropped on Hiroshima and Nagasaki, Nazism, South African apartheid, the genocides in Africa, and so on (see Peter Singer's review of Pinker's book in the *New York Times Book Review,* October 6, 2011). Two weeks after Singer's review, three letters to the editor were printed in the *New York Times Book Review* responding to both Singer and Pinker. All three letters make a similar point to the one I make above. In his letter, Robert Greenberg, a philosophy professor at Brandeis University, observes that Singer never mentions the *reason* violence is committed and thus he makes no distinction between the different kinds of violence, for example, violence that is cruel and might fall under the category of "evil" versus violence that is not. As a result, Singer's analysis, and if his analysis is accurate, Pinker's discussion, allow for no reason to consider the Holocaust more horrifying than Mongol conquests of the thirteenth century (letter to the editor, *The New York Times Book Review,* October 23, 2011, p. 6). The two other letters make similar points and ask both Singer and Pinker to respond to the historians and social scientists who refer to the twentieth century as "the most bellicose in human history" or "the most murderous era so far recorded in history" (cited by Peter Haidu in his letter). Indeed, when Levinas points out the violence that triggers his view that we are experiencing a crisis of humanism, the violence is almost completely state violence as we experienced it in the twentieth century.

14. And yet those who are professional philosophers are also subject to a series of jokes that imply the opposite, for example, those who work on applied ethics are not ethical, etc.

15. See Richard A. Cohen, *Ethics, Exegesis, and Philosophy: Interpretation after Levinas* (Cambridge: Cambridge University Press, 2001), 216–265. Chapter 7 of Cohen's book

focuses on Levinas's "humanism." He opens a subsection, titled "Biblical Humanism," with this statement: "Levinas—and not only Levinas—has been accused of humanism. As if this were an accusation!" He then provides an interesting reading of Levinas's humanism, by which Cohen means, "at the very least, a pragmatic and fundamental respect for the dignity and worth of each and every human being *qua* human being—is [humanism] not rather a great human good, and hence indirectly also a great *religious* good?" (218). Cohen's definition is certainly not controversial but he does add that for Levinas, humanism takes on a different meaning, one that is precisely positioned against the way it emerges from modernity. He writes, "For Levinas, humanism, respect for the human *qua* human, does not derive from or remain limited to some Greek or Renaissance or Enlightenment 'definition' of the human being: 'rational animal,' 'worker,' 'artist,' '*homo sapiens*,' '*homo politicus*,' 'language user.' Rather, more deeply it recalls and animates a central biblical teaching, the idea—and not *merely* an idea—that each and every human being, regardless of differences in wealth, power, talent, position or status, is 'created' in the 'image and likeness of God'" (219).

16. The novel *Sophie's Choice* comes to mind when thinking about the point Levinas makes. Sophie was given a choice that was not really a choice: choose one child to live (by implication, choose one child to die) or they will both be killed. She cannot help but feel herself responsible for the death of the other child even though in a sense, this choice was taken out of her hands. The mere posing of the "choice" brings into relief that saving one child, not having both children killed, does not relieve her of a responsibility that is seemingly not really in her control.

17. There is a similar argument made with regard to a crude utilitarianism—there is value in saving someone's life simply to continue torturing the person or for them to continue as a slave. Thus, the claim that the Other simply "makes my having a world possible" does not in itself yield an ethical responsibility for the Other, or even if it did, it could be a responsibility to save that person because I stand in a master relation to that person as a slave.

18. It is difficult not to sense a critique of Heidegger lurking in the background. Indeed, Heidegger seems to haunt much of Levinas's writings on humanism. Yet, this response is overdetermined. Insofar as Levinas also believes that Heidegger's philosophy runs counter to what he calls the message of the Hebrew Bible, namely a message of ethics and response to the other, then Levinas's invocation of humanism is both a critique of Heidegger and also a positive formulation.

19. My thanks to Boris Wolfson and Jennifer Cayer for their helpful suggestions on this point.

20. Indeed, he makes this point as early as 1935 in his essay "L'inspiration religieuse de l'Alliance," *Paix et Droit* 15, no. 8 (October 1935): 4. He indicates that assimilation was a problem both for Jews and for the communities they tried to join. For the Jews, this was a sign of betrayal; for those who would be anti-Semites, it was hypocrisy. Levinas makes the point again nearly forty years later when he says that assimilation did not smooth over anti-Semitism; instead, it might have fueled it. But he also argues that in spite of itself, the Alliance has a religious mandate that underlies it—and it needs to recall that religious dimension. Since Christianity has co-opted the Hebrew Bible, including its Jewish prophets, the moral mission of Judaism appears to have come to an end. Thus, it needs to find meaning in its religious dimension—what he describes later as that

which makes Judaism unique. Assimilation was too easy a solution and in fact it failed. The ghetto, or at least the memory of the ghetto, remains even in the diaspora.

21. My claim here is not that no philosopher prior to Levinas thought that parents needed to be responsible for or to their children. Rather, the educational models that are presented through European modernity replicate the ideals of modernity. Thus, for example, the education advanced by John Locke in *Some Thoughts Concerning Education*, although demonstrating a tutor's responsibility for a student (indeed, even a father's responsibility for his child), nonetheless sponsors an education that corresponds to the kind of subjectivity Locke advanced in the seventeenth century. In this case, the education was befitting a gentleman and was nowhere near as radical with regard to moral development as the subjectivity that Levinas suggests in his essays on Jewish education. My thanks to Adam Sitze for pushing me on this point.

22. Although his ethical project is often applied to the field of teaching, both in the primary grades and in the university, very little work has been done on Levinas's own ideas about education and its relationship to his philosophical project. The one notable exception is Annette Aronowicz, who wrote several essays mapping Levinas's work to his other writings on Judaism, most specifically his talmudic lectures. See, for example, Aronowicz, "Jewish Education in the Thought of Emmanuel Levinas," in *Research Perspectives on Jewish Education,* ed. Yisrael Rich and Michael Rosenak (Freund and Bar-Ilan University, 1999). Another version of this essay was published in French: Aronowicz, "L'éducation juive dans la pensée d'Emmanuel Levinas," *Pardes* no. 26 (1999): 195–210. For work that applies Levinas's project to education, see Sharon Todd, *Learning from the Other* (Albany: State University of New York Press, 2003); Denise Egea-Kuehne, *Levinas and Education* (London: Routledge, 2008); Paul Standish, "Education for Grownups, a Religion for Adults: Scepticism and Alterity in Cavell and Levinas," *Ethics and Education* 2, no. 1 (2007):73–91.

23. See Howard Caygill, *Levinas and the Political* (London: Routledge 2002), 8–15; Vicki Caron, "The 'Jewish Question' from Dreyfus to Vichy," in *French History Since Napolean,* ed. Martin S. Alexander (New York: Oxford University Press, 1999), 172–202; Emile Zola, *The Dreyfus Affair: 'J'accuse' and Other Writings,* ed. Alain Pagès, trans. Eleanor Levieux (New Haven, CT: Yale University Press, 1996).

24. Although the influence of Hermann Cohen's philosophy on Levinas's philosophical thought is not made explicit, it is difficult not to see at least some resonance between the two thinkers.

25. What does Levinas mean by the face? A difficult question to answer but in the negative, he indicates that he does not mean the actual face of a person. He does not mean the collection of eyes, nose, mouth, and so on. Rather, he means what the face conveys—vulnerability, openness, and mortality of the other. See *Totality and Infinity* for his early description of the face. See also the interviews with Philippe Nemo published as *Ethics and Infinity.*

26. Many have noted that Levinas's philosophical writings engage the performative dimension of what he expresses in the Jewish writings: the translation of the Hebrew into Greek. The performative dimension, then, of Levinas's own readings is transferred to his readers, who must also grapple with the stories and the lessons those stories ask us to bear in mind. Levinas refers to the relationship philosophy has to religion as "the Bible and the Greeks," and he refers to this tenuous relationship in several of his writ-

ings on Judaism. In several places, he claims that philosophy is subordinate to religion (ethical Judaism)—going so far as to claim that philosophy is the handmaiden to religion, even though he admits that biblical verse often displays a philosophical accent. His talmudic readings clearly have this philosophical accent, and it makes them unique. But the philosophy imposed on the biblical passages is often what motivates the criticism of his talmudic work by talmudic scholars. See the work of Robert Gibbs, but in particular see *Why Ethics? Signs of Responsibility* (Princeton, NJ: Princeton University Press, 2000). See also Richard A. Cohen, *Ethics, Exegesis, Philosophy* (Cambridge: Cambridge University Press, 2001).

27. When I consider the question about Levinas's ethical project and the possibility of what it might contribute to controversies that currently occupy discussions about the public schools, the most relevant one is the debate surrounding the teaching of values. My prima facie response is to say that the question is a silly one, since the schools teach, endorse, and promote values every day. For example, students are not allowed to cheat and there are serious consequences for doing so; students are expected to work together cooperatively; young students are asked to share school supplies; and fighting (at least physical violence and unacceptable language) is prohibited. These students are being taught values, even if there is no critical discussion that accompanies these lessons. To say that this is not what the school is doing is simply to be in bad faith. It is not a question, then, of whether values should be taught—they are taught. The question is which values and how do we teach them?

28. My argument takes seriously that Levinas's philosophy is phenomenological in that he describes the ethical relation and ethical subjectivity. We find an explicit statement on moral development in his essays on Jewish education where Levinas openly laments the lack of Jewish wisdom and rigorous Hebrew education in the Jewish education of the younger generations. However, to identify this account means making the necessary turn to his writings on Judaism and more significantly it means taking note of the implicit but fundamental role that education, and specifically, Jewish education, plays in the background of his philosophical project.

29. See Levinas, *Difficult Freedom*.

30. Martha Nussbaum makes this point in several of her books, most recently in *Not for Profit: Why Democracy Needs the Humanities* (Princeton, NJ: Princeton University Press, 2010).

31. In the same way that Merleau-Ponty's description of child development in his essay "The Child's Relations With Others" explains how the structures in the *Phenomenology of Perception* came to be, so too, we need an account of education to explain the subjectivity Levinas describes phenomenologically.

32. Like the rabbis of the Talmud, Levinas holds the Jewish community to a higher ethical standard than he holds those outside that community. We see him affirm this view not only in his talmudic lecture "Toward the Other," but also in several of his essays published in *Difficult Freedom*. The Jews are to be the light unto the nations but he cannot demand the same of others, even if it is hoped that they will follow. The subjectivity, the ethical obligation that is required of the community of Israel in "Toward the Other," is severe and uncompromising, but it is not expected of those who exist outside of the community of Israel. His affirmation of this rabbinic reading parallels exactly what he asks of the Jewish community and what he does not ask of others outside of it.

33. My point is not that Levinas was the first to have made such a claim—we can see resonances of his philosophy in Hermann Cohen, Moses Mendelssohn, and Franz Rosenzweig. Although there is no textual evidence that Levinas engaged Cohen's work in any sustained way, we do know that he claims to be deeply influenced by Rosenzweig's *Star of Redemption.* However, even with this relationship established, I have not found evidence that Levinas read Rosenzweig's essays on Jewish education, although Levinas appears to echo the concerns that Rosenzweig articulates in these essays. For an interesting perspective on Levinas's relationship to these modern philosophers, see Leora Batnitzky, *Leo Strauss and Emmanuel Levinas: Philosophy and the Politics of Revelation* (Cambridge: Cambridge University Press, 2007). In particular, see Batnitzky's fourth chapter, "An Irrationalist Rationalism"; see also Ephraim Meir, "Moses Mendelssohn's Jerusalem from Levinas's Perspective," in *In Proximity: Emmanuel Levinas and the 18th Century,* ed. Melvyn New (Lubbock: Texas Tech University, 2001), 243–260.

1. The Limits of the Humanities

This chapter benefited tremendously from the Association for Political Theory Virtual Reading Group in 2011, organized by Lisa Ellis and Peyton Wofford. That summer the group discussed on-line Martha Nussbaum's *Not for Profit.* The discussion was set up such that each chapter of the book was assigned to a particular scholar who posted a longish response and then the discussion was open to anyone who wanted to post a comment. I am grateful for the thoughtful, smart, eloquent posts that helped me think through my own concerns. Robert Watson's quote can be found here: "Bottom line shows humanities really do make money," Mar 23, 2010, accessed March 26, 2010 from *UCLA Today,* http://www.today.ucla.edu/portal/ut/bottom-line-shows-humanities-really-155771.aspx. A recent "report" designed to show the how the different disciplines fared economically at my current institution also demonstrated, even with its flawed methodology, that the humanities are quite the good investment for legislatures, parents, and of course the students themselves.

1. Stanley Fish, "The Last Professor," http://fish.blogs.nytimes.com/2009/01/18/the-last-professor/

2. In his remarks to the University of Texas Arts and Sciences Foundation at their 1979 meeting, the then President of the University of Texas, Austin, Peter Flawn, criticized this retrograde view of higher education, calling it a "Widget Theory of Higher Education." Standing firmly in contrast to such a view of higher education, Flawn said this:

> I stand on the reality that there is no way to measure the social benefit that derives from a cultivated mind. Even the very young mind of a recent graduate with just a few furrows broken in what may become a fertile intellectual field is a social asset of great potential worth. There is no way to measure the social benefit that comes from a first-class intelligence touching and awakening young minds in the classroom or in the laboratory or in the studio. There is no way to measure the social benefit that comes from enhancing the ability of a human being to think, and to adapt, and to function in society. There is no way in the accounting sense to put a value on knowledge and inquiry and judgment. But our inability to measure, our inability to quantify qualities, does not mean

that the value, the benefit of higher education is not real. What we produce in our colleges and universities is worth far more to society than a widget, or an individual to fill a particular job—what we produce is tomorrow's world—the people and the knowledge that in large part will shape what is to come. The Widget Theory of Higher Education, if accepted by the people, will mean that ultimately our highest form of education will be a Job Corps. But it will be cost-effective. We will be able to measure all the inputs and outputs. And, ironically, our enormous loss will not show up on any social balance sheet. History will simply record a society that came to less. (3–4) Peter Flawn, "The Widget Theory of Higher Education," http://alliancefortamu.org/op-eds-editorials/. Accessed May 13, 2012.

3. One need only look to the recent cuts made in universities across the United States and the UK, the latter including places like King's College, Cambridge, to see that this question is neither hypothetical nor simply academic, but pressing. Most recently the entire program in European Thought at Middlesex University was cut. Of importance to note is that Middlesex had been one of the older polytechnic schools that then tried to include a liberal arts education alongside of the technical one. But this experiment failed. If the board does not believe in a classical education from the beginning, they will simply see it as a valueless luxury taking up space and resources in an otherwise perfectly fine educational institution. And so the battle between technical and nontechnical education continues to rage, leaving students all the more impoverished.

4. See Fish, "A Classical Education: Back to the Future," *New York Times,* http://opinionator.blogs.nytimes.com/2010/06/07/a-classical-education-back-to-the-future/, accessed June 7, 2010, and June 22, 2010. In his essay "Deep in the Heart of Texas," published two weeks later, Fish responds to a set of "reforms" proposed by the Texas A&M Board of Regents. In response to a complaint that faculty act as though the colleges and universities belong to them, and thus criticizing that faculty write articles that seem of use only to their academic peers, Fish writes: "That is what academic research is all about: highly qualified scholars working on problems that may have no practical payoff except the unquantifiable payoff of advancing our understanding of something in philosophy or nature that has long been a mystery." See Fish, "Deep in the Heart of Texas," *New York Times,* accessed June 21, 2010. http://opinionator.blogs.nytimes.com/2010/06/21/deep-in-the-heart-of-texas/.

My point in citing this particular passage has less to do with the attack to which Fish responds—though the attack is dangerous to academia and Fish's response is spot on. Instead, my point is that Fish's position has changed over the years and where he once would argue that there is no discernible value in the humanities but the pleasure one gets from partaking in it, this current position is closer to my own—that there is value but it is not a value as we understand it in simple terms of commodity and exchange. See also Michael Bérubé, "The Science Wars Redux," *Democracy: A Journal of Ideas* 19 (Winter 2011), accessed January 6, 2011, http://www.democracyjournal.org/19/6789.php; David Brooks, "History of Dollars," *New York Times,* accessed June 7, 2010, http://www.nytimes.com/2010/06/08/opinion/08brooks.html?_r=1; Fish, "The Crisis of the Humanities Officially Arrives," *New York Times,* accessed October 7, 2010, http://opinionator.blogs.nytimes.com/2010/10/11/the-crisis-of-the-humanities-officially-arrives/; and Simon Head, "The Grim Threat to British Universities," *New York Review of Books,* accessed January

13, 2011, http://www.nybooks.com/articles/archives/2011/jan/13/grim-threat-british-universities/?pagination=false.

5. We can argue about why this is the case—e.g., that public school and higher education are accountable to different constituencies, most notably, the taxpayer who demands to see "something" for his or her money. As any educator of classical education will state, a classical education produces something that precisely cannot be seen or easily assessed.

6. "Studying Economics in College Can Influence Your Political Affiliation, Fed Study Says," *Huffington Post,* http://www.huffingtonpost.com/2010/06/07/studying-economics-in-col_n_603180.html, accessed June 21, 2010. See also Harry Brighouse, *On Education* (London: Routledge, 2006).

7. James Jarrett makes a similar point in his 1973 book *The Humanities and Humanistic Education* when he asks us to consider if there was any time when the humanities were not under siege. Indeed, going back to the inception of the humanities, we can see that they have always been viewed suspiciously. If we consider Socrates not only as a philosopher but his life as a metaphor for philosophy, we do not find a stronger image of that suspicion and fear than putting the philosopher—and philosophy—to death. The range of references in Jarrett's book is impressive, from Plato and Plutarch to Heidegger and Merleau-Ponty. It is a book worth reading, if for nothing else than a good survey of the literature at that time on the humanities. Two other interesting essays on teaching the humanities—and their crisis—are I. A. Richards, "The 'Future' of the Humanities," *The Journal of General Education* 1, no. 3 (April 1947): 232–237, and Richard McKeon, "The Nature and Teaching of the Humanities," *The Journal of General Education* 3, no. 4 (July 1949): 290–303. My thanks to Adam Sitze for these last two references.

8. Although not as far back as the nineteenth century, James Jarrett's aforementioned 1973 book *The Humanities and Humanistic Education* opens with an exploration of the crisis of the humanities—in this case, the sciences, feeling underprivileged and undervalued, were beginning to bear down on the humanities, and the criticisms of the humanities in 1973, the height of the explosion of university education, could easily be printed today without a date and no one would blink. Additionally, Jarrett's book reminds us that as academics we have nostalgia for a time when the humanities were never under siege. Each epoch sees itself as the crisis—not recognizing that there has not been a time when the humanities have ever enjoyed unfettered respect, admiration, and support.

9. Colleges of liberal arts, indeed even some particular programs (e.g., see how Women's and Gender Studies programs describe themselves), prominently display the word "leadership" in the description of the education it provides their students.

10. There is ever-growing literature on this topic. The collection *Debating Moral Education* stands out as particularly good. See Elizabeth Kiss and J. Peter Euben, eds., *Debating Moral Education: Rethinking the Role of the Modern University* (Durham, NC: Duke University Press, 2010). In particular, see the essays in that volume by Stanley Fish and Ruth W. Grant. See Fish, "I Know It When I See It: A Reply to Kiss and Euben," 76–91, and Grant, "Is Humanistic Education Humanizing?" 283–295. See also Peter Euben's essay, "Hannah Arendt on Politicizing the University and Other Clichés," in *Hannah Arendt and Education: Renewing Our Common World,* ed. Mordechai Gordon (Boulder, CO: Westview, 2001), 175–199.

11. This body of literature quite literally would extend as far back as Plato, including but not limited to his *Republic,* Plutarch and Cicero, the medievalists, and the moderns,

including Kant and Hegel through the twentieth century and into the twenty-first, where discussions about this question have yielded dangerous consequences for education at all levels but most significantly higher education where simply teaching the humanities is in jeopardy, not to mention the support for humanities research.

12. Like the prison system, which also suffers from an identity crisis resulting from aims that range from the lofty to the most expedient—is prison intended to punish, rehabilitate, or simply remove people from society?—the educational system has also taken on so many different tasks that even small communities can become deeply divided about its aims: is it to prepare children for civic engagement, learn a set of skills for job preparation, or instill a set of values to cultivate ethical people? The more cynical among us might fairly ask the additional question if the aim is to accomplish all three at once but with the express purpose of preparing people to hold particular values: to work in a capitalist economy or to be ready and willing to fight in a war.

13. Philosophy professor Michael Ruse captures the sentiment nicely when he concludes his *Chronicle of Higher Education* blog post describing his own ambivalence about German culture: "I found Die Walküre deeply satisfying and deeply troubling. And that I guess, after 60 years, is my answer to my stepmother. I find your culture deeply satisfying and deeply troubling. I am still trying to sort things out and come to adequate answers. And that ultimately is why I am so glad to be essentially a cultural and intellectual historian. *These are grown-up questions for grown-up people.* And that as [*sic*] ultimately is my answer to those Philistines at large today in our society who are so scornful and belittling of higher education and all that the universities embody" (emphasis added). "German Culture—Goethe, Wagner, Hitler?" May 15, 2011, http://chronicle.com/blogs /brainstorm/german-culture-goethe-wagner-hitler/35264. Accessed May 21, 2012.

14. For a lovely account of the history of the humanities and humanistic education, see James L. Jarrett, *The Humanities and Humanistic Education*.

15. Hannah Arendt, "The Crisis in Education," in *Between Past and Future: Eight Exercises in Political Thought* (New York: Viking Press, 1968). I have addressed Arendt's critique of progressive education in my essay "'The presence of the Other is a presence that teaches': Levinas, Pragmatism, and Pedagogy," *The Journal of Jewish Thought and Philosophy* 14, nos. 1–2 (2006): 91–108. For contemporary essays on Arendt's essay and on thinking about Arendt in relationship to questions concerning education, see Gordon, *Renewing Our Common World*. See also the work of Natasha Levinson, Aaron Schutz, and Wendy Kohli.

16. John Dewey, *Democracy and Education: An Introduction to the Philosophy of Education* (New York: Free Press, 1916).

17. Dewey, *Democracy and Education*, 359–360.

18. Ibid.

19. Ibid., 340–341. One can see the influence of Aristotle's *Nicomachean Ethics*. The *phronemos* cultivates *phronesis*, or practical wisdom, through experience—and indeed through friendship, which allows even someone who is already practically wise to gain still more insight into possible ways to act.

20. Though not as simplistic as the points I just mentioned, Kant's philosophy of education does focus more on the intellectual model than on a model that focuses on practice. See *The Metaphysics of Morals* and *On Education*.

21. John Dewey, *Philosophy of Education* (Totowa, NJ: Littlefield, Adams & Co., 1971), 34.

22. John Dewey, *Experience and Education* (New York: Collier Books, 1938).

23. See Aaron Schutz, "Is Political Action an Oxymoron? Hannah Arendt's Resistance to Public Spaces in Schools," in *Philosophy of Education 2001*, ed. Suzanne Rice (Urbana, IL: Philosophy of Education Society), 324–332; Natasha Levinson, "Hannah Arendt on the Relationship Between Education and Political Action" (a reply to Schutz), in *Philosophy of Education 2001*, 333–336; Natasha Levinson, "Beginning Again: Teaching, Natality and Social Transformation," *Philosophy of Education Yearbook*, 1996, accessed May 19, 2008: http://www.ed.uiuc.edu/eps/PES-Yearbook/96_docs/levinson.html.

24. We find elements of this ideology in contemporary models of democratic education, and indeed this point was made in response to Nussbaum's book *Not for Profit*. To promote a particular set of values, though not inherently wrong, undermines the main thrust behind a democratic society governing itself, namely, the pluralism of that society. I would be more inclined to label this model "character" or "moral" education rather than "democratic education." And here we come full circle and arrive back at our question about what education, or in this case, schooling, is intended to accomplish.

25. In a recent conversation with the parent of one of my daughter's friends, I lamented the sorry experience that my daughter was having in school. Her teachers for the previous school year had been smart, funny, and wise. A rare set of traits in anyone. This present year, her teachers seem not to exhibit any of these traits. To say that my daughter's experience in school has been frustrating would be an understatement. The other parent's response was that this was just another opportunity for rebellion, to assert one's own individual identity. I understood the point and the motivation for the response: sometimes one has to see the positive in these experiences or it becomes too easy to despair. However, my reply was that I did not think all of childhood should have to be a series of rebellions, that some places need to be safe spaces where a positive expression of oneself was allowed. One should be able to formulate a positive expression of identity, not only an expression as a negation of something else. I think that this is especially true of a child's experience in school. For this reason I am closer to Hannah Arendt's views about school than I would otherwise probably admit.

I bring up this discussion because this is precisely why the school needs to be a safe place for learning and not another site for rebellion, for having to assert one's independence, especially when the risk is simply too great. Arendt talks about the safety of the classroom precisely because she views the school—and education—as apolitical. As such, students should not be placed in a position where they are put at risk nor should they be put in a position where they must take these risks. I have disagreements with Arendt's position and I will explore those in more detail, but her claim opens up the question about the relationship that education has to the larger society in which it is situated.

26. One need look only to celebrities in our current culture to confirm Arendt's point—Brittany Spears, Lindsay Lohan, et al. Arendt herself noted the children of celebrities—though we now have celebrities who are children themselves. I can only imagine the horror that Arendt would express at the proliferation of "public" space that enables very young children to expose themselves to the entire world via the internet. If we recall the new ways that bullying now manifests itself on the internet, we can begin to understand what Arendt means by the need to protect the privacy of young children and not expose them to the political—the public space—so early in their development. For a wonderful video that explores this particular point, see: "Hannah Arendt reads

from "The Crisis in Education,'" http://www.youtube.com/watch?v=ouj5fklnzks, accessed September 25, 2011.

27. One of Arendt's arguments against turning education into a public space is that we must practice self-restraint in public or political spaces. This would have the effect of stymieing education. Here I think Arendt is a bit out of touch if she believes that children in American education do not need to practice self-restraint, independent of the question of progressive education.

28. See Aaron Schutz's lovely essay "Contesting Utopianism: Hannah Arendt and the Tensions of Democratic Education," in *Hannah Arendt and Education*, 93–125.

29. Stacy Smith offers a insightful discussion of this point in her essay "Education for Judgment: An Arendtian Oxymoron?" in *Hannah Arendt and Education*, 67–91.

30. Dewey, *Experience and Education*, 23.

31. Nonetheless, depending on how we view the nature-nurture battle, we can claim that education frees the mind in some ways while also cultivating it in others. This is the point that I believe some who promote humanities education wish to underscore. I recognize that I am painting with broad strokes. My aim is not to deliver a treatise on the history of humanities education or even modern humanism. Instead, I wish to highlight certain dominant views of subjectivity and humanism that have been appropriated, rightly or wrongly, accurately or inaccurately, by contemporary approaches to both education (here read as schooling) and moral development.

32. Scanning any number of mission or philosophy statements about a school—public, private, or independent—one finds this phrase in common: "Our curriculum is child-centered." Unless the school is teaching in the old Latin School tradition—developed long before Piaget, indeed even before Rousseau's educational treatise became influential, nearly every school is child-centered in some form or other.

33. Most recently when I was taking a walk on the track outside of my daughters' elementary school, a group of second graders emerged for recess. Apparently, they had not exited or reentered the school correctly the previous week when a substitute was in charge of the class. So they were going to be punished that day. The punishment consisted of the whole group walking around the perimeter of a hardcourt. They were to walk in a single-file line with hands clasped behind their backs and a "bubble in their mouth." The expression is used to indicate that if their cheeks are puffed as if there is a bubble in it, then they cannot talk. I continued my walk for ten more minutes and then left for home. When I left the kids were still walking. Admittedly, I was unsure about what to do. Even without having read Foucault or Althusser, I would have thought that this Stalag-type punishment seemed a bit excessive. So, they did not enter or exit the building correctly. So what? So, show them again how to do this and then let them go play. They are seven years old, after all. How many times do I forget how to do something? And what is the lesson that in the end is being taught to these kids? More obviously, public schools simply display an extraordinary number of mixed messages—kids learn to share in kindergarten only to be taught a bit later that knowledge is not shared. Property is not to be shared; in fact, it is to be guarded dearly. Kids are supposed to say they are sorry and make amends, only to learn that the goal of corporate America is to get away with not doing these things. Exactly why are these lessons taught? The public schools seem torn between teaching knowledge and teaching wisdom, and in the end I am not sure they are good at either (though without question, individual teachers are excellent at both and my daughters have been lucky enough to have them).

34. Martha Nussbaum, *Not For Profit: Why Democracy Needs the Humanities* (Princeton, NJ: Princeton University Press, 2010), 1–2.

35. Ibid., 2.

36. Ibid., 7.

37. Ibid., 29.

38. Or at least not before the age of reason, as Rousseau determines it—somewhere around twelve years of age or after.

39. I hold a Master's degree in the Philosophy for Children program. I received it in 1987 when the M.A.T. program was still quite young. I absolutely believe in this program to help students develop critical reasoning skills, a community of inquiry with their classmates, and self-esteem. Recalling the example I described in the Introduction, we need to remember that if philosophy is to be taught as philosophy and not ideology, then we must risk that students, even of this program, will not all arrive at the moral answers we believe are correct, nor can we be assured that whatever beliefs they come to, they will act on them. I find myself critical of this approach and the conclusions that Nussbaum draws, in part, because I also find them tempting.

40. For a particularly good formulation of the question and an answer, see Grant, "Is Humanistic Education Humanizing?"

41. Belot was one of the scholars who posted to the Association for Political Theory Virtual Reading Group, organized by Lisa Ellis, a political theorist at Texas A&M. Belot's post can be found here: http://aptvrg2011.blogspot.com/2011/06/chpt-4-socratic -pedagogy.html. I accessed this post Monday June 27, 2011, and again Tuesday June 28, 2011.

42. And it is precisely because of the limits of humanities education that Levinas intentionally turned to Jewish education to accomplish his task of cultivating an ethical subject.

43. Although this view is often presented as part of the ancient Greek model, I am hesitant to agree with this interpretation of Aristotle. There is enough dispute regarding interpretations of Aristotle's *Nicomachean Ethics* and even his *Politics* to claim that philosophy was simply pleasurable navel-gazing.

44. Peter Euben advances a compelling argument about the politicization of the university that reveals how the political, in an Aristotelian sense of the term, has always characterized both education and the university—unless the education has been sanitized of anything of interest to the participant. See Euben, "Hannah Arendt on Politicizing the University and Other Clichés," in *Hannah Arendt and Education,* 175–199.

45. See Louis Menand's article "Debating the Value of College in America," *The New Yorker,* accessed May 31, 2011. http://www.newyorker.com/arts/critics/atlarge/2011/06 /06/110606crat_atlarge_menand.

46. I suspect that many colleges of liberal arts suffer from bad press simply because they are called colleges of liberal arts rather than colleges of arts and letters or humanities and social science, or some other name that does not include "liberal."

47. See Max Horkheimer and Theodor Adorno, "The Concept of Enlightenment," in *The Dialectic of Enlightenment: Philosophical Fragments,* ed. Gunzelin Schmid Noerr and trans. Edmund Jephcott (Palo Alto, CA: Stanford University Press, 2002), 1–34. Most striking in this essay is the clever way that Horkheimer and Adorno expose the ideology that underlies what they call Enlightenment thinking and the manner in which it has succumbed to instrumental reason. See also Jacques Derrida, "The future of the profession

or the university without condition (thanks to the 'Humanities,' what *could take place tomorrow*)," in *Jacques Derrida and the Humanities: A Critical Reader,* ed. Tom Cohen (Cambridge: Cambridge University Press, 2002), 24–57.

48. Most recently, this article appeared in the local College Station, TX, newspaper: http://www.theeagle.com/am/Perry-views-create-a-stir.

In this article, the current governor, an alumnus of Texas A&M University, drew criticism for recent remarks that indicated he in fact knew very little about higher education, though he is responsible for policies that deeply affect the ethos of the university.

49. See Wes Davis, "The 'Learning Knights' of Bell Telephone," *New York Times,* June 15, 2010. http://www.nytimes.com/2010/06/16/opinion/16davis.html?_r=1.

50. This particular view of the humanities dates back to the development of the first Ivy League universities (e.g., Harvard and Yale) in the northern colonies of what became the United States. The original purpose of these colleges was to educate and produce clergy for their respective denominations, since it was the clergy who functioned as leaders of the community. With the exception of Dartmouth and the University of Pennsylvania, each Ivy League school corresponded to a particular Protestant denomination. Though originally training the clergy, the Ivy League schools, which initially offered only a liberal arts education, came to symbolize the educational institutions into which the best and brightest would enter and from which would emerge the most effective and creative leadership. That is, the theological dimension moved into the background—and into the divinity schools—but the view that the liberal arts trained leaders remained. It was assumed that upon receiving their degree, these graduates would enter the political arena and use their education to better American society. Not surprisingly, those who attended these universities were not always the best and the brightest when they entered. Rather, they were typically the wealthiest or the most well-connected. When they left these universities, there were not necessarily any brighter than when they entered, nor did they become the civil servants and do the public service work that had been expected of them. Instead, they became doctors, lawyers, and bankers and thereby reproduced or expanded the wealth they already possessed. For an interesting discussion on the democratization of the Ivy League universities, see Nicholas Lemann, *The Big Test: The Secret History of the American Meritocracy* (New York: Farrar, Straus and Giroux, 1999).

51. Pierre Hadot, *Philosophy as a Way of Life* (Oxford: Blackwell, 1995). For an interesting twist on Hadot's reading of Western philosophy, see Hilary Putnam, *Jewish Philosophy as a Guide to Life* (Bloomington: Indiana University Press, 2009).

52. Ibid., 265.

53. Ibid., 265–266.

54. Ibid., 266.

55. I suspect that many will be surprised by Levinas's reversal of terms.

56. The irony of course is that even modernity's humanism failed to keep the human—or at least human experience—central to the study of philosophy, hence the emergence of existentialist philosophers such as Nietzsche and Kierkegaard in the nineteenth century, and Sartre, et al., in the twentieth. We find ourselves now in the twenty-first century with the discipline of philosophy actually engaged in a battle over what counts as philosophy. It is nothing short of alarming that a tradition in philosophy that keeps the *human* experience central to its study is deemed not even philosophy by those whose philosophical interests lie elsewhere.

57. For interesting arguments about Judaism and universality, see Moses Mendels-sohn's *Jerusalem* (Part I), and Hermann Cohen, *Religion of Reason Out of the Sources of Judaism,* trans. Simon Kaplan (Atlanta: Scholars Press, 1995). See also Cohen, "Affinities Between the Philosophy of Kant and Judaism," in *Reason and Hope: Selections from the Jewish Writings of Hermann Cohen,* trans. and ed. Eva Jospe (Cincinnati: Hebrew Union College Press, 1971), 77–89.

2. Solitary Men

1. Another way of reading the development of *Émile* is Rousseau's focus on self-preservation. Hence, his insistence that the only book *Émile* should read before becoming an adult is *Robinson Crusoe.* For an interesting reading of this book in light of Levinas's philosophy, see John Llewelyn, "What is Orientation in Thinking? Facing the Facts in *Robinson Crusoe,*" in *In Proximity: Emmanuel Levinas and the 18th Century,* ed. Melvyn New (Lubbock: Texas Tech Press, 2001), 69–90.

2. Emmanuel Levinas, *Humanism of the Other,* trans. Nidra Poller (Urbana: University of Illinois Press, 2006), 45.

3. Jean-Jacques Rousseau, *The Social Contract,* trans. G. D. H. Cole. Internet/Public Domain. Rousseau's dates are 1712–1778.

4. I realize that some will see Rousseau as too late to be considered an Enlightenment thinker, but I nonetheless place him within this tradition of thought. See, for example, Zeev Sternhell, *The Anti-Enlightenment Tradition,* trans. David Maisel (New Haven, CT: Yale University Press, 2010), and Jonathan Israel, *Radical Enlightenment: Philosophy and the Making of Modernity 1650–1750* (Oxford: Oxford University Press, 2001).

5. Thomas Hobbes, *Leviathan,* chapter 13, "Of the Natural Condition of Mankind as Concerning Their Felicity and Misery," public domain: http://www.publicliterature .org/books/leviathan/1. Emphasis added.

6. Pufendorf also held this view.

7. For an interesting reading of the two different types of self-love identified by Rousseau, see Frederick Neuhouser, *Rousseau's Theodicy of Self-Love: Evil, Rationality, and the Drive for Recognition* (Oxford: Oxford University Press, 2008). For my purposes, even if Neuhouser is correct and *amour-propre* is simply a dangerous form of self-love that needs to be managed, my claim about the relationship between the educational treatise and the political one still stands.

8. Though not without restrictions or suspicion. See *The Jew in the Modern World: A Documentary History,* ed. Paul Mendes-Flohr and Jeuda Reinharz, 2nd ed. (Oxford: Oxford University Press, 1995), 114–118.

9. See Mendelssohn's *Jerusalem,* written in response to the question of Judaism and German citizenship. But also see many of Mendelssohn's letters, written in response to the edicts restricting the rights of Jews during his lifetime. Additionally, see ibid.

10. Jean-Jacques Rousseau, *Émile,* trans. Barbara Foxley (London: Everyman, 1993). Although published in the same year as his *Social Contract, Émile* was published several months later. Jonathan Israel refers to *Émile* as Rousseau's most mature statement of his thought. See Israel, *Radical Enlightenment,* 718.

11. Moses Mendelssohn makes a similar point twenty years later in a letter to August Hennings where he describes the relationship between the individual and the state, or in this case specifically, the proper development of the child and the integrity of the state.

Society needs to be structured so that the proper development of the individual can be achieved. Of course, Rousseau's project points to the circular problem: how can we have a proper state if we do not cultivate the individuals properly, thus leading him to decide that education is best done when the child is removed from society. Alexander Altmann et al., eds., *Gesammelte Schriften. Jubliäumsausgabe*, 27 vols., trans. Matt Erlin (Stuttgart, 1971–), 13:64. Cited in Matt Erlin, "Reluctant Modernism: Moses Mendelssohn's Philosophy of History," *Journal of the History of Ideas* 63, no. 1 (January 2002): 83–104.

12. There are a number of books by feminist theorists that chart the defining traits of what it means to be human in terms of male and female. See, for example, Genevieve Lloyd, *The Man of Reason: "Male" and "Female" in Western Philosophy* (London: Routledge, 1993); Simone de Beauvoir, *The Second Sex,* trans. Constance Borde and Sheila Malovany-Chevalier (New York: Vintage, 2011); Carol Gilligan, *In a Different Voice: Psychological Theory and Women's Development* (Cambridge, MA: Harvard University Press, 1993).

13. It is significant that this view of gendered behavior and the definition of human subjectivity that emerged from it characterized much of modernity and influenced the status of women within European—and North American—culture. If being a human subject, now read as a political subject, is defined by one's rationality, independence, and autonomy, and if this view in turn is connected to a particular gender, then by default women cannot be viewed as political subjects. Thus, in turn, rather than trying to redefine how the human subject should be defined, much of the response to this view was to demonstrate that women could be just like men.

14. Rousseau, *Émile,* 5.

15. This time period unsurprisingly saw the rise of questions about women's inequality, just as questions about natural law and equality among men were also being discussed. The audience for this book could be men, but Rousseau could also be speaking to those women, particularly those with some education, who were beginning to question certain assumptions about men, and women whom Rousseau himself still clung to. See for example, Mary Wollstonecraft's 1792 treatise, *A Vindication of the Rights of Women* (London: Penguin, 1982).

16. Matt Erlin's superb essay "Reluctant Modernism: Moses Mendelssohn's Philosophy of History" illustrates the tension between Mendelssohn and Lessing precisely on the question of historical progress. The essay includes a nice discussion of Mendelssohn's critique of Rousseau's view of the role of sociality in human development as Rousseau articulates this view in *The Discourse on Inequality.* Erlin, "Reluctant Modernism," 83–104.

17. Certainly this is not the first time a philosophical treatise encounters the problem of origins. We also find this in Plato's *Republic* and Aristotle's *Nicomachean Ethics.*

18. Rousseau, *Émile,* 393.

19. Ibid., 387.

20. Mary Wollstonecraft uses this point to undo Rousseau's argument. Woman, or Sophie, must be an independent thinker, indeed a thinker capable of reason, in order to fulfill the task that he has assigned to her. Thus, in his zeal to make woman the male's "caretaker" because she lacks intellectual traits that he has, Rousseau inadvertently ascribes characteristics to her that at the very least would warrant her equality. See *A Vindication of the Rights of Women.*

21. See Claire Elise Katz, *Levinas, Judaism, and the Feminine: The Silent Footsteps of Rebecca* (Bloomington: Indiana University Press, 2003).

22. Roussaeu, *Émile*, 532.

23. Ibid., 533.

24. See Rousseau, *Émile et Sophie ou Les Solitaires* (Paris: Rivages poche Petite Bibliothèque, 1994). The sequel to *Émile*, this story follows Émile and Sophie to Paris. The tragic ending of the story indicates that neither Émile nor Sophie, nor the two of them as a couple, can function without the presence of the tutor. When Sophie is grieving the loss of their daughter, Émile is unable to console her. He takes her to Paris because he believes she needs the distractions of the city. Émile, however, is corrupted by the temptations of the city. He is not only unable to respond adequately to Sophie's need for an intimate relationship with another person, but he also turns his attentions to women outside of his marriage. Rejected and hurt, Sophie must also turn to another to allay her grief. The story continues to its sad ending—Sophie becomes pregnant by another man and Émile must eventually abandon her. One wonders if the tutor has been successful; one also wonders if Rousseau realizes the failure of his own educational project. See Susan Moller Okin, "The Fate of Rousseau's Heroines," in *Feminist Interpretations of Jean-Jacques Rousseau* (University Park: Pennsylvania State University Press, 2002), 92–93.

25. Emmanuel Levinas's conception of ethical subjectivity emphasizes an obligation that is not chosen and from which we cannot recuse ourselves. It emphasizes our obligation and response to the Other that cannot be discussed in terms of failure—we are already obligated. But in spite of this claim, certainly it is the case that this obligation to others is violated, betrayed, and ignored. In other words, we often fail in our response to the Other. Additionally, it is not clear how this response occurs or why it fails. I suggest that Levinas's philosophical project needs to be supplemented by a discussion of how to cultivate this response. I thus turn to themes in education and schooling, in particular. If Levinas's view of subjectivity is "universal," that is, if it applies to everyone, and if this conception of response can be or needs to be cultivated, then we need a conception of that cultivation that is also universally applicable.

26. My claim here is not that this is an accurate reading of Socrates, but it is the one that is carried through to contemporary readings of him as a figure in Plato's dialogues.

27. For an expanded discussion on the role of this phrase in both Plato and contemporary education, see my essay "Teaching our Children Well: Pedagogy, Religion, and the Future of Philosophy," *Cross Currents* 53, no. 4 (Winter 2004), 530–547.

28. See Bettina Bergo and Jill Stauffer, *Nietzsche and Levinas: After the Death of a Certain God* (New York: Columbia University Press, 2008).

29. Martin Heidegger, "Who is Nietzsche's Zarathustra," in *The New Nietzsche*, ed. David Allison (Boston: MIT Press, 1985), 64–79.

30. Friedrich Nietzsche, "Thus Spoke Zarathustra," in *The Portable Nietzsche*, trans. Walter Kaufmann (New York: Penguin Press, 1977) , 103–449. TZ100.

31. This view is supported by Gilles Deleuze's reading of Zarathustra in *Nietzsche and Philosophy*, trans. Hugh Tomlinson (New York: Columbia University Press, 1962). *Nietzsche et la philosophie* (Paris: PUF). Hereafter cited by the English and the French page number unless otherwise specified.

32. Deleuze, *Nietzsche and Philosophy*, 146 (not in the French version).

33. Ibid., 172/198.

34. See Daniel Conway, "Nietzsche *contra* Nietzsche: The Deconstruction of Nietzsche," in *Nietzsche as Postmodernist,* ed. Clayton Koelb (Albany: State University of New York Press, 1990), 91–110, 304–311.

35. Ibid., 95.

36. See for example, Nietzsche, "Homer's Contest," in *The Portable Nietzsche.*

37. Nietzsche, "The Antichrist" 25, in *The Portable Nietzsche.*

38. For more on this "ambivalence," see Yirmiyahu Yovel, *Dark Riddle: Hegel, Nietzsche, and the Jews* (University Park: Pennsylvania University Press, 1998). In particular, see pages 145–148. In this discussion, Yovel asserts that Nietzsche is clear—all ambivalence is gone and Nietzsche "decries" the priestly period just as he decried anti-Semitism and Christianity (145). However, even here we see a more complex ambivalence. For Nietzsche, the Jews of the Diaspora are the "promise" of the cure for Christianity. While Nietzsche blames the Jews—precisely for bringing Christianity into being—it is the Jews of the modern period who he believes can cure modernity of its ills. Thus, the children are to cure what the ancestors wrought. My intent here is not to solve the problem of Nietzsche's ambivalence, or his attitude toward the Jews. Rather, I call attention to it and ask us to think about the ways in which Nietzsche remained trapped within the very system he hoped to escape.

39. Although Judaism recognizes dietary restrictions and rules governing sexual activity, the enjoyment of both food and sexuality for its own sake is neither prohibited nor frowned upon. Admittedly, there are conflicting rabbinic views on sexual activity—to be sure, Judaism is not monolithic. Nonetheless the canon explicitly maintains the minority views precisely to indicate the nuances of Jewish tradition.

40. See Claire Elise Katz, "Teaching the Other: Levinas, Rousseau and the Question of Education," *Philosophy Today* 49, no. 2 (Summer 2005): 200–207; Claire Elise Katz, "Educating the Solitary Man: Dependence and Vulnerability in Levinas and Rousseau," *Levinas Studies: An Annual Review,* vol. 2 (Pittsburgh: Duquesne University Press, 2007), 133–152.

41. Bonnie Honig, *Emergency Politics: Paradox, Law, Democracy* (Princeton, NJ: Princeton University Press, 2009).

42. Levinas refers to the talmudic and midrashic rabbis as "doctors." See various references in *Difficult Freedom,* trans. Seán Hand (Baltimore, MD: Johns Hopkins University Press, 1990).

3. The Crisis of Humanism

1. Martin Buber, "Biblical Humanism," in *On the Bible: Eighteen Studies,* trans. Nahum N. Glatzer (Syracuse, NY: Syracuse University Press, 2000), 211–216.

2. Ibid., 212.

3. Ibid., 212–213.

4. The original site of the ENIO. It later moved to Rue la Bruyère.

5. *"La réouverture de l'Ecole Normale Israélite Orientale," Cahiers l'Alliance Israélite Universelle,* no. 9 (July 1946): 1–2. All translations from this essay are mine; emphasis added.

6. Emmanuel Levinas, *Humanism of the Other,* trans. Nidra Poller (Urbana and Chicago: University of Illinois Press, 2006). Originally published in French as *Humanisme*

de l'Autre Homme (Montpellier: Fata Morgana, 1972). The individual essays collected in *Humanisme de l'Autre Homme* were originally published as follows: "La Signification et le Sens," *Revue de métaphysicque et de morale*, 1964; "Humaism et an-archie," *Revue international de philosophie*, 1968; "Sans identité," *L'Éphémère*, 1970.

7. For an interesting context in which to place Levinas's essay on Hitlerism, see Joëlle Hansel, "Paganisme et 'philosophie de l'hitlérisme," *Cités: Philosophie, Politique, Histoire* 25 (2006): 25–29.

8. In July 2003, I participated in the 2003 *Collegium Phaenomenologicum*, where Robert Bernasconi gave a fascinating week-long course on Levinas. The question concerning the primacy of transcendence vs. the primacy of ethics emerged from his course. The question is certainly warranted. However, this chapter will explore the possibility that Levinas's initial concern with transcendence does not oppose his concern with ethics. Rather, he saw the problem of immanence and transcendence *as* an ethical concern.

9. A similar theme is explored in more detail in *De l'evasion*, published in 1935, just one year after the "Hitlerism" essay. See the recent English translation, *On Escape*, trans. Bettina Bergo (Palo Alto, CA: Stanford University Press, 2002).

10. "Ethics" is alluded to in *Existence and Existents* and in *Time and the Other*, where Levinas conceives of time as a social relation. And he uses the term "ethics" in his essay "Ethics and Spirit," published in the 1950s. However, this term does not appear in his philosophical work until much later.

11. Emmanuel Levinas, "Some Reflections on the Philosophy of Hitlerism," trans. Seán Hand, *Critical Inquiry* 17 (Autumn 1990): 63–71. Originally published as "Quelques Réflexions sur la Philosophie de L'Hitlérisme," *Esprit* 2 (1934): 199–208. For an illuminating discussion of this essay, see Stefanos Geroulanos, *An atheism that is not humanist emerges in French thought* (Stanford, CA: Stanford University Press, 2010).

12. Levinas, "Some Reflections on the Philosophy of Hitlerism," 71 ("Quelques Réflexions sur la Philosophie de L'Hitlérisme," 208).

13. Levinas wrote this essay only five years after attending the 1929 Davos debate between Heidegger and Cassirer. It is thought that Heidegger "won" the debate—though that declaration has come to mean many things, ranging from his position being more persuasive at showing the problems in Cassirer's view to being the philosophy that was the most influential. Certainly, we can say the latter is true, and yet, much of Levinas's essays indicate that he laments this outcome. Although he did not think Cassirer's humanism went far enough, he came to see that Heidegger's anti-humanism was far more dangerous. For an excellent, nearly line-by-line analysis of the Davos debate, see Peter Gordon, *Continental Divide: Heidegger, Cassirer, Davos* (Cambridge, MA: Harvard University Press, 2010).

14. As I mentioned, he continues this discussion in *On Escape*. However, he does not arrive at the solution.

15. The agreements the Church made when Hitler came to power betray it and the political forces that work on it. See Susannah Heschel, *The Aryan Jesus: Christian Theologians and the Bible in Nazi Germany* (Princeton, NJ: Princeton University Press, 2008).

16. Similar to the argument Horkheimer and Adorno make regarding the residue of myth in Enlightenment. See Theodor Adorno and Max Horkheimer, *The Dialectic of Enlightenment: Philosophical Fragments* (1947), ed. G. S. Noerr, trans. E. Jephcott (Stanford, CA: Stanford University Press, 2002).

17. For an illuminating discussion of this essay see Martin Kavka's analysis of it in his essay co-authored with David Kangas, "Hearing, Patiently: Time and Salvation in Kierkegaard and Levinas," in *Kierkegaard and Levinas: Ethics, Politics and Religion,* ed. Aaron Simmons and David Wood (Bloomington: Indiana University Press, 2008), 125–152. Kavka writes, "While Hitlerism is opposed to liberalism insofar as they have opposing hierarchies of the mind/body relation, they are mirrors of each other insofar as they are both monist ways of looking at the world. Levinas' task, then, is to develop a mode of thinking that takes account both of the embodied nature of human selfhood and of the 'escape from self' that both Christianity and liberalism promise but cannot fulfill. He wants both metaphysics and historicity, yet, there is nothing in Levinas' breakneck tour through the history of Western philosophy in this essay that makes such a double affirmation possible. Nowhere in this early essay does Levinas pose a philosophical answer to the problem of how to reclaim the liberal world after the turn to materialism, a turn which was justified under the weight of all existence (UH, 40/20)—by the inability to free oneself from being determined by one's body and one's history—then no individual has the strength to lessen his own burden, and no other individual has the strength that would enable her to come to his rescue. Levinas ends this essay by saying that racism 'is contrary to the very humanity of humankind' (UH, 41/21), but this contest is one in which liberal and Christian humanism seem to be losing to Hitlerism because there has been no account of humanism which could out-think Hitlerism on the issue of the body, its philosophical trump card" (140).

18. What is less apparent in this essay is Levinas's view that at the root of liberalism, indeed at the root of secularity, is in fact a religious structure that those tethered to the non-religious refuse to acknowledge. Levinas makes this point more strongly and more explicitly in his essays on Judaism. Not surprisingly, the point appears in those essays because it is in the attempts to live a Jewish life that one feels the pull of assimilation and the resistance of the larger population—i.e., the state. Paul Kahn brilliantly makes a similar point when he observes, "[Modern liberalism] is the replication of the two sides of our Christian inheritance: separation and empire." And he continues with this striking accusation: "Failure to recognize the quasi-religious character of the modern nation-state as the context within which liberalism operates is the single largest failure of liberal political theorists. Reading them, one would never know that the modern nation-state has been the site of endless passion and of sacrifice for ultimate meanings . . . In one direction, liberalism traces its origins to the separation of religion and state; in the other direction, liberalism understands itself as situated within a state that is itself a successor to the church. . . ." Paul Kahn, *Putting Liberalism in its Place* (Princeton, NJ: Princeton University Press, 2005), 93.

19. Levinas makes a similar point in "L'inspiration religieuse de l'Alliance," published in the same year that he publishes *On Escape*. Blending themes from both the essay on "Hitlerism" and *On Escape,* Levinas refers to Hitlerism as an incomparable event that Judaism must cross. The moral and physical challenges that Hitlerism presents go straight to the very core of Judaism. Additionally, Hitlerism presented an anti-Semitism of a different kind, one in which the plight of simply being Jewish became a fatality. "The Jew cannot escape being Jewish. The Jew is ineluctably riveted [*rivé*] to his Judaism." See Levinas, "L'inspiration religieuse de l'Alliance," *Paix et Droit* 15, no. 8 (October 1935): 4 (translations are mine). Thus, it is interesting to note that while Levinas describes "being

enchained" or riveted more generally—or as part of the general human condition—he makes a specific point about the Jew being "enchained" or "riveted" to his Judaism as a result of Hitler's version of anti-Semitism, which tied Judaism to a race.

20. Levinas, *On Escape*, trans. Bettina Bergo (Palo Alto, CA: Stanford University Press, 2003).

21. One could easily characterize the Jewish religion as making the everyday sacred, or hallowing the everyday. For example, the laws of *kashrut* and the observance of the Sabbath are examples of how immanence is brought together with transcendence, how daily practice is made sacred. Abraham Joshua Heschel's *The Sabbath* is specifically about how the meaning of the Sabbath is found in the transcending of time.

22. I am reminded here of Levinas's criticism of Buber's I-Thou relation as too ethereal, too spiritual. He says, "Misery and poverty are not properties of the Other, but the modes of his or her appearing to me, way of concerning me, and mode of proximity. One may wonder whether clothing the naked and feeding the hungry do not bring us closer to the neighbor than the rarefied atmosphere in which Buber's Meeting sometimes takes place . . . Before the face of God one must not go with empty hands" (*Outside the Subject*, 1993, 18–19 / *Hors Sujet*, 31). This essay was first published in French in 1968, although a similar view was published in 1965. I realize that this view appears thirty years after Levinas first approaches this philosophical problem, but the ideas are not discontinuous from what we see first concerning him in 1934. More recently, Judith Butler made the following statement when she spoke at Occupy Wall Street: "It matters that as bodies we arrive together in public. As bodies we suffer, we require food and shelter, and as bodies we require one another in dependency and desire. So this is a politics of the public body, the requirements of the body, its movement and its force." Cited from: http://flexner.blogs.brynmawr.edu/2011/10/27/the-only-place-for-women-in-the-movement-is-%E2%80%98prone%E2%80%99–2/, accessed November 6, 2011. Original source can be found here: http://www.youtube.com/watch?v=rYfLZsb9by4.

23. This point is famously made in one of Levinas's epigraphs to *Otherwise than Being*. Yet, it appears that this structure of violence and hatred is found much earlier in Levinas's writings.

24. See also Adorno/Horkheimer, *The Dialectic of Enlightenment*.

25. Levinas, "L'actualité de Maïmonide," *Paix et Droit*, no. 4 (1935): 6–7. Translations are mine unless otherwise noted.

26. Levinas, *Difficult Freedom*, trans. Seán Hand (Baltimore, MD: Johns Hopkins University Press, 1990). *Difficile liberté* (Paris: Albin Michel, 1976).

27. *DF*, 236. Unfortunately, Hegel's characterization of the Jews has influenced not only non-Jews but also Jews themselves. For more on anti-Semitism in both Hegel and Nietzsche see Yirmiyahu Yovel, *Dark Riddle: Hegel, Nietzsche, and the Jews* (University Park: Pennsylvania State University Press, 1998).

28. See Moses Mendelssohn, "Open Letter to Deacon Lavater of Zurich," Moses Mendelssohn, "Reply to Johann Caspar Lavater (1769)," in *German History in Documents and Images: Volume 2 From Absolutism to Napoleon, 1648–1815*, trans. Richard Levy. Source of original German text: Moses Mendelsohn, *Gesammelte Schriften, Jubiläumsausgabe* [*Collected Writings. Anniversary Edition*], ed. I. Elbogen, J. Guttmann, and E. Mittwoch (Berlin: Akademie-Verlag, 1930), 7–17. General website: http://germanhistorydocs.ghi-dc.org/Index.cfm?language=english. Website to document: http://germanhistorydocs

.ghi-dc.org/sub_doclist_s.cfm?s_sub_id=28&sub_id=329&section_id=8. Accessed April 2, 2012.

29. Levinas, *On Escape,* trans. Bettina Bergo (Stanford, CA: Stanford University Press, 2003), 50. Published in French as *De l'évasion* (Montpellier: Fata Morgana 1982), 91.

30. When thinking about Rousseau's *Émile,* it is difficult not to think about one's own practical experience with children. Levinas's insight here could not ring more true. I can think of only too many conversations with my elder daughter when she was five years old. These conversations began with her complaint that she does not like the rules (as few as there are!) and that she does not have to listen to us. Instead, she tells us, she's going to live in the wild (her exact words). Images of Itard's *The Wild Child* abound. So, we remind her that she will have to find food, clothing, and that there are no soft beds in the wild. Although her first inclination is to want to say "so what?" she gets the point— thus providing her with a different sense of who we are as parents—our position, while also one of making rules, affords her a certain freedom insofar as we provide her with clothes, food, and shelter, not to mention love, warmth, and fun—and safety.

31. Levinas is clearly not the first Jewish thinker to reveal this ambivalence, or to situate himself between the poles of particularity and universality, between Judaism and the Enlightenment—see Matt Erlin, "Reluctant Modernism: Moses Mendelssohn's Philosophy of History," *Journal of the History of Ideas* 63, no. 1 (January 2002): 83–104. See also the work of Leora Batnitzky.

32. See Levinas, *Time and the Other,* trans. Richard Cohen (Pittsburgh: Duquesne University Press, 1987), originally published as *Le Temps et l'autre* (Montpellier: Fata Morgana, 1979; 1st ed. 1947); and *Totality and Infinity,* trans. Alphonso Lingis (Pittsburgh: Duquesne University Press, 1969), originally published as *Totalité et infini: Essai sur l'exteriorité* (The Hague: Martinus Nijohff, 1971; 1st ed. 1961). See also Claire Elise Katz, *Levinas, Judaism, and the Feminine: The Silent Footsteps of Rebecca* (Bloomington: Indiana University Press, 2003).

33. See Levinas, *Otherwise than Being; or, Beyond Essence,* trans. Alphonso Lingis (The Hague: Martinus Nijhoff, 1981). Originally published as *Autrement qu'être, ou, Au-delà de l'essence* (Dordrecht: Martinus Nijhoff, 1974).

34. See *OB,* 67. Translation altered: "Psychisme comme un corps maternel" (*AE,* 107).

35. Levinas, "The Transcendence of Words: On Michel Leiris's *Biffures,*" in *Outside the Subject,* trans. Michael B. Smith (Palo Alto, CA: Stanford University Press, 1993), 144–150. First published in French in *Les Temps Moderns* 44 (1949): 1090–1095. Reprinted as "La Transcendance des Mosts. À propos des biffures," in *Hors Sujet* (Fata Morgana, 1987), 195–204.

36. *OS,* 148.

37. Levinas, "The Transcendence of Words," 148/201.

38. Seán Hand, Introduction to "The Transcendence of Words," in *The Levinas Reader,* edited by Seán Hand (Oxford: Blackwell, 1996), 144.

39. *LR,* 144.

40. Levinas's reference to holiness confuses many readers of his work. Holiness evokes the sacred, an "other" world, religious experience in a traditional sense. But for Jews, holiness is often equated with the ethical, with mitzvot or ethical obligations. Rabbi Steven Carr Reuben writes: "Judaism has never seen holiness primarily in such otherworldly terms. To be 'holy' in Judaism means to act in such a way as to bring our highest and

noblest ideals and values into play in our everyday lives. It's about mystic meditation, it's about clothing the naked, housing the homeless, caring for the elderly and frail, treating people with dignity and compassion and justice. That's holiness for Jews" (36). See Rabbi Steven Carr Reuben, *Raising Jewish Children in a Contemporary World: The Modern Parent's Guide to Creating a Jewish Home* (Rocklin, CA: Prima Publishing, 1992).

41. In his interview with Michaël de Saint-Cheron, Levinas says, "What is entirely original to holiness . . . is also its greatest misery. It's the strength to want what is good for the other in the misery that can come from him" (24). And then a few pages later, Levinas admits that "God's coming to mind is certainly contemporaneous with the responsibility assumed by the other's face" (33). See Michaël de Saint-Cheron, *Conversations with Emmanuel Levinas,* trans. Gary D. Mole (Pittsburgh: Duquesne University Press, 2010).

42. One can quibble about what Levinas means by "holiness," and if it has an abstract meaning that relates to something like virtue. It is not a stretch to refer back to Hillel who was asked by a non-Jew to teach him the whole of Torah on one foot. Hillel responds: "That which is hateful to you, do not do to others. This is the whole Torah. All the rest is commentary. Now go and study" (*Shabbat* 31a). Joseph Telushkin argues that this response affirms two things. The first is that ethics is the core of Judaism and the second is that without study, without knowing what Judaism says in all its contradictions, inconsistencies, and richness, one cannot really come to know what Judaism asks of those who claim it for a religion. This lack of knowledge leaves Judaism without content: we might know that Judaism demands of us to act ethically, but we will never know what that actually means. See Telushkin, *Hillel: If Not Now, When?* (New York: Schocken, 2010).

43. In the interview published as "On Jewish Philosophy," he responds to a question about Maimonides and Judah Halevi by describing how he understands what it means to be in relation to or with God: "[Each person answering for the lives of all the others seems] fundamental to the Jewish faith, in which the relation to God is inseparable from the Torah; that is, inseparable from the recognition of the other person. The relation to God is already ethics; or, as *Isaiah 58* would have it, the proximity to God, devotion itself, is devotion to the other man" (*ITN,* 169–171).

44. The second essay in *Humanism of the Other.* See note above.

45. See Levinas, *Ethics and Infinity: Conversations with Philippe Nemo,* trans. Richard A. Cohen (Pittsburgh: Duquesne University Press, 1985), 89.

46. Levinas writes, "the Ego, in relation with Infinity, is the impossibility of stopping the forward march, the impossibility, as Plato expressed it in the *Phaedo,* of deserting one's post; it is, literally, no time to look back, no way to escape responsibility, no inner hiding place to go back into self; it is marching straight ahead without concern for self. Increase of obligations with regard to self: the more I face up to my responsibilities the more I am responsible. Power made of 'powerlessness'—that is the challenge to consciousness and its entry into a contingency of relations that clash with unveiling" (*HO,* 34). But I think it is important to note that throughout this essay Levinas implies that responsibility is not simply that which claims me—it is a way of being in relationship to the Other. It is not that I am responsible but can then say, I choose to do otherwise. Levinas seems to imply that responsibility is at once the same as being for the Other, acting for the Other.

47. See Carl Cederberg's extensive treatment of humanism/anti-humanism. Cederberg, *Resaying the Human: Levinas Beyond Humanism and Antihumanism,* Södertörn doctoral dissertation, 52. Stockholm, 2010.

48. Nietzsche, *Thus Spoke Zarathustra,* prologue, part 4, in *The Portable Nietzsche,* trans. Walter Kaufmann (New York: Penguin, 1982). Quoted in Levinas, *Humanism of the Other,* 45/73.

49. These essays are also directed at the philosophy of Ernst Cassirer. However, where Levinas is critical of Heidegger's philosophy as fundamentally opposed to ethics, his criticism of Cassirer falls along the lines that Cassirer's humanism is not radical enough. For an illuminating discussion on the background of these essays, see Richard A. Cohen's introduction in *Humanism of the Other.* For a detailed discussion of the Davos debate between Heidegger and Cassirer, see Peter E. Gordon, *Continental Divide* (Cambridge, MA: Harvard University Press, 2010).

50. This concern is neither new nor resolved. It continues into the twentieth century and we see it most recently in the discussions about contemporary moral theory, in particular the work that Patricia Churchland does in which she argues that morality can be reduced to neuroscience. See the article on her work in *The Chronicle of Higher Education,* http://chronicle.com/article/The-Biology-of-Ethics/127789/, accessed June 19, 2011.

51. A similar argument is made by Adorno and Horkheimer in "The Concept of Enlightenment," in which they provide a narrative for the totalitarian thinking that is central to reason—a foundation of the Enlightenment. Their criticism is directed at scientific thinking and the manner in which this kind of thinking obtains power precisely by the distance we create between ourselves and the object that we study. In the social sciences, the "object of study" is the human, thus one can only imagine how this critique of knowledge would be directed at those disciplines. See Adorno/Horkheimer, *The Dialectic of Enlightenment,* 1–34.

52. As we saw previously, "spiritualism" refers to paganism, or any religion that is not transcendent.

53. I am not going to rehearse in this book the debate at Davos. Others have done that far better than I could do in a brief space. For the most recent and comprehensive treatment of the debate see Peter Eli Gordon, *Continental Divide: Heidegger, Cassirer, Davos* (Cambridge, MA: Harvard University Press, 2010). I do however wish to draw attention to one line in Gordon's book. Gordon concludes his chapter "Philosophy and Memory" with the following observation: "The true danger in allegory, however, is that by dissolving the philosophical into the political, it threatens to divest us of any remaining criteria by which to decide intellectual debate other than the anti-intellectual contingencies of sheer power. For the ultimate tragedy of the Davos encounter is not that it ended in victory for politics of the wrong kind. The deeper tragedy is that it ended in politics at all" (357). I sympathize with the worry that Gordon expresses here and yet there is a nagging feeling that he has characterized philosophy naively—or maybe idealistically. The history of philosophy bears out that philosophy has always been political, that there have always been warring ideas. Some of these ideas hold sway and influence the time period while others are muted. In light of the effects that the winner of the debate had for decades to come, I think that indeed it is the deeper tragedy that the wrong politics won.

54. See Gordon, *Continental Divide.*

55. *DF,* 281. In January 1963, the *Cahiers d'Alliance* published an announcement of Levinas's participation as the external examiner for Bill Richardson's dissertation defense at Louvain on November 29, 1962. As is commonly known, Richardson's dissertation was titled "Heidegger: Through Phenomenology to Thought," which was dedicated to Heidegger's philosophy. Although the announcement reveals that those who work at the AIU are proud of this invitation for Levinas, we also see that the controversial subject matter of the dissertation does not escape them. They write: "Philosophy does not guarantee wisdom. . . . In 1933, Heidegger was a supporter of Hitler, and the magazine, *Mediations,* recently published the translation of some Heidegger texts of that period. . . . [Levinas's participation in Richardson's thesis defense included] an attempt to denounce [in Heidegger's philosophy] a fundamentally foreign and hostile message to the great biblical tradition. . . ." ("M. Emmanuel Levinas invite de l'Universite Catholique de Louvain," *Cahiers de l'Alliance Isaélite Universelle,* no. 139 [1963]: 5. Archived document, all translations are mine). Levinas participated in Richardson's defense only one year after the publication of *Totality and Infinity,* which is frequently read or interpreted as a critique of Heidegger's philosophy. That seems an uncontroversial statement. What the last point of this announcement makes clear, however, is that the critique of Heidegger's philosophy is linked to a critique of the message that is fundamental to Heidegger's philosophy *and also* opposed to "the great biblical tradition." That is, the critique of Heidegger is a philosophical critique that turns on a religious base.

4. Before Phenomenology

1. Phenomenology tends to describe structures of existence or behavior that apply to the human adult. One can look at both Husserl's writings and those of Merleau-Ponty for these descriptions. Yet, both also offer generative or developmental accounts that provide support for these descriptions. See, for example, Merleau-Ponty's essay "The Child's Relations with Others" for a developmental account of the structures that he addresses in his *Phenomenology of Perception,* trans. William Cobb, ed. James M. Edie (Evanston, IL: Northwestern University Press, 1964). See also Claire Elise Katz, "The Significance of Childhood," *International Studies in Philosophy* 34, no. 4 (2002): 77–101, for a reading of both the developmental and the static accounts of phenomenology in Merleau-Ponty.

2. See Rabbi Steven Carr Reuben, *Raising Jewish Children in a Contemporary World: The Modern Parent's Guide to Creating a Jewish Home* (Rocklin, CA: Prima Publishing, 1992).

3. There is a general set of arguments that can fall under the category "phenomenological." I believe Diane Perpich's book *The Ethics of Emmanuel Levinas* offers one of the strongest and clearest examinations not only of Levinas's phenomenology but also of a phenomenological reading of Levinas's philosophical project. See Perpich, *The Ethics of Emmanuel Levinas* (Palo Alto, CA: Stanford University Press, 2008).

4. Levinas, *Totality and Infinity,* trans. Alphonso Lingis (Pittsburgh: Duquesne University Press, 1969), 21.

5. Perpich, *The Ethics of Emmanuel Levinas,* 79.

6. See also John Drabinski, *Sensibility and Singularity: The Problem of Phenomenology in Levinas* (Albany: State University of New York Press, 2001).

7. Howard Caygill, *Levinas and the Political* (London: Routledge, 2002), 99.

8. See Maurice Merleau-Ponty, "The Child's Relations With Others." For a detailed discussion that tracks precisely this relationship between a developmental account and an ontological account of intersubjectivity, see Katz, "The Significance of Childhood."

9. I am quoting with permission of the author from a manuscript which is at the time of this writing (June 15, 2010) unpublished. The paper is forthcoming in the *European Journal of Philosophy*. The paper was presented as part of a keynote address to the inaugural meeting of the Southwest Seminar in Continental Philosophy, hosted by the University of New Mexico, Albuquerque, May 28–29, 2010. I wish to thank Steve Crowell for sending me the paper and allowing me to quote from it, and Iain Thomson who organized the conference and invited both me and Steve to present keynote addresses, enabling our work to come into productive conversation.

10. Crowell, ibid..

11. De Beauvoir's *Ethics of Ambiguity* improves on Sartre's ethics and in fact comes strikingly close to the ethics described in Levinas, an ethics that is based on the view that we are intersubjective and that relations with others free us, allow us to flourish in ways that are not possible when we are alone. Indeed, published in 1947 and written while the author was living in Nazi-occupied Paris, this book cannot escape the circumstances in which it was written. In an attempt to correct Sartre's inconsistencies, de Beauvoir's book is a brilliant analysis of an ethical relation and an ethical life from a theoretical perspective. She softens the radical freedom that Sartre presses. But, once again, the developmental component is missing. Additionally, Levinas would counter de Beauvoir by claiming that this view of ethics still assumes an ethical responsibility that has not been articulated. I believe Levinas would agree with the view of ethical ambiguity that de Beauvoir describes, including her claims to responsibility for the choices that we do make. He would, however, reject the position that an originary view of ethics is founded on freedom.

12. In his essay "Being Jewish," Levinas takes on the Sartrean concept of facticity and the idea that one simply chooses oneself. He writes, "But a fact will be a fact in an absolutely passive manner if it is a creature. The imperative of the creation that is continued in the imperative of the commandment and of the law inaugurates a total passivity. To do the will of God is in this sense the condition of facticity. The fact is possible only if, beyond its power to choose itself, which cancels out its facticity, it has been chosen, that is, elected. . . . Quite to the contrary, the past that creation and election introduce into the economy of being communicates to the present the gravity of a fact, the weight of an existence, and a sort of base. Thus, even if it is true that the Jewish fact exists bare, indeterminate in its essence, and called to choose an essence for itself according to the Sartrean framework, this fact is, in its very facticity, inconceivable without election. *The Jewish fact is not like this because he was plumped full of holy history, he refers to holy history because he is a fact like this.* In other words, the Jew is the very entrance of the religious event into the world; better yet, he is the impossibility of a world without religion." Levinas, "Being Jewish," trans. Mary Beth Mader, *Continental Philosophy Review* 40 (2007): 209, emphasis in original. Originally published as "Être Juif," *Confluences*, nos. 15–17 (1947 année 7): 253–264. Reprinted in *Cahiers d'Etude Lévinassiennes*, 2003, Numéro 1, pp. 99–106.

13. Levinas, "The Temptation of Temptation," in *Nine Talmudic Readings*, trans. Annette Aronowicz (Bloomington: Indiana University Press, 1990), 30–50; *Quatre Lectures Talmudiques* (Paris: Les Éditions de Minuit, 1968), 65–109.

14. We can note that this talmudic commentary might signal an important difference in thought between Levinas and Hermann Cohen.

15. This passage paraphrases Rashi's gloss cited in Avivah Gottlieb Zornberg, *The Beginning of Desire: Reflections on Genesis* (New York: Image/Doubleday, 1995), 4. These next few paragraphs are a version of material I published in my book *Levinas, Judaism, and the Feminine: The Silent Footsteps of Rebecca* (Bloomington: Indiana University Press, 2003). They are important to repeat since they tie together Levinas's talmudic reading and the discussion offered by Michael Fagenblat.

16. B. Shabbat 88a. See Zornberg's discussion in *The Beginning of Desire*, 27.

17. *Pesikta Rabbati*, 21 (100a). Zornberg writes,

"to be or not to be" is a question that is "suspended or standing" till Mount Sinai. . . . The world, till Sinai, awaits its true creation . . . This is not simply a matter of a shotgun commitment being demanded of the people at Mount Sinai. Their standing at the mountain is an experience *in extremis* of the instability, the terror, not only what would have happened had Israel not stood before Mount Sinai but also emphasizing the relationship between God and Israel: "Earth and all its inhabitants dissolve: 'it is I who keeps its pillars [*amudeha*, standing supports] firm'" (Psalms 75:4). The world was in the process of dissolving. Had Israel not *stood* before Mount Sinai and said, "'All that God has spoken, we will faithfully do'" [lit., we will do and we will listen (Exodus 24:7)] the world would already have returned to chaos. And who made a foundation for the world? "'It is I—*anokhi*—who keeps its pillars firm—in the merit of I—*anokhi*—am the Lord your God who brought you out of the Land of Egypt.'"

18. Deuteronomy 5:4 reads: "Face to face the Lord spoke to you on the mountain out of the fire." The phrase "face-to-face" permeates Levinas's work as a way of describing the ethical relation. We should find it no coincidence that this phrase is also used in this ancient Jewish text to describe the relationship between God and the Jewish people when the latter were to receive the Torah—God's ethical commandments—itself.

19. See Zornberg, *The Beginning of Desire*, 31.

20. Levinas, "Damages Due to Fire," in *Nine Talmudic Readings*, 182; *Du Sacré du Saint: Cinq Nouvelles Lectures Talmudiques* (Paris: Les Éditions de Minuit, 1977), 156.

21. Salomon Malka, *Emmanuel Levinas: His Life and Legacy*, trans. Michael Kigel and Sonja M. Embree (Pittsburgh: Duquesne University Press, 2006), 136.

22. Rosenzweig, *On Jewish Learning*, 122.

23. Ibid., 123.

24. Bonnie Honig, *Emergency Politics* (Princeton, NJ: Princeton University Press, 2009), 172n61. There is a typo in Honig's citation. When she provides page numbers for the Rosenzweig reference, it should read 122–123 and not 22–23 as it is printed in her book.

25. See Michael Fagenblat, *A Covenant of Creatures: Levinas's Philosophy of Judaism* (Stanford, CA: Stanford University Press, 2010). Jon D. Levenson, *Creation and the Persistence of Evil: The Jewish Drama of Divine Omnipotence* (Princeton, NJ: Princeton University Press, 1994).

26. Fagenblat, *A Covenant of Creatures*, citing Levenson, 12, emphasis added by Fagenblat. In his endnote, Fagenblat confides that Levenon's reading provides the "herme-

neutic inspiration" for the chapter in his book on creation. See Fagenblat, *A Covenant of Creatures*, 211n9.

27. Emmanuel Levinas, "Il y a," *Daucalion* 1 (1946): 141–154. As Fagenblat notes, this essay was Levinas's first publication after World War II, the Shoah, and the murder of his family (Fagenblat, *A Covenant of Creatures*, 211n12).

28. Fagenblat, *A Covenant of Creatures*, 37. See also, Katz, *Levinas, Judaism, and the Feminine*.

29. Ibid. See also Katz, *Levinas, Judaism, and the Feminine*.

30. Fagenblat, *A Covenant of Creatures*, 65.

31. Ibid., 66.

32. Ibid., 140.

33. Ibid., 140.

34. Ibid., 151–152.

35. Ibid., 152.

36. Levinas, "Nameless," in *Proper Names,* trans. Michael B. Smith (Palo Alto, CA: Stanford University Press, 1996), 119–123. This essay was originally published in 1966.

37. Levinas, "Israel and Universalism," in *Difficult Freedom: Writings on Judaism,* trans. Seán Hand (Baltimore, MD: Johns Hopkins University Press, 1990), 175–177.

38. In "Martin Buber's Thought and Contemporary Judaism," Levinas says, "Saying 'Thou' thus passes through my body to the hands that give, beyond the speech organs—which is in a good Biranian tradition and in keeping with the biblical truths. Before the face of God one must not go with empty hands." Cited in *Outside the Subject,* trans. Michael Smith (Palo Alto, CA: Stanford University Press, 1994), 18–19.

5. The Promise of Jewish Education

1. Levinas made this statement in 1986 on the occasion of a celebration for his eightieth birthday, which brought together several of his former students, including Malka. The celebration issued a publication, *Levinas—Philosophe et Pédagogue* (Alliance Israélite Universelle, 1998) (Paris: Les Editions du Nadir, 1998). The essays were contributed by David Banon, Ami Bouganim, and Catherine Chalier. Additionally, Ady Steg provided a brief story at the beginning and the collection included a discussion between Levinas and Paul Ricoeur. Salomon Malka, *Emmanuel Levinas: His Life and Legacy,* trans. Michael Kigel and Sonja M. Embree (Pittsburgh: Duquesne University Press, 2006), 84. Published in French as *Levinas, la vie et la trace* (Paris: Albin Michel, 2005), 99.

2. Adorno, "Education After Auschwitz," in *Critical Models: Interventions and Catchwords,* trans. Henry W. Pickford (New York: Columbia University Press, 1998), 191.

3. Adorno, "Education After Auschwitz," 191–204.

4. If we recall my point in the introduction and chapter 1, simply having "critical reflection" to resist authority will not be enough if there is not already a turn toward the Other.

5. See Rosenzweig, *On Jewish Learning,* ed. N. N. Glatzer (Madison: University of Wisconsin Press, 1995).

6. For a few sources, see the following: Richard A. Cohen, *Elevations: The Height of the Good in Rosenzweig and Levinas* (Chicago: University of Chicago Press, 1994); Robert Gibbs, *Correlations in Rosenzweig and Levinas* (Princeton, NJ: Princeton Univer-

sity Press, 1992); Martin Kavka, *Jewish Messianism and the History of Philosophy* (Cambridge: Cambridge University Press, 2004), especially chapter 4; Hilary Putnam, *Jewish Philosophy as a Guide to Life* (Bloomington: Indiana University Press, 2009).

7. Here, Rosenzweig means in the language that still contains the plethora of meanings not yet removed by translation.

8. For a remarkable discussion of Rosenzweig's writings on Jewish education, see Martin Kavka, "What Does it Mean to Receive the Tradition? Jewish Studies in Higher Education," *Cross Currents* (Summer 2006), http://www.crosscurrents.org/kavkasummer2006.htm.

9. Rosenzweig's view of Jewish education is inspiring, and not unlike the way we understand a classical liberal arts education—as enflaming the mind and transforming those engaged in the process. His essays reflect his own concerns regarding Jewish assimilation, though he could not have anticipated how the world would change for the Jews. Writing well before World War II, the ghettos, the camps, and Hitler's final solution, Rosenzweig is able to make the claim that one can be German and Jewish, that being German is contingent on national boundaries while being Jewish is how one lives. For Rosenzweig, the nation-state is neutral.

10. Kavka, "What Does it Mean to Receive Tradition?" 192.

11. Levinas, "Reflections on Jewish Education," in *Difficult Freedom: Writings on Judaism,* translated by Seán Hand (Baltimore, MD: Johns Hopkins University Press, 1990). First published in French as *"Réflexions sur l'éducation juive," Cahiers de l'Alliance Israélite Universelle* 58 (December 1951). Reprinted in *Difficile liberté* (Paris: Albin Michel, 1976), 368–373. Hereafter cited as *DF* followed by the English page numbers.

12. See Levinas, "L'inspiration religieuse de l'Alliance," *Paix et Droit* 15, no. 8 (October 1935), 4. Written in 1935, the themes Levinas covers in this essay reverberate throughout his writings on Judaism.

13. It is interesting to note how differently Jewish Studies is viewed today in the year 2012. Jewish Studies programs continue to increase, though the number of Jews is not increasing at a proportional rate. Certainly, there are many explanations for the number of Jewish Studies programs, and a bonafide interest in studying things Jewish might be the least among them. Most Jewish Studies programs—and the faculty lines that populate them—are funded through generous external endowments; thus they create a financial opportunity for many universities. Recently, there has been a turn in the university to Islamic Studies. There is without question a very real and very necessary practical necessity to this turn, in light of the ignorance and prejudice directed toward Muslim populations around the world. Levinas's concern is that the younger generations of Jews turn to that which appears more exotic than that which is familiar or old. That said, it is interesting to note that Jewish Studies has itself benefited from this turn to the exotic.

14. Levinas uses the term *cerveaux* and Seán Hand translates this term as "brains." It is certainly possible that if Levinas had meant "minds" he would have used "l'esprit." However, "brains" sounds too clinical. I do however think that Levinas intended to make the distinction between soul—as that which is the ethical part of us—and intellect. And I think he meant to do this without sounding either reductive or dualist.

15. "For a Jewish Humanism," in *Difficult Freedom,* 273–276. See esp. 273.

16. Levinas does not refer to Hermann Cohen, but his claim resonates with those made by Cohen in *Religion of Reason, Out of the Sources of Judaism.*

17. Levinas will repeat this exact phrase, "Ethics is an optics," in the Preface to *Totality and Infinity* (29/xvii).

18. Levinas, "The State of Israel and the Religion of Israel," in *Difficult Freedom*, 216–220.

19. Grinberg (sometimes spelled "Greenberg") was a member of the Labor Zionist movement. He was also part of the Zionist Organization that helped found the network of Tarbut Hebrew schools, which were also secular, that were developed in Eastern European countries before the Holocaust. See the pdf file under the title "Zionism and Zionist Parties," on the YIVO website: http://www.yivoinstitute.org/index.php?tid=109&aid =534, accessed July 20, 2010.

20. There is an argument to be made that the anti-Semitism of the Vichy government was a deeper violation of the French Republic than previous anti-Semitisms, including the Dreyfus Affair. As Vicki Caron points out, one difference between the two is that the anti-Semitism of the Vichy regime was state-sponsored. See Caron, "The 'Jewish Question' from Dreyfus to Vichy," in *French History Since Napolean*, ed. Martin Alexander (New York: Oxford University Press, 1999), 198.

For more on the context of France in which the Dreyfus Affair occurred, see Albert S. Lindemann, *The Jew Accused: Three Anti-Semitic Affairs—Dreyfus, Beilis, Frank, 1894–1915* (Cambridge: Cambridge University Press, 1991).

21. This is not the first time that Levinas refers to the separation of church and state as simply a veneer. In 1947 he writes, "Perhaps the most striking feature of Christianity is its capacity to become a state religion and to remain one after the separation of Church and State, to supply the State not only with its legal holidays but also with the entire framework of everyday life." Levinas, "Being Jewish," trans. Mary Beth Mader, *Continental Philosophy Review* 40 (2007): 207. Originally published as "Être Juif," *Confluences*, nos. 15–17 (1947 année 7): 253–264. Reprinted in *Cahiers d'Etude Lévinassiennes*, 2003, Numéro 1, pp. 99–106.

22. I cannot help but point out here the irony I see in many self-proclaimed atheist, agnostic, or areligious people who engage in "secularized" Christian practices such as having a Christmas tree or giving Easter baskets. This is a pervasive, and somewhat disturbing, phenomenon in the United States, and an excellent example of the ways in which Christianity is such a deeply ingrained part of secular American culture.

23. Catherine Chalier, *What Ought I to Do? Morality in Kant and Levinas*, trans. Jane Marie Todd (Ithaca, NY: Cornell University Press, 2002).

24. Ibid., 154.

25. Ibid., 164–175. Chalier's analysis offers a powerful contrast to Hermann Cohen's discussion of the affinities between Judaism and Kantian philosophy.

26. Levinas, "Antihumanism and Education," in *Difficult Freedom*, 277–288. This essay was originally published in *Hamoré*—a journal for Jewish teachers and educators. Reprinted in *Difficile liberté* (Paris: Albin Michel, 1976), 385–401. I would like to thank Michael Gottsegen for his very helpful answers to my questions about this essay. Although Michael's answers confirmed my own interpretation of the article, his elegant phrasing certainly made the philosophical points much clearer to me.

27. For a twenty-first-century discussion of this same theme, see Paul Kahn, *Putting Liberalism in its Place* (Princeton, NJ: Princeton University Press, 2005).

28. Richard Kearney, *Anatheism* (New York: Columbia University Press, 2009).

29. Levinas's remarks recall not only Hillel's response to Shammai's challenge to teach him all of Judaism on one foot but also the words from Isaiah 58, which have become central to the Yom Kippur service. Hillel's response to Shammai concluded with, "Now go and study." As I mentioned in a note to chapter 3, these words indicate that while

ethics is the core of Judaism, without study, without knowledge, one will never come to understand what Judaism asks of us or be challenged to rise to that occasion. See Joseph Telushkin, *Hillel: If Not Now, When?* (New York: Schocken, 2010). Isaiah 58, which can be found scattered throughout Levinas's writings, is a powerful speech to the Jewish community that the prophet believes has lost its way. His speech rebukes the community for being too focused on ritual and not focused enough on the meaning behind the ritual. The members of the community are treating ritual as the end rather than as the means to a greater end. In this particular speech, Isaiah demands of the community to examine why it fasts and if their actions (and non-actions) during the fast are the kind of fast that God wants. He then says this:

> [6] "Is not this the kind of fasting I have chosen:
> to loose the chains of injustice
>   and untie the cords of the yoke,
> to set the oppressed free
>   and break every yoke?
> [7] Is it not to share your food with the hungry
>   and to provide the poor wanderer with shelter—
> when you see the naked, to clothe them,
>   and not to turn away from your own flesh and blood?
> [8] Then your light will break forth like the dawn,
>   and your healing will quickly appear;
> then your righteousness will go before you,
>   and the glory of the LORD will be your rear guard.
> [9] Then you will call, and the LORD will answer;
>   you will cry for help, and he will say: Here am I. (Isaiah 58:6–9).

For Levinas's deployment of this particular passage from Isaiah see, for example, *Is it Righteous To Be? Interviews with Emmanuel Levinas,* trans. Jill Robbins (Palo Alto, CA: Stanford University Press, 2002), 256; "Demanding Judaism," in *Beyond the Verse: Talmudic Readings and Lectures,* trans. Gary D. Mole (Bloomington: Indiana University Press, 1994), 5.

30. Again, it is interesting to note the convergence with Hermann Cohen's work. Cohen emphasizes a shift from Isaiah to Ezekiel as development in prophetic thinking.

31. It is worth noting that Levinas is concerned primarily with the events of Paris in the 1960s. He makes no mention of the movements in the United States. In particular, it is interesting that he does not comment on the U.S. Civil Rights movement, which has religious roots. Indeed, Martin Luther King's "Letter from a Birmingham Jail" refers to both St. Augustine and Martin Buber. It is also worth mentioning that Abraham Joshua Heschel marched hand in hand with MLK, and refers to that experience as "praying with his legs."

32. As we saw in chapter 3, in *Humanism of the Other* (2006), a collection of essays initially published separately, Levinas addresses the problem of humanism produced in modernity's wake—and the critique of that humanism offered by Heidegger. Levinas does not support either and in turn he argues that we do not find our humanity through mathematics, metaphysics, or introspection, but instead we find it in the recognition that the suffering and mortality of others are the obligations and morality of the self (see, in particular, "Humanism and An-archy" and "No Identity"). It is interesting to note that

twenty years prior to publishing these essays, he praises Sartre in a 1947 essay, "Existentialism and Anti-Semitism," for his important contribution to the humanist cause: "The presence of an existentialist humanism, that is to say … of a humanism that would assimilate the fundamental experiences of the modern world—this is Sartre's essential contribution to our cause, the cause of humanity." Levinas, "Existentialism and Anti-Semitism," trans. Denis Hollier and Rosalind Krauss, *Translation (October Magazine)* 87 (Winter 1999): 27–31.

33. Chalier, "Lévinas maître," in *Levinas—Philosophe et Pédagogue,* 69. Translated and published as "Emmanuel Levinas: School Master and Pedagogue," in *Levinas and Education,* ed. Denise Egéa-Kuehne (London: Routledge, 2008), 14.

34. Ibid.

35. Ibid., 15.

6. Teaching, Fecundity, Responsibility

1. In "Morris R. Cohen, The Teacher," Leonora Cohen Rosenfield, *Journal of the History of Ideas* 18, no. 4 (October 1957): 552–571.

2. Levinas, *Carnets de Captivité et autres inédits, Oeuvres 1* (450, emphasis added, my translation; written on the back of a card, dated 1960).

3. Howard Caygill, "The Prison Notebooks," *Radical Philosophy* 160 (March/April 2010), accessed July 27, 2010, http://www.radicalphilosophy.com/default.asp?channel _id=2188&editorial_id=28975.

4. Ady Steg, "A Fable," in *Levinas: Philosophe et Pédagogue (Éditions du Nadir de l'alliance Israélite Universelle,* 1998), 7. All translations are mine. For more information, see chapter 5, n. 1.

5. It is important to note that Levinas continued his directorship of the ENIO long after he had obtained a university position. His first university position came in 1961 at the Univeristy of Nanterre and then in 1973 he was given a professorship at the Sorbonne. He did not leave his position as director until 1979. See André Kaspi, *Histoire de l'Alliance Israélite Universelle de 1860 À Nos Jours* (Paris: Armand Colin, 2010), 417–420.

6. My thanks to Martin Kavka for suggestions about phrasing this point.

7. See Levinas's short piece "L'École Normale Israélite Orientale," which he presented at the reunion of the Alliance Israélite Universelle on June 19, 1961. It was subsequently published in *Les Cahiers de l'Alliance Israélite Universelle,* no. 34 (September–October 1961): 9–10. Levinas explains that the the work of the AIU is to fight against anti-Semitism, "in other words, the rights of man," and it cannot handle a clearing or a disappearance of Judaism. The source of such immortal ideas as "revolution" is found in Jewish civilization—carnal Judaism (Judaism's material existence) is where these ideas are experienced as feelings. But Jewish society is formed in the spirit of need for masters, teachers, who will educate and nourish the Jewish values that are so important to this fight. In this short piece, Levinas declares that the ENIO bears the responsibility for responding to these needs.

8. See Bouganim's contribution in Chalier and Bouganim, "Emmanuel Levinas: School Master and Pedagogue," in *Levinas and Education,* ed. Denise Egéa-Kuehne (New York: Routledge, 2008), 15.

9. Ibid., 16.

10. These are overnight camps that served the Conservative Jewish movement. See Riv-Ellen Prell, *Jewish Summer Camping and Civil Rights: How Summer Camps Launched a Transformation in American Jewish Culture* (Ann Arbor, MI: Jean and Samuel Frankel Center for Judaic Studies, 2006).

11. Bouganim, "Emmanuel Levinas," 16, emphasis added.

12. Translation altered. The quote continues: ". . . Levinas was interested in Talmud, and more especially in the *aggada,* diving once again in the raging sea of controversies, sweeping along behind him disciples from all nations who could be filled with wonder at his obstinacy—wholly Judaic—in persisting in humanism, simply humanism. . . . He spoke Greek only to better reach listeners and readers who had lost their Hebrew, not to mention their Aramaean, and only because he understood a discourse on Judaism which was articulated according to the snares of philosophical reason. Perhaps Levinas was not so much from Maimonides's school, which installed the Greek science under 'the tents of the Torah' as from Philo's school—less deceived and more experienced than the historical Philo—who carried the Judaic diversion to the very heart of Greek wisdom. In fact, he was mostly 'Lithuanian,' irremediably so, locating Judaism 'at the intersection of faith and reason,' pushing it in its secular entrenchments only to better tap into a Jewish secularism [*laïcité*] which could vie with a secularism [*laïcité*] readily masking its Christian motives." Bouganim, "Emmanuel Levinas," 16–17, translation altered. See also Bouganim's essay "The School Ghetto in France," in *Jewish Day Schools / Jewish Communities,* ed. Alex Pomson and Howard Deitcher (Oxford: Littman Library, 2009), 222–234. In this essay, Bouganim notes the need for Jewish schools to respond to / protect themselves from the threat of assimilation.

13. Levinas, *Totality and Infinity: An Essay on Exteriority,* trans. Alphonso Lingis (Pittsburgh: Duquesne University Press, 1969). *Time and the Other,* trans. Richard A. Cohen (Pittsburgh: Duquesne University Press, 1987).

14. Martin Kavka, "Phenomenology," in *The Cambridge History of Jewish Philosophy: The Modern Era,* ed. Kavka, Zachary Braiterman, and David Novak (Cambridge: Cambridge University Press, 2012), 97–127. See also chapter 4.

15. For two instances where Levinas's ethical project has been examined in relationship to Judaism and also education, see Richard A. Cohen, *Ethics, Exegesis and Philosophy: Interpretation after Levinas* (Cambridge: Cambridge University Press, 2001), and Robert Gibbs, *Why Ethics? Signs of Responsibilities* (Princeton, NJ: Princeton University Press, 2000). See also Egéa-Kuehne, *Levinas and Education.* This edited collection brings together eighteen essays engaging Levinas's work with themes central to educational theory and practice. The book is important for alerting scholars and practitioners to this connection. However, with the exception of the first essay which was translated from *Levinas: Philosophe et Pédagogue,* none of the essays written for this collection engage Levinas's own essays on education and only the essay by Gert Biesta makes any mention of these essays whatsoever.

16. Totality and Infinity, 51–77.

17. Ibid., 194–219.

18. Robert Bernasconi has argued that this final section of *Totality and Infinity,* "Beyond the Face," which includes the discussions of eros and fecundity, is a holdover from *Time and the Other,* a discussion that Levinas drops in his later work because it reads too much like a family structure. Bernasconi might be right that Levinas had personal reasons to include it and philosophical reasons to discard it. However, one could also

argue that inclusion of this section was less about something idiosyncratically personal and more about a generic indication of how the ethical subject is formed. In this regard, Levinas's description calls us to think about what it means to be a parent who is responsible for raising a child. Thus, Levinas can offer a mechanism for explaining how the ethical subject comes into being—by the way in which the child obligates the parent to respond to her and thus the parent responds by feeding her, clothing her, and caring for her. The parent is called to respond to the child but in so doing one could argue that the parent is part of the cultivation of that child to respond to other others.

19. One criticism in particular stands out. Luce Irigaray's essay "The Fecundity of the Caress" offers a rereading of two sections of Emmanuel Levinas's *Totality and Infinity*—"The Phenomenology of Eros" and "Fecundity." See Irigaray, "Fecundity of the Caress," in *Ethics of Sexual Difference*, trans. Carolyn Burke and Gillian Gill (Ithaca, NY: Cornell University Press, 1993), 185–217. For a critical discussion of Irigaray's reading of Levinas, see Claire Elise Katz, *Levinas, Judaism, and the Feminine: The Silent Footsteps of Rebecca* (Bloomington: Indiana University Press, 2003).

20. *Ethics and Infinity: Conversations with Philippe Nemo*, trans. Richard A. Cohen (Pittsburgh: Duquesne University Press, 1985), 70/62–64.

21. Levinas's emphasis on fecundity underscores the importance of asymmetrical responsibility that is unique to the parent-child relation. It should be noted that Robert Gibbs disagrees with characterizing this relationship as *strictly* asymmetrical and which is not a characteristic of the erotic relationship that Levinas describes in the preceding section. See Gibbs, *Why Ethics*. Nonetheless, Levinas describes love as bringing us out of ourselves through the desire that cannot be fulfilled, but that longs for eternity. The birth of the son represents this eternity. The parent's responsibility for the child is joined to the child's role as the parent's teacher. Insofar as the child is unique, the child teaches the parent, instructs her to be attentive to the child's own growth. And it is in turn the parent's responsibility to help the child become responsible for others. And so our hope that our children will be responsible to others opens onto the hope that others will be responsible for other others. This movement from love to fecundity opens finally into fraternity, as the first micro-community, and then to a larger community.

22. I maintain that the subtext of Levinas's ethical project, manifested in Levinas's use of the feminine throughout his work, also serves a pedagogical end. The feminine becomes the example, that to which the masculine, the virile, should aspire to become. A close reading of the feminine from Levinas's earliest work, *Time and the Other*, to his last philosophical book, *Otherwise than Being*, reveals an instructive dimension. For a longer discussion of this point, see Claire Elise Katz, *Levinas, Judaism, and the Feminine: The Silent Footsteps of Rebecca* (Bloomington: Indiana University Press, 2003).

23. In his interview with François Poirié, Levinas tells us that "Judaism is not the Bible; it is the Bible seen through the Talmud, through the rabbinical wisdom, interrogation, and religious life." See *Is it Righteous To Be? Interviews with Emmanuel Levinas*, ed. Jill Robbins (Stanford, CA: Stanford University Press, 2001), 76. In an interview published under the title "On Jewish Philosophy," Levinas tells his interlocutor, "it seems to me essential to consider the fact that the Jewish reading of Scripture is carried out in the anxiety, but also the hopeful expectation, of midrash." Levinas goes on to name Rashi's commentary in particular as that which brings the Chumash to light: "the Pentateuch—*Chumash*—never comes to light without Rashi." See "On Jewish Philosophy," in *In the*

Time of the Nations, trans. Michael B. Smith (Bloomington: Indiana University Press, 1994), 169. Reprinted in *Is It Righteous to Be?* 239–254.

24. See Katz, "Teaching Our Children Well: Pedagogy, Religion and the Future of Philosophy," *Cross Currents* 53, no. 4 (Winter 2004): 530–547, and Katz, "Levinas—Between Philosophy and Rhetoric: The 'Teaching' of Levinas's Scriptural References," *Philosophy and Rhetoric* 38, no. 2 (2005): 159–172.

25. This, for example, is the argument offered by Allan Bloom when he suggests that the Bible should be viewed as the core text of American culture. See Allan Bloom, *The Closing of the American Mind: How Higher Education Has Failed Democracy and Impoverished the Souls of Today's Students* (New York: Simon and Schuster, 1987).

26. Cohen, *Ethics, Exegesis, and Philosophy,* 251–252. Levinas makes this point repeatedly. See, for example, his interviews with Michaël de Saint Cheron.

27. Levinas, LR, 263; Cohen, *Ethics, Exegesis, and Philosophy,* 252.

28. My use of "rhetoric" here refers to Levinas's style of writing and the performative dimension that his use of this particular language has in the context of his philosophical work.

29. In any number of places Levinas refers to midrash as an example of his philosophical term "the saying," that which remains unthematized. In Levinas's view, midrash opens up the voices in the Torah that are muted in the text, either because they are explicitly absent from the narrative structure or because the narrative structure lacks clarity. Midrash lifts these voices out of the text and then brings them to bear on the narrative. By enabling our access to these others, midrash brings us closer to the ethical. To approach the Torah Jewishly, then, is precisely to approach it through rabbinic commentary. Thus, midrash keeps the Torah alive by preventing its easy thematization. And it prevents this thematization by posing questions and offering alternative readings of the text. Further, the interpretative model of midrash is similar to Levinas's saying insofar as the saying is an excess, that which lies beyond the said. In Levinas's words, the saying opens me to the Other. The saying expresses the infinite quality of the other person. Philosophy, then, is derivative of religion because it is what allows us to take the ethical message of Judaism and project it into a universal language. See "God and Philosophy," in *Of God Who Comes to Mind,* trans. Bettina Bergo (Stanford, CA: Stanford University Press, 1998), 74.

30. I use the term "pedagogy" with care. It is not clear what other word can be used to refer to an educational model or method, yet Levinas makes several negative comments about pedagogy in *Totality and Infinity.* I suspect that his comments there are specific to the kind of teaching he believes takes place between the self and the Other, which he would want to distance from the standard use of pedagogy as a didactic hegemonic practice that is associated with traditional schools.

31. See Claire Elise Katz, "'The presence of the Other is a presence that teaches': Levinas, Pragmatism, and Pedagogy," *Journal of Jewish Thought and Philosophy* 14, no. 1–2 (2007): 91–108. See also Katz, "Thus Spoke Zarathustra; Thus Listened the Rabbis: Nietzsche, Education, and the Cycle of Enlightenment," *New Nietzsche Studies* 7, nos. 3–4 (Fall 2007 / Winter 2008).

32. For more on Levinas and Russian literature see Val Vinokur, *The Trace of Judaism: Dostoevsky, Babel, Mandelstam, Levinas* (Evanston, IL: Northwestern University Press, 2009).

33. Jeffrey S. Kress and Marjorie Lehman, "The Babylonian Talmud in Cognitive Perspective: Reflections on the Nature of the Bavli and its Pedagogical Implications," *Journal of Jewish Education* 69, no. 2 (Winter 2003): 58–78.

34. Ibid., 58.

35. The Talmud comprises two parts. The Mishnah, which is the oral law, and the Gemara, which is the commentary on the Mishnah. *Sugyot* is the plural of *sugya*, which is a passage from the Gemara.

36. Kress and Lehman, "The Babylonian Talmud," 58.

37. Ibid., 58.

38. Ibid., 59.

39. Ibid.

40. Ibid.

41. Ibid.

42. Ibid.

43. Ibid.

44. Ibid.

45. This model of teaching is not unique to Levinas. We see appropriations of this communal model in Buber's essays on education. Franz Rosenzweig also describes a similar model in his essays on education. See Rosenzweig, *On Jewish Learning*, ed. N. N. Glatzer (Madison: University of Wisconsin Press, 1955).

46. As mentioned earlier, Levinas is critical of the term "pedagogy" (see Levinas, *Totality and Infinity*), since for him it signals all that is wrong with education and ethics, primarily that it is simply a didactic relationship. It also has an unfortunate Greek etymology, which ties it to the *paidagógos*, the slave who escorted the children to school. Worse, it can reference a dull or pedantic teacher. But of course pedagogy can also simply refer to "instruction" or "learning," which is how I employ this term.

47. Lee S. Shulman, "Professing Understanding and Professing Faith: The Midrashic Imperative," in *The American University in a Postsecular Age,* ed. Douglas Jacobsen and Rhonda Jacobsen (Oxford: Oxford University Press, 2008), 203.

48. Shulman, "Professing Understanding and Professing Faith," 204.

49. Ibid.

50. See, for example, the objections and replies to Descartes's *Meditations.*

51. Shulman, "Professing Understanding and Professing Faith," 215.

52. Levinas, *Of God Who Comes to Mind,* trans. Bettina Bergo (Stanford, CA: Stanford University Press, 1998).

53. See Robert Gibbs, *Why Ethics?* See also Oona Eisenstadt, "Levinas versus Levinas: Hebrew, Greek, and Linguistic Justice," *Philosophy and Rhetoric* 38, no. 2 (2005), 145–158.

54. Cohen, *Ethics, Exegesis and Philosophy,* 241.

55. David Stern, *Midrash and Theory* (Evanston, IL: Northwestern University Press, 1996), 15. For a contemporary reading of this view, see Rabbi Steven Carr Reuben, *Raising Jewish Children in a Contemporary World: The Modern Parent's Guide to Creating a Jewish Home* (Rocklin, CA: Prima Publishing, 1992).

56. Ibid., 15.

57. See Katz, "'The presence of the Other is a presence that teaches.'"

58. Levinas's talmudic reading, *The Temptation of Temptation,* references the acceptance of the covenant at Sinai. I believe this is what he has in mind when he thinks about

what his ethics means in reality and for a community. But I am not sure how this covenant translates into terms that make sense outside the Jewish community.

7. Humanism Found

1. Abraham Joshua Heschel, *The Prophets* (New York: Harper Perennial Modern Classics Readers, 2001). Readers might think it odd to pair the hasidic thinker Abraham Joshua Heschel with Emmanuel Levinas. However, there are several points of intersection between these two men. The first is that each sees Judaism as a path to bring about social justice. Their writings are strikingly similar on several themes: for example, Judaism having lost its way and become focused too much on ritual and not the meaning behind the ritual, and the role of prayer as that which alerts us to injustice and positions us to do something about it. Finally, they both wrote about Judaism and education. When I was in the archives of the Alliance Israélite Universelle (AIU), I came across a letter, dated March 29, 1962, written by Morris Laub, the director of the World Council of Synagogues. It was addressed to Jules Braunschvig, the vice president of the AIU. The letter invited Emmanuel Levinas to the convention of the World Council of Synagogues, to be held in Jerusalem, May 1962, in order to be a discussant for the paper on Jewish education that Abraham Joshua Heschel would be presenting. The letter mentioned that having met Levinas at the Paris conference that previous year, they believed he was the perfect person to participate in this capacity. The reply by Jules Braunschvig indicates that Levinas would be unable to attend because he needed to be in Paris at that time to oversee the move of the ENIO to its new building. See the Alliance files during the years that Levinas was the director of the ENIO. (These are unpublished documents. See the folders containing Levinas's correspondence while he was directing the ENIO—these folders are dated 1961 and 1962.)

2. Heschel, *The Prophets,* xviii. In a biographical note about Heschel, we find him struggling to find an academic home where he fits in both intellectually and spiritually. His colleagues at the Jewish Theological Seminary did not welcome his belief that academics also have a responsibility to be activists for social causes. The JTS faculty later lamented this disagreement with Heschel and conceded that they should have followed his lead. At this present time, Heschel's concern rings all too true.

3. Heschel, *The Prophets,* xxi.

4. Ibid., xxvii.

5. Ibid., xxvi.

6. Susannah Heschel, "Looking Back, Looking Forward: A Forum," *The Nation,* December 2, 2004, http://www.thenation.com/doc.mhtml?i=20041220&s=forum.

7. A. J. Heschel, *The Prophets,* xxix.

8. In A. J. Heschel, *Moral Grandeur and Spiritual Audacity,* ed. Susannah Heschel (New York: Farrar, Straus and Giroux, 1997).

9. Heschel, *Moral Grandeur,* 101.

10. Ibid., 108.

11. Ibid.

12. Ibid.

13. Ibid., 109.

14. Ibid.

15. Ibid., 110.

16. Ibid., 111.

17. Ibid.

18. The simplest definition of *kavanah* would be mindset or disposition, the direction of the heart, meaning here that the prayer is recited not as a simple mouthing of the words but with the person's full attention and the person's heart directed at what the prayer means. Although his use of *kavanah* takes him in a different direction from my interest here, the work of Roger I. Simon provides a helpful connection between kavanah and education.

19. Heschel, *Moral Grandeur,* 112.

20. Ibid., 114.

21. Ibid., 108.

22. Levinas, "Education and Prayer," in *Difficult Freedom: Writings on Judaism,* trans. Seán Hand (Baltimore, MD: Johns Hopkins University Press, 1990); first published as "Philosophie et Prière," in "Bulletin intérieur du Consistoire Central des Israélites de France," July 1964, 196–197, exposition on pp. 57–59 (dedicated to the "Assises du judaïsme français" of June 1964). Reprinted in *Difficile liberté: essays sur le judaïsme* (Paris: Éditions Alban Michel, 1976). I am grateful to Georges Hansel for finding the citation for the original French publication.

23. It has become a popular, even if uncritical position, to oppose religion (read as superstition or myth) to modernity (read as science and truth), assuming the two must be mutually exclusive.

24. This positive view of reason should be noted. Levinas sees reason tempered by Jewish wisdom in the Talmud as different from the reason that defines philosophy.

25. Michaël de Saint Cheron, *Conversations with Emmanuel Levinas,* trans. Gary D. Mole (Pittsburgh: Duquesne University Press, 2010), 25.

26. The French reads as follows: ". . . et voici que dans ces blocs uniformes qui devraient préfigurer une humanité égale, se manifest—étrange germination dans matière aussi homogène!—la Différence, sous laquelle remue, obstinée et difficile, la liberté" (*DL,* 379). It could be translated as follows: "and in these uniform bricks, which should prefigure an equal humanity, we find *Difference*—a strange germination in a homogenous material—under which moves an obstinate and difficult freedom."

27. Let me also state here that without question, my own relationship to Judaism and its prayers is unorthodox—both literally and figuratively. My Reform upbringing by two socially activist and intellectually minded grandparents informs my relationship to Judaism as a religion that at its heart promotes social justice, requires us to respond to those who are most needy among us, and encourages our minds to be critically engaged. I do not doubt that this informs my own interpretation of Judaism. That is, I understand Judaism as a relationship to God that mirrors precisely what one is asked when one recites the Shema—to approach it with all one's mind, heart, and body. Thus, this engagement with Judaism, God, and the Shema are neither mindless nor are they indicative of blind faith. Rather, this relationship requires one to be fully engaged.

28. Heschel, *The Prophets,* xviii.

29. See Levinas, *Beyond the Verse: Talmudic Readings and Lectures,* trans. Gary D. Mole (Bloomington: Indiana University Press 1994), xiii. See also the discussion in chapter 6.

30. Levinas, *Is it Righteous To Be?* ed. Jill Robbins (Stanford, CA: Stanford University Press, 2001), 64.

31. See Levinas, *Difficult Freedom*, 271.

32. The title for this section is taken from an essay by Lee S. Shulman: "Professing Understanding and Professing Faith: The Midrashic Imperative," in *The American University in a Postsecular Age*, ed. Douglas Jacobsen and Rhonda Jacobsen (Oxford: Oxford University Press, 2008), 203–217. I would like to thank Martin Kavka for calling this essay to my attention.

33. Levinas, "On Religious Language and the Fear of God," *Beyond the Verse*, trans. Gary D. Mole (Bloomington: Indiana University Press, 1994), 86–98. Published in French as "Du Langage Religieux et de la Crainte de Dieu," *L'Au-dela du Verset* (Paris: Éditions de Minuit, 1982), 107–122.

34. Levinas, *Outside the Subject*, trans. Michael Smith (London: Athlone, 1993), 94. *Hors Sujet* (Monpellier: Fata Morgana, 1987), 130.

35. See Levinas's discussion of Kierkegaard's reading of Abraham and the Akedah. "A propos of 'Kierkegaard vivant," in *Proper Names*, trans. Michael B. Smith (London: Athlone, 1996), 75–79. See my discussion of this same topic in Claire Elise Katz, *Levinas, Judaism, and the Feminine: The Silent Footsteps of Rebecca* (Bloomington: Indiana University Press, 2003), 108–125.

36. Levinas, Is it Righteous To Be? 62.

37. See Claire Elise Katz, "Teaching our Children Well: Pedagogy, Religion, and the Future of Philosophy," *Cross Currents* 53, no. 4 (Winter 2004): 530–547.

38. Hegel's *Phenomenology of Spirit* had an enormous impact on scholars, Jewish and otherwise, who came to understand Judaism in these terms. I find this particularly troubling, not that so many scholars were influenced by this view, but that so many scholars who had very little information about Judaism in the first place came to understand what Judaism is from Hegel.

39. I would like to thank Martin Kavka who simply asked me, "Why service? Why not election?" Why not indeed?

40. Rosenzweig, *On Jewish Learning*:

> [d]esires are the messengers of confidence . . . For who knows whether desires such as these—real, spontaneous desires, not artificially nurtured by some scheme of education—can be satisfied? But those who know how to listen to real wishes may also know perhaps how to point out the desired way . . . For the teacher able to satisfy such spontaneous desires cannot be a teacher according to a plan; he must be much more and much less, a master and at the same time a pupil. It will not be enough that he himself knows or that he himself can teach. He must be capable of something quite different—he must be able to "desire." He who can desire must be the teacher here. The teachers will be discovered in the same discussion room and the same discussion period as the students. And in the same discussion hour the same person may be heard as both master and student. In fact, only when this happens, will it become certain that person is qualified to teach. (69)

41. See also Claire Elise Katz, "'The Presence of the Other is a Presence that Teaches': Levinas, Pragmatism, and Pedagogy," *Journal of Jewish Thought and Philosophy* 14, nos. 1–2 (2006): 91–108.

42. We see this demonstrated by the very substance of the Talmud, which raises questions about all aspects of daily life from the food we eat to our obligations in marriage.

43. See also Levinas, "Reflections in the Philosophy of Hitlerism," trans. Seán Hand, *Critical Inquiry* 17 (Autumn 1990), 63–71.

44. He makes this reference explicit in his writings on Jewish education, some of which are collected in *Difficult Freedom*.

45. We do find in Levinas's writings occasional references to God's covenant with Noah and the Noahide commandments. However, this covenant is very different from the one at Sinai where those who became Jews said, "We will do and we will hear."

46. It might mean turning to the Jewish philosophers who wrote on the political. Additionally, one might turn to contemporary philosophers who have also become frustrated with the same insufficient toolbox. See for example Bonnie Honig, *Emergency Politics*.

47. Carl Cederberg wrote a lovely dissertation tracing the concept of the human in Levinas. At the end he discusses what is at stake politically in Levinas's concept. Like most recent political theory, he turns to philosophers like Agamben and Rancière. I do not know if either of these thinkers will be successful at offering a politics comparable to Levinas's ethics. Nor do I think that Honig's work is immune to criticism. But it seems that any account of the political that will allow for the radical ethics Levinas suggests must also stretch beyond the tools in the Western philosophical toolbox. See Cederberg, *Resaying the Human: Levinas Beyond Humanism and Antihumanism* (Stockholm: Södertörn högskola, 2010). My thanks to Hans Ruin for introducing me to this work.

Bibliography

Adorno, Theodor. 1998. "Education After Auschwitz." In *Critical Models: Interventions and Catchwords*, trans. Henry W. Pickford, 191–204. New York: Columbia University Press.

Arendt, Hannah. 1968. *Between Past and Future: Eight Exercises in Political Thought*. New York: Viking Press.

Aronowicz, Annette. 1999. "Jewish Education in the Thought of Emmanuel Levinas." In *Research Perspectives on Jewish Education*, ed. Yisrael Rich and Michael Rosenak, Freund and Bar-Ilan University.

Arum, Richard, and Josipa Roksa. 2011. *Academically Adrift: Limited Learning on College Campuses*. Chicago: University of Chicago Press.

Baker, Keith Michael. 1990. *Inventing the French Revolution*. Cambridge: Cambridge University Press.

Batnitzky, Leora. 2006. "Jewish Vengeance, Christian Compassion?—or the misunderstanding that won't go away." *Character: A Journal of Everyday Virtues* (September 1). http://incharacter.org/archives/justice/jewish-vengeance-christian-compassion-or -the-misunderstanding-that-wont-go-away/ (accessed August 23, 2010).

———. 2007. *Leo Strauss and Emmanuel Levinas: Philosophy and the Politics of Revelation*. Cambridge: Cambridge University Press.

Bell, David. 2010. "Does This Man Deserve Tenure?" Review of *Crisis on Campus*, by Mark C. Taylor. http://www.tnr.com/book/review/mark-taylor-crisis-campus-colleges -universities. Accessed June 1, 2011.

Bergo, Bettina, and Jill Stauffer. 2008. *Nietzsche and Levinas: After the Death of a Certain God*. New York: Columbia University Press.

Bernasconi, Robert. 2005. "No Exit: Levinas' Aporetic Account of Transcendence." *Research in Phenomenology* 35:101–117.

———. 2008. "Sartre and Levinas: Philosophers Against Racism and Antisemitism." In *Race after Sartre*, ed. Jonathan Judaken, 113–128. Albany: State University of New York Press.

Bérubé, Michael. 2011. "The Science Wars Redux." *Democracy: A Journal of Ideas*, no. 19 (Winter). http://www.democracyjournal.org/19/6789.php (accessed January 6, 2011).

Brenner, Michael. 1998. *The Renaissance of Jewish Culture in Weimar Germany*. New Haven, CT: Yale University Press.

Brooks, David. 2010. "History of Dollars." *New York Times*, June 7, 2010. http://www .nytimes.com/2010/06/08/opinion/08brooks.html?_r=1 (accessed June 7, 2010).

Buber, Martin. 1958. *I and Thou*. London: Continuum.

———. 2000. *On the Bible: Eighteen Studies*, trans. Nahum N. Glatzer. Syracuse, NY: Syracuse University Press.

Burch, Kerry. 2000. *Eros as the Educational Principle of Democracy*. New York: Peter Lang Publishing.

Butler, Judith. 2011. Speech at Occupy Wallstreet: http://www.youtube.com/watch?v=rYfLZsb9by4 (accessed November 6, 2011).

Caron, Vicki. 1999. "The 'Jewish Question' from Dreyfus to Vichy." In *French History Since Napolean*, ed. Martin Alexander, 172–202. New York: Oxford University Press.

Cassirer, Ernst. 1978. *An Essay on Man*. New Haven, CT: Yale University Press.

———. 2009. *The Philosophy of the Enlightenment*, trans. Fritz C. A. Koelln and James Pettegrove. Princeton, NJ: Princeton University Press.

Caygill, Howard. 2002. *Levinas and the Political*. London: Routledge.

Cederberg, Carl. 2010. *Resaying the Human: Levinas Beyond Humanism and Antihumanism*. PhD diss., Södertörn högskola, Stockholm.

Chalier, Catherine, 1998. *Levinas: Philosophe et Pédagogue*. Alliance Israélite Universelle. Paris: Les Editions du Nadir.

———. 2002. *What Ought I to Do? Morality in Kant and Levinas*, trans. Jane Marie Todd. Ithaca, NY: Cornell University Press.

Chalier, Catherine, and Miguel Abensour. 2006. *Levinas: Les Cahiers de L'Herne*. Paris: Éditions de l'Herne.

Cohen, Hermann. 1971. *Reason and Hope: Selections from the Jewish Writings of Hermann Cohen*, trans. and ed. Eva Jospe. Cincinnati: Hebrew Union College Press.

———. 1995. *Religion of Reason Out of the Sources of Judaism*, trans. Simon Kaplan. Atlanta: Scholars Press.

Cohen, Richard A. 1994. *Elevations: The Heights of the Good in Rosenzweig and Levinas*. Chicago: University of Chicago Press.

———. 2001. *Ethics, Exegesis and Philosophy*. Cambridge: Cambridge University Press.

Connolly, William. 2000. *Why I'm Not a Secularist*. Minneapolis: University of Minnesota Press.

Conway, Daniel. 1990. "Nietzsche *contra* Nietzsche: The Deconstruction of Nietzsche." In *Nietzsche as Post-Modernist*, ed. Clayton Koelb, 91–110, 304–311. Albany: State University of New York Press.

Crowell, Steven Galt. Forthcoming. "Why Is Ethics First Philosophy? Levinas in a Phenomenological Context." *European Journal of Philosophy*.

Davis, Wes. 2010. "The 'Learning Knights' of Bell Telephone." *New York Times,* June 15, 2010. http://www.nytimes.com/2010/06/16/opinion/16davis.html?_r=1. Accessed June 20, 2010.

de Beauvoir, Simone. 2000. *The Ethics of Ambiguity*. New York: Citadel.

———. 2011. *The Second Sex,* trans. Constance Borde and Sheila Malovany-Chevalier. New York: Vintage.

de Saint-Cheron, Michaël. 2010. *Conversations with Emmnanuel Levinas*, trans. Gary D. Mole. Pittsburgh: Duquesne University Press.

Deleuze, Gilles. 1962. *Nietzsche and Philosophy,* trans. Hugh Tomlinson. New York: Columbia University Press. Originally published in French as *Nietzsche et la philosophie*. Paris: PUF.

Derrida, Jacques. 2002. "The future of the profession or the university without condition (thanks to the 'Humanities,' what *could take place* tomorrow)." In *Jacques Derrida and the Humanities: A Critical Reader,* ed. Tom Cohen, 24–57. Cambridge: Cambridge University Press.

Dewey, John. 1916. *Democracy and Education*. New York: Free Press.

———. 1938. *Experience and Education.* New York: Collier Books.

Donoghue, Frank. 2009. *The Last Professors.* New York: Fordham.

Drabinski, John. 2001. *Sensibility and Singularity: The Problem of Phenomenology in Levinas.* Albany: State University of New York Press.

Egéa-Kuehne, Denise, ed. 2008. *Levinas and Education: At the Intersection of Faith and Reason.* London: Routledge.

Erlin, Matt. 2002. "Reluctant Modernism: Moses Mendelssohn's Philosophy of History." *Journal of the History of Ideas* 63 (January): 83–104.

Fagenblat, Michael. 2010. *A Covenant of Creatures: Levinas's Philosophy of Judaism.* Stanford, CA: Stanford University Press.

Fish, Stanley. 2009. "The Last Professor," http://fish.blogs.nytimes.com/2009/01/18/the-last-professor/. Accessed June 7, 2010.

———. 2010. "A Classical Education: Back to the Future." *New York Times,* June 7, 2010. http://opinionator.blogs.nytimes.com/2010/06/07/a-classical-education-back-to-the-future/ (accessed June 7, 2010).

———. 2010. "Deep in the Heart of Texas." *New York Times,* June 21, 2010. http://opinionator.blogs.nytimes.com/2010/06/21/deep-in-the-heart-of-texas/ (accessed June 21, 2010).

———. 2010. "The Crisis of the Humanities Officially Arrives." *New York Times,* October 11, 2010. http://opinionator.blogs.nytimes.com/2010/10/11/the-crisis-of-the-humanities-officially-arrives/ (accessed October 11, 2010).

Flawn, Peter. 1979. "The Widget Theory of Higher Education." http://alliancefortamu.org/op-eds-editorials/. Accessed May 13, 2012.

Fox, Seymour, Israel Scheffler, and Daniel Marom, eds. 2003. *Visions of Jewish Education.* Cambridge: Cambridge University Press.

Galston, William. 2005. *Community Matters.* Lanham, MD: Rowman and Littlefield.

Gay, Peter. 2001. *Weimar Culture.* New York: Norton.

Geroulanos, Stefanos. 2010. *An Atheism that is not Humanist Emerges in French Thought.* Stanford, CA: Stanford University Press.

Gibbs, Robert. 2000. *Why Ethics? Signs of Responsibilities.* Princeton, NY: Princeton University Press.

Gilligan, Carol. 1993. *In a Different Voice: Psychological Theory and Women's Development.* Cambridge, MA: Harvard University Press.

Gordon, Mordechai, ed. 2001. *Hannah Arendt and Education: Renewing Our Common World.* Boulder, CO: Westview Press.

Gordon, Peter Eli. 2010. *Continental Divide: Heidegger, Cassirer, Davos.* Cambridge, MA: Harvard University Press.

Gosse, Johanna. 2011. "The only place for women in the movement is 'prone.'" http://flexner.blogs.brynmawr.edu/2011/10/27/the-only-place-for-women-in-the-movement-is-%E2%80%98prone%E2%80%99-2/ (accessed November 6, 2011).

Hadot, Pierre. 1995. *Philosophy as a Way of Life.* Oxford: Blackwell.

Hammerschlag, Sarah. 2010. *The Figural Jew: Politics and Identity in Postwar French Thought.* Chicago: University of Chicago Press.

Handelman, Susan. 1983. *Slayers of Moses.* Albany: State University of New York Press.

Hansel, Joëlle. 2006. "Paganisme et 'philosophie de l'hitlérisme.'" *Cités: Philosophie, Politique, Histoire* 25:25–29.

Head, Simon. 2011. "The Grim Threat to British Universities." *New York Review of Books,* January 13, 2011. http://www.nybooks.com/articles/archives/2011/jan/13/grim-threat -british-universities/?pagination=false (accessed January 13, 2011).

Heidegger, M. 1985. "Who is Nietzsche's Zarathustra?" In *The New Nietzsche,* ed. David Allison, 64–79. Cambridge, MA: MIT Press.

———. 1993. "Letter on Humanism." In *Basic Writings,* ed. David Farrell Krell. San Francisco: HarperCollins.

Heschel, Abraham Joshua. 1997. *Moral Grandeur and Spiritual Audacity,* ed. Susannah Heschel. New York: Farrar, Straus and Giroux.

———. 2001. *The Prophets.* New York: Harper Perennial Modern Classics.

Heschel, Susannah. 2008. *The Aryan Jesus: Christian Theologians and the Bible in Nazi Germany.* Princeton, NJ: Princeton University Press.

Hirsch, E. D. 1987. *Cultural Literacy.* Boston: Houghton Mifflin.

Hobbes, Thomas. *Leviathan.* Public domain: http://www.publicliterature.org/books /leviathan/1. Accessed September 15, 2011.

Honig, Bonnie. 2009. *Emergency Politics: Paradox, Law, Democracy.* Princeton: Princeton University Press.

Horkheimer, Max, and Theodor Adorno. 2002. "The Concept of Enlightenment." *The Dialectic of Enlightenment: Philosophical Fragments,* ed. Gunzelin Schmid Noerr and trans. Edmund Jephcott, 1–34. Palo Alto, CA: Stanford University Press.

Hyman, Paula. 1979. *From Dreyfus to Vichy: The Remaking of French Jewry, 1906–1939.* New York: Columbia University Press.

———. 1979. *The Jews of Modern France.* Berkeley: University of California Press.

Israel, Jonathan. 2001. *Radical Enlightenment: Philosophy and the Making of Modernity 1650–1750.* Oxford: Oxford University Press.

Kahn, Paul. 2005. *Putting Liberalism in its Place.* Princeton, NJ: Princeton University Press.

Kangas, David, and Martin Kavka. 2008. "Hearing, Patiently: Time and Salvation in Kierkegaard and Levinas." In *Kierkegaard and Levinas: Ethics, Politics and Religion,* ed. Aaron Simmons and David Wood, 125–152. Bloomington: Indiana University Press.

Kant, Immanuel. 2003. *On Education.* Mineola, NY: Dover Classics.

Kaspi, André. 2010. *Histoire de l'Alliance israélite universelle de 1860 À nos jours.* Paris: Armand Colin.

Katz, Claire Elise. 2002. "The Significance of Childhood," *International Studies in Philosophy* 34:77–101.

———. 2003. *Levinas, Judaism, and the Feminine: The Silent Footsteps of Rebecca.* Bloomington: Indiana University Press.

———. 2004. "Teaching Our Children Well: Pedagogy, Religion and the Future of Philosophy." *Cross Currents* 53 (Winter): 530–547.

———. 2005. *Emmanuel Levinas: Critical Assessments.* Vols. 1–4. London: Routledge.

———. 2005. "Levinas—Between Philosophy and Rhetoric: The 'Teaching' of Levinas's Scriptural References." *Philosophy and Rhetoric* 38:159–172.

———. 2005. "Teaching the Other: Levinas, Rousseau and the Question of Education." *Philosophy Today* 49, no. 2 (Summer): 200–207.

———. 2006. "Before the face of God one must not go with empty hands: Transcendence and Levinas's Prophetic Consciousness." *Philosophy Today* 50, nos. 1/5 (Spring), 57–68.

———. 2007. "Educating the Solitary Man: Dependence and Vulnerability in Levinas and

Rousseau." In *Levinas Studies: An Annual Review* 2:133–152. Pittsburgh: Duquesne University Press.

———. 2007. "'The Presence of the Other is a Presence that Teaches': Levinas, Pragmatism, and Pedagogy." *Journal of Jewish Thought and Philosophy* 14:91–108.

———. 2007. "On a word and a prayer," published on-line in the *Journal for the Society of Textual Reasoning* 5, no. 1.

———. 2008. "Thus Spoke Zarathustra; Thus Listened the Rabbis: Philosophy, Education, and the Cycle of Enlightenment," *New Nietzsche Studies* 7, nos. 3 and 4. Reprinted in *After the Death of a Certain God: Nietzsche and Levinas,* ed. Bettina Bergo and Jill Stauffer, 81–95. New York: Columbia University Press.

———. 2008. "'The Eternal Irony of the Community': Prophecy, Patriotism, and the Dixie Chicks." *Shofar: An Interdisciplinary Journal of Jewish Studies* 26, no. 4 (Summer):139–160.

———. 2011. "The Stirrings of a Stubborn and Difficult Freedom: Assimilation, Education, and Levinas's Crisis of Humanism." *Journal of French and Francophone Philosophy* 53, no 1, 86–105.

———. 2011. "Jew-Greek redux: Knowing what we do not know—on Diane Perpich's *The Ethics of Emmanuel Levinas*." *PhiloSOPHIA: A Journal of Continental Feminism* 1, no. 1 (January 2011):103–111.

———. 2012. "Turning toward the Other," in *Totality and Infinity at 50,* ed. Scott Davidson and Diane Perpich, 209–226. Pittsburgh: Duquesne University Press.

———. Forthcoming. Review of Michael Fagenblat, *A Covenant of Creatures. Shofar: An Interdisciplinary Journal of Jewish Studies.*

Kavka, Martin. 2004. *Jewish Messianism and the History of Philosophy.* Cambridge: Cambridge University Press.

———. 2006. "What Does it Mean to Receive Tradition?" *Cross Currents* (Summer).

Kearney, Richard. 2009. *Anatheism.* New York: Columbia University Press.

Kitcher, Philip. 2011. "Philosophy Inside Out." *Metaphilosophy* 42 (April): 248–260.

Kress, J., and M. Lehman. 2003. "The Babylonian Talmud in Cognitive Perspective: Reflections on the Nature of the Bavli and its Pedagogical Implications." *Journal of Jewish Education* 69 (Winter): 58–78.

Levinson, Natasha. 1996. "Beginning Again: Teaching, Natality and Social Transformation." *Philosophy of Education Yearbook.* http://www.ed.uiuc.edu/eps/PES-Yearbook /96_docs/levinson.html (accessed May 19, 2008).

———. 2002. "Hannah Arendt on the Relationship Between Education and Political Action." In *Philosophy of Education 2001,* ed. Suzanne Rice, 333–336. Urbana, IL: Philosophy of Education Society.

Lloyd, Genevieve. 1993. *The Man of Reason: "Male" and "Female" in Western Philosophy.* London: Routledge.

Malino, F., and B. Wasserstein, eds. 1985. *The Jews in Modern France.* Hanover, NH: University of New England Press.

Malka, Salomon. 2002. *Emmanuel Levinas: la vie et la trace.* Paris: J-C Lattès.

Menand, Louis. 2010. *The Marketplace of Ideas: Reform and Resistance in the American University.* New York: Norton.

———. 2011. "Debating the Value of College in America." *The New Yorker,* June 6, 2011. http://www.newyorker.com/arts/critics/atlarge/2011/06/06/110606crat_atlarge_menand (accessed June 6, 2011).

Mendelssohn, Moses. 1983. *Jerusalem*. Waltham, MA: Brandeis University Press.

Mendes-Flohr, Paul, and Jehuda Reinharz, eds. 1995. *The Jew in the Modern World*. Oxford: Oxford University Press.

Merleau-Ponty, Maurice. 1964. "The Child's Relations With Others," trans. William Cobb, in *The Primacy of Perception*, ed. James M. Edie. Evanston, IL: Northwestern University Press.

Montessori, Maria. 1988. *The Montessori Method*. New York: Schocken.

Moyn, Samuel. 2007. *Origins of the Other: Emmanuel Levinas Between Revelation and Ethics*. Ithaca, NY: Cornell University Press.

———. 2010. *The Last Utopia: Human Rights in History*. Cambridge, MA: Harvard University Press.

Neuhouser, Frederick. 2008. *Rousseau's Theodicy of Self-Love: Evil, Rationality, and the Drive for Recognition*. Oxford: Oxford University Press.

New, Melvyn, ed. 2001. *In Proximity: Emmanuel Levinas and the 18th Century*. Lubbock: Texas Tech Press.

Nietzsche, Friedrich. 1982. *The Portable Nietzsche*, ed. Walter Kaufmann. New York: Penguin.

Nussbaum, Martha. 1998. *Cultivating Humanity*. Cambridge, MA: Harvard University Press.

———. 2010. *Not for Profit: Why Democracy Needs the Humanities*. Princeton, NY: Princeton University Press.

Okin, Susan Moller. 2002. "The Fate of Rousseau's Heroines." In *Feminist Interpretations of Jean-Jacques Rousseau*, ed. Lynda Lange, 92–93. University Park: Penn State University Press.

Perpich, Diane. 2008. *The Ethics of Emmanuel Levinas*. Palo Alto, CA: Stanford University Press.

Pinker, Steven. 2011. *The Better Angels of Our Nature: Why Violence has Declined*. New York: Viking.

Pomson, Alex, and Howard Deitcher, eds. 2009. *Jewish Day Schools / Jewish Communities: A Reconsideration*. Oxford: Littman Library.

Putnam, Hilary. 2009. *Jewish Philosophy as a Guide to Life*. Bloomington: Indiana University Press.

Rancière, Jacques. 1991. *The Ignorant Schoolmaster*. Palo Alto, CA: Stanford University Press.

Ravitch, Diane. 2010. *The Death and Life of the Great American School System*. New York: Basic Books.

Rosenfeld, Leonora Cohen. 1957. "Morris R. Cohen, The Teacher." *Journal of the History of Ideas* 18 (October): 552–571.

Rosenzweig, Franz. 1995. *On Jewish Learning*, ed. N. N. Glatzer. Madison: University of Wisconsin Press.

Rosenstock-Huessy, Eugen. 2008. Collected works on DVD.

Rousseau, J. J. 1993. *Émile*, trans. Barbara Foxley. London: Everyman.

———. 1997. *The Social Contract and Other Later Political Writings*. Cambridge: Cambridge University Press.

———. 2004. *Émile et Sophie ou Les Solitaires*. Paris: Rivages poche Petite Bibliothèque.

Ruse, Michael. 2011. "German Culture—Goethe, Wagner, Hitler?" *The Chronicle of Higher*

Education. May 15, 2011. http://chronicle.com/blogs/brainstorm/german-culture -goethe-wagner-hitler/35264. Accessed May 21, 2012.

Schutz, Aaron. 2002. "Is Political Action an Oxymoron? Hannah Arendt's Resistance to Public Spaces in Schools." In *Philosophy of Education 2001,* ed. Suzanne Rice, 324– 332. Urbana, IL: Philosophy of Education Society.

Shea, Christopher. "Rule Breaker." *The Chronicle of Higher Education,* June 12, 2011. http://chronicle.com/article/The-Biology-of-Ethics/127789/ (accessed June 19, 2011).

Shulman, Lee S. 2008. "Professing Understanding and Professing Faith: The Midrashic Imperative." In *The American University in a Postsecular Age,* ed. Douglas Jacobsen and Rhonda Jacobsen, 203–217. Oxford: Oxford University Press.

Simmons, J. Aaron, and David Wood, eds. 2008. *Kierkegaard and Levinas: Ethics, Politics, and Religion.* Bloomington: Indiana University Press.

Simon-Nahum, Perrine. 2005. "'Penser le judaïsme'. Retour sur les Colloques des intellectuels juifs de langue française (1957–2000)." *Archives Juives: Revue d'histoire des Juifs de France* 38:79–106.

Spatscheck, Christian. 2010. "Theodor W. Adorno on Education." In *The Encyclopaedia of Informal Education.* www.infed.org/thinkers/adorno_on_education.htm (accessed September 26, 2011).

Standish, Paul. 2007. "Education for Grownups, a Religion for Adults: Skepticism and Alterity in Cavell and Levinas." *Ethics and Education* 2:73–91.

Stern, David. 1996. *Midrash and Theory.* Evanston, IL: Northwestern University Press.

Sternhell, Zeev. 2010. *The Anti-Enlightenment Tradition,* trans. David Maisel. New Haven, CT: Yale University Press.

Taylor, Mark C. 2010. *Crisis on Campus: A Bold Plan for Reforming Our Colleges and Universities.* New York: Knopf.

Thomson, Iain. 2005. *Heidegger on Ontotheology: Technology and the Politics of Education.* New York: Cambridge University Press.

Todd, Sharon. 2003. *Learning from the Other.* Albany: State University of New York Press.

Vinokur, Val. 2009. *The Trace of Judaism: Dostoevsky, Babel, Mandelstam, Levinas.* Evanston, IL: Northwestern University Press.

Wollstonecraft, Mary. 1982, first published 1792. *A Vindication of the Rights of Women.* London: Penguin.

Yovel, Yirmiyahu, 1998. *Dark Riddle: Hegel, Nietzsche, and the Jews.* University Park: Penn State University Press.

Zarader, Marlene, 2006. *The Unthought Debt: Heidegger and the Hebraic Heritage,* trans. Bettina Bergo. Stanford, CA: Stanford University Press.

Zornberg, Avivah Gottlieb. 1995. *The Beginning of Desire: Reflections on Genesis.* New York: Image/Doubleday.

———. 2001. *The Particulars of Rapture: Reflections on Exodus.* New York: Image.

Index

economy, vii, 36, 178n12; of being, 194n12

education: humanities, xi, xii, 6, 14, 15, 18–39, 116, 123, 180n31, 181n42; Jewish, xii, 1, 8, 9–17, 22, 23, 38, 39, 57–60, 78, 81, 90–92, 96–103, 105–24, 126–27, 131, 132–34, 136, 148–49, 150, 155, 160, 161–64, 165, 173n21, 173n22, 174n28, 175n33, 181n42, 197n9, 205n1; philosophy of, xi, xviii, 3–4, 23–26, 31, 54, 178n20. *See also individual philosophers*

ego: and ethics, 128; and infinity, 191n46; and philosophy, 95, 99; sovereignty of, 6–13, 91; and subjectivity, 102; turning away from, 71–85, 115, 131, 133–34

election, 59, 75, 102, 144, 160, 163, 166, 194n12, 207n39

Émile/Émile, 29–31, 42–47, 52–57, 70, 91, 132, 183n1, 183n10, 185n24, 190n30

escape, 186; and Hitlerism, 188n17; "On Escape," 124, 165, 188n19; and responsibility, 191n46, 194n11

essence: Christian, 114; of consciousness, 63; Jewish, 106–108, 194n12; man's, 64; of the modern world, 200n32; of morals, 24; of the soul, 80

eternity, 202n21

experience, 40, 83, 200n7; of alterity, 69; Aristotle, 178n19; of our bodies, 63–66; with children, 190n30; of creation, 195n17; and education, 24–29, 167; of the ethical, 133; everyday, 81; human, 182n56; of human inefficacy, 73; and the humanities, 34–36; learning, 140, 179n25; lived, 107–108, 137, 170n8; mystical, 58; and obligation, 81; of praying, 199n31; pre-linguistic, 85; of the real, 70, 130; religious, 96–97, 159, 190n40; of revenge, 50; and Sartre, 87–89; of secularity, 115; and violence, 171n13; of wisdom, 54

evil, vii, xiii, 1, 10, 60, 89, 95, 171n13; duped by, 100, 116; face of, 151, 155; good and, 121, 150

face, 61, 95, 129, 201n18; of Abel, 146; of evil, 151; face-to-face, 6, 94, 163, 195n18; of God, 102, 189n22, 196n38; of the Good, 72; Levinas's definition of, 173n25; meaning of, 159; nakedness of, 72; of the Other, 11, 76, 77, 86–87, 89–90, 102, 112, 113, 130, 133, 134, 135, 147, 149, 159, 160, 191n41; phenomenology of, 83–86, 129, 133; relation with, 72

Fagenblat, Michael, 97–99, 195n15, 195n25, 195n26, 196n27

fecundity, 125, 130–32, 201n18, 202n19, 202n21

femininity / the feminine, 17, 42, 44, 46, 69, 202n22

Fisch, Menachem, 138–39

Fish, Stanley, 18–21, 33, 39, 123, 176n4, 177n10

Flawn, Peter, 175n2

Foucault, Michel, 120, 141, 180n33

France, 10, 11; anti-Semitism, 198n20; French Republic, 69, 121; Jewish education in, 9, 126, 201n12

freedom, 1, 6, 47, 93, 99, 190n30, 206n26; Arendt on, 27–28; and Christianity, 62–63, 128; and existentialism, 194n11; Hadot on, 37; and Judaism, 122, 155; and liberalism, 64–69, 164; and modernity, 123, 165; political, 61; Rousseau on, 42, 47; the state, 116, 122; and subjectivity, 74–77

Gibbs, Robert, 174n26, 196n6, 202n21, 204n53

God, 52–53, 67, 71–76, 80–84, 92–102, 104, 111–18, 122, 124, 133, 142, 144–48, 150–60, 172n15, 189n22, 191n41, 191n43, 194n12, 195n17, 195n18, 196n38, 199n29, 203n29, 206n27, 208n45

Gordon, Peter Eli, 187n13, 192n49, 192n53

Greek, 37, 48, 54, 61–63, 68, 127–28, 131, 134, 142, 145, 172n15, 173n26, 181n43, 201n12, 204n45

Grinberg, Chaim, 111–14, 198n19

Hadot, Pierre, 37
Hand, Sean, 70
Hebrew (language), 8, 10–15, 106–17, 118, 127–31, 140, 145, 148, 156, 173n26, 201n12
Hebrew Bible: and Christianity, 172n20, 173n26, 187n15; and humanism, 39, 58, 71, 75–78, 157; and Martin Buber, 186n1, 203n25; message of the Bible and Heidegger, 172n18; and midrash, 130–36, 142–47; and Nietzsche, 53; the Other, 8, 159; and prayer, 155; and Rosenzweig, 106–109, 112; and Talmud, 112, 202n23
Hegel, 3, 6, 15, 46, 63, 68, 88, 178n11, 189n27, 207n38
Heidegger, Martin, 7, 119, 125, 127, 156, 172n18, 177n7, 199n32; and Cassirer, 187n13, 192n49, 192n53, 193n55; on Nietzsche, 49, 73, 76–78, 185n29
Heschel, Abraham Joshua, 38, 150–53, 155–56, 158, 189n21, 199n31, 205n1, 205n2
Heschel, Susannah, 187n15
Hillel, 154
hineni (Here I am), vii, 124, 146, 155, 156
Hitler (Hitlerism), 40, 59–77, 117, 119, 124, 156, 178n13, 187n7, 187n15, 188n17, 188n19, 193n55, 197n9
Hobbes, Thomas, 2, 42, 171n13
holiness, 71, 72, 83, 84, 147, 190n40, 191n41, 191n42
Holocaust, 1, 104, 171n13, 198n19
Honig, Bonnie, 55–57, 97, 186n41, 195n24, 208n46, 208n47
Horkheimer, Max, 181n47, 187n16, 192n51
humanism, 58–79, 172n15; and anti-humanism, 57, 115–23, 134, 160, 187n13; and Cassirer, 187n13, 192n49; Christian, 188n17; crisis of, 6, 11, 12, 13, 23, 40, 96, 102, 124, 128, 133, 148, 150, 161, 171n13; and education, 57; and Heidegger, 199n32; Jewish, 8, 11, 12, 16, 38, 133, 135, 136, 201n12; and Jewish education, 14–15, 17, 83, 90, 109, 110–15; modern, 9,

11, 14, 38, 40, 180n31, 182n56; new, 6, 8, 12, 16, 133–34; and the Other, 83, 86, 172n18; and Sartre, 200n32; secular, 14, 160. *See also* Hebrew Bible
"Humanism and An-archy," 199n32
Husserl, Edmund, 85–89, 125, 156, 193

immanence, 59–61, 65–68, 156, 187n8, 189n21. *See also* transcendence
independence, 29, 46, 52, 79, 179n25, 184n13
injustice, xii, 23, 152, 155–57, 199n29, 205n1
Isaiah, vii, 10, 71–72, 104, 130, 136, 149, 150, 152, 155, 156, 191n43, 198n29, 199n30
Israel, 16, 54, 58, 59, 92–94, 101, 111–12, 114, 127, 149, 153–54, 174n32, 195n17
Israel, Jonathan, 183n4, 183n10

James, William, 96
Jeremiah, 101
Judaism. *See* education; Hebrew Bible; humanism; midrash; prayer

Kahn, Paul, 188n18
Kant, Immanuel, 3, 5, 19, 35, 37, 61, 67, 114, 115, 123, 134, 140, 141, 148, 178n20, 183n57, 198n23
Kavka, Martin, 188n17, 196n6, 197n8, 197n10
Kearney, Richard, 117
Kierkegaard, Søren, 207n35
King, Martin Luther, 199n31
King Lear, 36
Kitcher, Philip, 170n8

Laub, Morris, 205n1
Levenson, Jon D., 97
liberalism, 8, 15, 41, 43, 61–65, 119, 122, 164, 188n17, 188n18
Lipman, Matthew, 30

Maimonides, Moses, 111, 119, 153, 191n43, 201n12
Malka, Salomon, 96, 104, 196n1

Mann, Horace, 170n9
Marrano, 113
Marx, Karl, 62–63, 67, 127
Mendelssohn, Moses, 175n33, 183n57
Merleau-Ponty, Maurice, 85, 88, 90, 132, 170n10, 174n31, 177n7, 193n1, 194n8
midrash, 8, 12, 13, 53, 99, 109, 134, 136–37, 139–47, 157, 163–64, 186n42, 202n23, 203n29
Milgram, Stanley, 30
Mill, John Stuart, 170n7
Montaigne, Michel de, vii, 1, 41, 80, 169
Montessori, Maria, 28–29, 41, 42, 57

National Socialism (Nazi), 1, 35, 66, 100, 105, 113, 128, 148, 156, 171n13, 194n11
Neuhouser, Frederick, 183n7
Nietzsche, Friedrich, 8, 11, 40–42, 48–57, 58, 73, 76, 78, 79, 138, 164, 165, 182n56, 185n31, 186n34, 186n38, 189n27
Nussbaum, Martha, 21–23, 30–32, 33, 36, 39, 174n30, 175 chapter 1, 179n24, 181n39

ontology, 7–8, 85, 95, 98, 145

pagan/paganism, 60, 66–68, 192n52
passivity, 74–77, 99, 194n12
peace, vii, 84, 100, 102, 116, 130, 141, 144
Perpich, Diane, 84–85, 193n3, 193n5
phenomenology. See Crowell, Steven Galt; Husserl, Edmund; Kavka, Martin; Perpich, Diane
philosophy. See humanism; religion, and philosophy
Philosophy for Children, xi, 30, 31, 181n39
Pinker, Steven, 171n13
Plato, 3, 19, 37, 51, 52, 55, 72, 140, 141, 177n7, 177n11, 184n17, 185n26, 191n46
political. See Arendt, Hannah; democracy; education; humanism; Nietzsche, Friedrich; Nussbaum, Martha; Rousseau, Jean-Jacques

prayer, 106, 124, 135, 152–55, 157–59, 205n1, 206n18, 206n27
Principles of 1789, 41, 113–14, 118
prophetic. See prophets
prophets, xii, 53, 71–72, 116, 120, 133, 149, 150–67, 172n20, 198n29, 199n30

race, 7
racism, 66, 188n17
Rancière, Jacques, 208n47
Ravitch, Diane, 21
religion, 14–15, 38, 57, 60, 71, 76, 83, 85, 90, 101, 117–19, 134, 151, 154, 157, 188n18, 198n21, 206n23; as the ethical, 134, 141, 144, 159–61; Jewish, 109–13, 147, 154, 189n21, 191n42, 194n12, 206n27; and philosophy, 91–98, 100, 143, 145, 153, 173n26, 203n29; and transcendence, 159, 192n52
responsibility: anarchic, 76–80; asymmetrical, 7, 12, 89, 202n21
revelation, 82, 85, 91, 93–95, 97, 147, 153, 175n33
Ricoeur, Paul, 157
Robinson Crusoe, 70, 130, 183n1
Rosenzweig, Franz, 10, 96–97, 105–108, 118, 163, 175n33, 195n24, 197n7, 197n9, 204n45
Rousseau, Jean-Jacques, 41–47, 51, 52–57, 68–69, 73, 76, 79, 91, 132, 138, 170n6, 170n7, 180n32, 181n38, 183n1, 183n4, 183n7, 183n10, 184n11, 184n15, 184n16, 184n20, 185n24, 190n30
Ruse, Michael, 178n13

Schlink, Bernard, 1
Shoah, xiii, 196n27
Shulman, Lee S., 139–41, 207n32
Socrates, 48–52, 54, 63, 70, 130, 177n7, 185n26
Sophie, 43, 45–47, 184n20, 185n24
Sophie's Choice, 172n16
Spinoza, 111, 170n6
subjectivity. See humanism

CLAIRE ELISE KATZ is Associate Professor of Philosophy and Women's and Gender Studies at Texas A&M University. She is the author of *Levinas, Judaism, and the Feminine* (Indiana University Press, 2003).